WBI LEARNING RESOURCES SERIES

Beyond Economic Growth

An Introduction to Sustainable Development

Second Edition

Tatyana P. Soubbotina

The World Bank
Washington, D.C.

For more information and classroom materials on issues of sustainable development, visit our web sites at www.worldbank.org/depweb and www.worldbank.org/wbi/developmenteducation.

Please send comments to dep@worldbank.org.

Tatyana P. Soubbotina is a consultant at the World Bank Institute.

Cover and chapter opener design by Patricia Hord Graphic Design. Typesetting by Precision Graphics.

Library of Congress Cataloging-in-Publication Data has been applied for.

Contents

Acknowledgments   vi

Introduction   1
   Difficult Questions, Different Answers   2
   Development Data   2
   About This Book   3
   How to Use The Book   4

1. **What Is Development?**   7
   Goals and Means of Development   7
   Sustainable Development   8

2. **Comparing Levels of Development**   12
   Gross Domestic Product and Gross National Product   12
   Grouping Countries by Their Level of Development   15

3. **World Population Growth**   17

4. **Economic Growth Rates**   23

5. **Income Inequality**   28
   Cross-country Comparisons of Income Inequality   28
   Lorenz Curves and Gini Indexes   29
   Costs and Benefits of Income Inequality   31

6. **Poverty and Hunger**   33
   The Nature of Poverty   33
   The Geography of Poverty   34
   The Vicious Circle of Poverty   35
   The Challenge of Hunger   38

7. **Education**   43
   Education and Human Capital   43
   Primary Education and Literacy   46
   Issues in Secondary and Tertiary Education   48

8. **Health and Longevity   53**
    Global Trends   53
    Population Age Structures   55
    The Burden of Infectious Disease   57
    Lifestyle Challenges   61

9. **Industrialization and Postindustrialization   63**
    Major Structural Shifts   63
    Knowledge Revolution   65
    Implications for Development Sustainability   67

10. **Urban Air Pollution   69**
    Particulate Air Pollution   70
    Airborne Lead Pollution   73

11. **Public and Private Enterprises: Finding the Right Mix   76**
    The Dilemma of Public-Private Ownership   77
    Is There a Trend toward Privatization?   80

12. **Globalization: International Trade and Migration   83**
    Waves of Modern Globalization   83
    Costs and Benefits of Free Trade   85
    Geography and Composition of Global Trade   87
    International Migration   91

13. **Globalization: Foreign Investment and Foreign Aid   95**
    Private Capital Flows   96
    Official Development Assistance   99

14. **The Risk of Global Climate Change   102**
    Whose Responsibility Is It?   103
    Will the North-South cooperation work?   107

15. **Composite Indicators of Development   110**
    "Development Diamonds"   110
    Human Development Index   111

16. Indicators of Development Sustainability   113
Composition of National Wealth   113
Accumulation of National Wealth As an Indicator of Sustainable Development   114
Material Throughput and Environmental Space   117
Social Capital and Public Officials' Corruption   119

17. Development Goals and Strategies   123
Millennium Development Goals   123
The Role of National Development Policies   127
Difficult Choices   129

Glossary   131

Annex 1: Classification of Economies by Income and Region   145

Annex 2: Data Tables   149
Table 1. Indicators to Chapter 1–5   150
Table 2. Indicators to Chapter 6–7   160
Table 3. Indicators to Chapter 8–9   170
Table 4. Indicators to Chapter 10–13   180
Table 5. Indicators to Chapter 14–16   192

Annex 3: Millennium Development Goals   203

Acknowledgments

The preparation of this book benefited greatly from the support and valuable contributions of many colleagues in the World Bank Institute (WBI) and in other parts of the World Bank.

I am particularly indebted to the head of WBI, Frannie Leautier, for her support of the second edition of this book and to two successive managers of the WBI Development Education Program (DEP), Katherine Sheram and Danielle Carbonneau, for the inspiration and important inputs they provided to this challenging multiyear project. The work on this book was also greatly facilitated by close collaboration with the other DEP team members, including Evi Vestergaard, Kelly Grable, and Brooke Prater.

Next I would like to express my sincere appreciation to those World Bank experts who provided extremely useful comments, suggestions, and inputs during the drafting of the first and second editions of this book: Carl Dahlman, Dusan Vujovic, Gregory Prakas, Joanne Epp, John Oxenham, John Middleton, Kirk Hamilton, Ksenia Lvovsky, Magda Lovei, Peter Miovic, Philip Karp, Simon Commander, Tatyana Leonova, Thomas Merrick, Tim Heleniak, Vinod Thomas, Vladimir Kreacic, and William Prince. Special thanks go to John Didier for his dedicated help with the final editing of the first edition and unfailing support during the preparation of the second edition.

I am also grateful to all of my colleagues in Russia, Latvia, and Belarus for their knowledgeable advice during our joint work on the respective country adaptations of this book, particularly Vladimir Avtonomov, Andrei Mitskevitch, Erika Sumilo, and Mikhail Kovalev.

An important role in pilot-testing and distributing the first edition and its three country adaptations was played by DEP partners in the US National Council on Economic Education (NCEE), in Russia's State University–Higher School of Economics, in the Latvian Association of Teachers of Economics (LATE), and in the Belarusian Institute for Post-Diploma Teacher Training.

Introduction

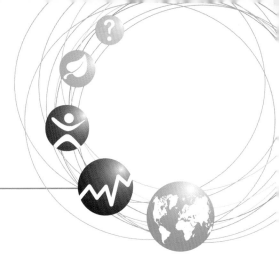

The underlying premise of this book is that in order for development to be sustainable, it has to be comprehensive—it has to successfully balance economic goals with social and environmental. "Development" is really much more than simply economic growth. The understanding of development can differ among countries and even among individuals, but it usually goes far beyond the objective of increased average income to include things like freedom, equity, health, education, safe environment, and much more. Hence the title of this book: "Beyond Economic Growth."

By publishing this book, the Development Education Program (DEP) of the World Bank Institute (WBI) seeks to help more people understand that in the present-day globalized world international development should be everyone's concern because it affects everyone's life. Ordinary people including youth—not just economists and development experts—should be prepared to discuss and participate in making decisions on the most pressing issues of sustainable development, proceeding from their own cherished values and based on reliable data and information from reputable international sources (like the World Bank and the UN specialized development agencies).

This book is designed to introduce readers to some major challenges in today's sustainable development (from the global to the national and perhaps even to the local level) and help them gain a more holistic and realistic view of their country's situation in a global context. Because development is a comprehensive process involving economic as well as social and environmental changes, this book takes an interdisciplinary approach. It attempts to explain some complex relationships among various aspects of development, including population growth, economic growth, improvements in education and health, industrialization and postindustrialization, environmental degradation, and globalization. Young people and learners of all ages, teachers and students, are invited to explore these relationships even further—using the statistical data and theoretical concepts presented in this book—and to engage in informed discussions of the controversial development issues closest to their hearts. "An Invitation to a Global Discussion" could be another appropriate subtitle for this book.

1

Difficult Questions, Different Answers

The book starts with three difficult questions: What is development? How can we compare the levels of development achieved by different countries? And what does it take to make development sustainable? The author does not claim to have all the answers to these and other controversial questions posed directly or indirectly in the book. Instead, readers are encouraged to suggest their own answers based on facts—necessary for understanding the constraints of reality—but inevitably rooted in personal value judgments determining different relevant weights attached to certain goals and costs of development by different people. For example, for some people development means primarily higher incomes, for others, a cleaner environment. Some are most interested in personal security, others, in personal freedom. Note that these goals and values are not always easily compatible—faster economic growth may be more damaging to the natural environment and a strengthening of personal security may require limiting some personal freedoms. The abundance of such tradeoffs in development is one of the reasons why there are so many open questions in this book.

Acknowledging that many answers inevitably involve value judgments, which makes absolute objectivity impossible, the author has based this book on one simple ideological principle: development should be a tool for improving the lives of all people. It is up to people (including the readers of this book) to define for themselves the meaning of a better life and to prioritize the goals of development and the means of their achievement.

Development Data

Perhaps the main attraction of this book is that it is based on plentiful statistical data for most countries, presented in data tables in Annex 2 as well as in figures, maps, and references in the text. Statistics can be powerful tools for learning about development. They can help paint a more accurate picture of reality, identify issues and problems, and suggest possible explanations and solutions. But statistics have their limitations too. They are more reliable for some countries than for others. They often allow very different interpretations, particularly when considered in isolation from other important statistics. And because it takes a long time to collect and verify some statistics (particularly on a global scale), they may seem to be or really be out of date before they are even published. It is also important to remember that many aspects of development cannot be accurately measured by statistics. Examples include people's attitudes, feelings, values, ideas, freedoms, and cultural achievements. Thus statistical data can tell us only part of the story of development—but it is an important part.

Note that comparing development data on your country with those on other countries can be extremely revealing for several reasons. First, seeing one's country in a global context and learning how it is different from or similar to other countries can improve understanding of the country's present-day status and of its development prospects and priorities. Second, because the economies of the world are becoming increasingly interdependent, development processes in each country can usually be better understood when studied in the context of their interaction with related processes in other countries. The author hopes that this book will help satisfy popular demand for information about global development and at the same time help readers gain some new insights into their own country's recent past, present, and future.

The statistics presented here were the most recent available when this book was written. Most of the data in the data tables, figures, and maps are from World Bank publications, including the *World Development Indicators* (2000, 2001, 2003), the *World Development Report* (various years), and other statistical and analytical studies. Figures 4.4 and 9.2 have been included with the permission of the International Monetary Fund. Some data were also borrowed from the

specialized United Nations agencies, such as the UN Development Program, World Health Organization, and UN Food and Agriculture Organization (as noted in the text).

About This Book

This book was prepared as part of an international project under the World Bank Institute's Development Education Program (DEP). The main objective was to create a template text about the global issues of sustainable development—social, economic, and environmental—that could then be customized for various countries by teams of local educators and published in their respective national languages. It was also expected that students and other readers interested in development issues could use this international template without adaptation as a source of relatively current statistical data and widely accepted development concepts for further research and discussions.

The first edition was published in 2000 and simultaneously posted on the DEP website in the original English and in French and Spanish translations. The print copies were distributed in the USA and internationally, mostly in countries where students were prepared to read in English (in Sri Lanka and India, in Ghana and Uganda, in Lithuania and Estonia).

In addition, the first national adaptation was developed and published in Russia as *The World and Russia student book,* officially approved by the Russian Ministry of General and Professional Education for secondary students in the 10th and 11th grades studying economics, social studies, geography, and environmental studies. The three local coauthors of the Russian adaptation represented three leading research and educational institutions in Moscow.

The Latvian adaptation, *The World and Latvia,* was prepared in coauthorship with Erika Sumilo, a professor and department head at the University of Latvia, and published in Latvian. The book was awarded a national prize as the best Latvian book on economics published in 2002.

The latest national adaptation was undertaken in Belarus in coauthorship with Mikhail Kovalev, a professor and department head at Belarus State University, and was published as *The World and Belarus* in 2003. Most of these Russian-language books were distributed among secondary schools specializing in social and humanitarian studies.

Thanks to the rich history of this book, the author has had many opportunities to receive feedback from students and educators in many countries, developed as well as developing. Many of their com-

ments were taken into account in the course of preparing this second edition.

As compared with the first edition, the second one is completely updated and revised. All the data and charts are more current by 4–5 years and new materials are included on a number of issues such as Millennium Development Goals, the nature of poverty, global hunger, the burden of infectious diseases (HIV/AIDS, TB, malaria), the knowledge revolution, stages of modern globalization, international migration, and the costs of government corruption. Additional controversial questions for further discussion are included as well. The Development Education Program hopes that this new edition will find its way into classrooms as well as family rooms in many countries.

How to Use The Book

Because all development issues are intricately interrelated, there is no single, best sequence in which to study them. Thus the structure of this book allows the readers to start with almost any chapter that they might find the most intriguing. The author, however, would advise not skipping Chapters 1 and 2 since they serve as a general introduction to the book and present some important basic concepts on which the following chapters build. Note also that Chapters 15, 16, and 17 can be read as a continuation of the conceptual discussion started in the first two chapters. The other chapters, devoted to particular development issues, will then allow you to continue considering the same general issues in a more concrete manner.

As you read this book, you should keep in mind the multiplicity of interconnections among all aspects of sustainable development. In some cases, these interconnections will be explicitly pointed out in the text (see cross references to other chapters), while in others readers may need to identify them on their own. Questions in the margins are intended to help readers see the larger and more complex picture behind the specific data.

Suppose you are most interested in environmental issues. Chapters 10 and 14 are devoted to two different environmental challenges: local particulate air pollution in large cities and global air pollution from carbon dioxide emissions. But to gain a better understanding of these issues you will also need to read about population growth and economic growth (Chapters 3 and 4), industrialization and postindustrialization (Chapter 9), income inequality and poverty (Chapters 5 and 6), and health and longevity (Chapter 8). These are the most obvious links, and they are relatively easy to identify while reading the environmental chapters. You could also, however, look into links with all the other chapters in the book. For example, how does global-

ization (Chapters 12 and 13) affect air pollution in large cities in developed and developing countries? Or how does globalization help international efforts to minimize the risk of global climate change? You could then explore the links between privatization and energy efficiency (Chapter 11) or between education (Chapter 7) and environmental protection. Eventually, it becomes clear that development is so comprehensive that understanding any one issue inevitably requires studying all the rest.

Although teachers of various school subjects can use this book to help their students understand specific development issues, students should always be made aware that no single issue exists in isolation from the others. Ideally, teachers would use most or all of the book's content to build one or more learning modules centered around given curricular topics. For example, an Air Pollution module might look like this:

Air Pollution

1. Introduction: Concepts of "development" and "sustainable development"—Chapters 1, 2, and 16.
2. Local and global air pollution—Chapters 10 and 14.
3. What are the major causes of the increasing air pollution?
   - Population growth—Chapter 3
   - Economic growth—Chapter 4
   - Industrialization—Chapter 9

- Urbanization—Chapter 10
- Income inequality—Chapter 5
- Poverty—Chapter 6

4. Aggravating factors or new opportunities?
    - International trade—Chapter 12
    - Foreign investment—Chapter 13
    - Foreign aid—Chapter 13
    - Privatization—Chapter 11

5. Air pollution as a threat to development sustainability:
    - Healthy environment as one of the goals of development—Chapters 1 and 17
    - Natural capital as a component of national wealth—Chapter 16
    - The role of government policies—Chapter 17.

You will notice that most of a module's components can be formulated as questions for discussion. It is up to the reader to conclude whether, for example, the effects of economic growth are more detrimental to the environment than are the effects of poverty or whether foreign investment in developing countries contributes to pollution rather than helps reduce it. The book provides helpful (although not exhaustive) data and concepts but does not provide any easy answers.

When discussing questions arising from this book, it is important to make full use of the statistics contained in the data tables (at the end of this book). Comparing data on different countries and looking for correlation among various indicators can often provide more insights and food for thought than simply reading a text.

The author hopes that the discussions generated by this book will help readers understand how global and national development relate to issues in their own lives, and that this understanding will lead to practical action at the local level. Teachers, youth leaders, and other educators can use this book to inform discussion about local development challenges not only among their students but also among parents and other community members. Students can use the knowledge gained to make better-informed life choices and to become more active, involved citizens of their country as well as global citizens.

***

The World Bank Institute's Development Education Program encourages young people and educators around the world to visit its web site and send us their feedback including queries, opinions, and concerns.

For more information and learning materials on issues of sustainable development, visit our web sites at www.worldbank.org/depweb and www.worldbank.org/wbi/developmenteducation

Please send comments to dep@worldbank.org

1
What Is Development?

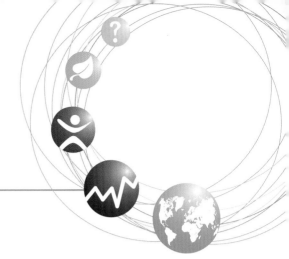

Are you sure that you know what "development" really means with respect to different countries? And can you determine which countries are more developed and which are less?

It is somewhat easier to say which countries are richer and which are poorer. But indicators of wealth, which reflect the quantity of resources available to a society, provide no information about the allocation of those resources—for instance, about more or less equitable distribution of income among social groups, about the shares of resources used to provide free health and education services, and about the effects of production and consumption on people's environment. Thus it is no wonder that countries with similar average incomes can differ substantially when it comes to people's **quality of life**: access to education and health care, employment opportunities, availability of clean air and safe drinking water, the threat of crime, and so on. With that in mind, how do we determine which countries are more developed and which are less developed?

Goals and Means of Development

Different countries have different priorities in their development policies. But to compare their development levels, you would first have to make up your mind about what development really means to you, what it is supposed to achieve. Indicators measuring this achievement could then be used to judge countries' relative progress in development.

Is the goal merely to increase national wealth, or is it something more subtle? Improving the well-being of the majority of the population? Ensuring people's freedom? Increasing their economic security?[1]

Recent United Nations documents emphasize "human development," measured by life expectancy, adult literacy, access to all three levels of education, as well as people's average income, which is a necessary condition of their freedom of choice. In a broader sense the notion of human development incorporates all aspects of individuals' well-being, from their health status to their economic and

How do we determine which countries are more developed and which less?

---

[1]If you think that the "simple" answer to this question is something like "maximizing people's happiness," think of the different factors that usually make people feel happy or unhappy. Note that a number of special surveys in different countries appear to show that the average level of happiness in a country does not grow along with the increase in average income, at least after a certain rather modest income level is achieved. At the same time, in each country richer people usually reported slightly higher levels of happiness than poorer people, and people in countries with more equal distribution of wealth appeared to be generally happier.

political freedom. According to the *Human Development Report 1996,* published by the United Nations Development Program, "human development is the end—economic growth a means."

It is true that **economic growth,** by increasing a nation's total wealth, also enhances its potential for reducing poverty and solving other social problems. But history offers a number of examples where economic growth was not followed by similar progress in human development. Instead growth was achieved at the cost of greater inequality, higher unemployment, weakened democracy, loss of cultural identity, or overconsumption of **natural resources** needed by future generations. As the links between economic growth and social and environmental issues are better understood, experts including economists tend to agree that this kind of growth is inevitably unsustainable—that is, it cannot continue along the same lines for long. First, if environmental and social/human losses resulting from economic growth turn out to be higher than economic benefits (additional incomes earned by the majority of the population), the overall result for people's well-being becomes negative. Thus such economic growth becomes difficult to sustain politically. Second, economic growth itself inevitably depends on its natural and social/human conditions. To be sustainable, it must rely on a certain amount of natural resources and services provided by nature, such as pollution absorption and resource regeneration. Moreover, economic growth must be constantly nourished by the fruits of human development, such as higher qualified workers capable of technological and managerial innovations along with opportunities for their efficient use: more and better jobs, better conditions for new businesses to grow, and greater democracy at all levels of decisionmaking (see Fig. 1.1).

Conversely, slow human development can put an end to fast economic growth. According to the *Human Development Report 1996,* "during 1960–1992 not a single country succeeded in moving from lopsided development with slow human development and rapid growth to a virtuous circle in which human development and growth can become mutually reinforcing." Since slower human development has invariably been followed by slower economic growth, this growth pattern was labeled a "dead end."

Sustainable Development

Sustainable development is a term widely used by politicians all over the world, even though the notion is still rather new and lacks a uniform interpretation. Important as it is, the concept of sustainable development is still being developed and the definition of the term is constantly being revised, extended,

Figure 1.1	Economic growth and human development

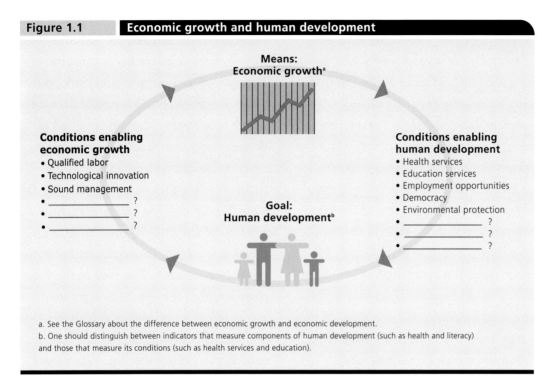

Means:
Economic growth[a]

Conditions enabling economic growth
• Qualified labor
• Technological innovation
• Sound management
• _____ ?
• _____ ?
• _____ ?

Goal:
Human development[b]

Conditions enabling human development
• Health services
• Education services
• Employment opportunities
• Democracy
• Environmental protection
• _____ ?
• _____ ?
• _____ ?

a. See the Glossary about the difference between economic growth and economic development.
b. One should distinguish between indicators that measure components of human development (such as health and literacy) and those that measure its conditions (such as health services and education).

Why is equity important for sustainable development?

and refined. Using this book, you can try to formulate your own definition as you learn more about the relationships among its main components—the economic, social, and environmental factors of sustainable development—and as you decide on their relative significance based on your own system of values.

According to the classical definition given by the United Nations World Commission on Environment and Development in 1987, development is sustainable if it "meets the needs of the present without compromising the ability of future generations to meet their own needs." It is usually understood that this "intergenerational" equity would be impossible to achieve in the absence of present-day social equity , if the economic activities of some groups of peo-

ple continue to jeopardize the well-being of people belonging to other groups or living in other parts of the world. Imagine, for example, that emissions of **greenhouse gases,** generated mainly by highly industrialized countries, lead to global warming and flooding of certain low-lying islands—resulting in the displacement and impoverishment of entire island nations (see Chapter 14). Or consider the situation when higher profits of pharmaceutical companies are earned at the cost of millions of poor people being unable to afford medications needed for treating their life-threatening diseases.

"Sustainable" development could probably be otherwise called "equitable and balanced," meaning that, in order for development to continue indefinitely, it should balance the interests of different groups of people, within the same generation and among generations, and do so simultaneously in three major interrelated areas—economic, social, and environmental. So sustainable development is about equity, defined as equality of opportunities for well-being, as well as about comprehensiveness of objectives. Figure 1.2 shows just a few of the many objectives, which, if ignored, threaten to slow down or reverse development in other areas. You are invited to add more objectives and explain how, in your opinion, they are connected to others. In the following chapters you will find many examples of such interconnections.

Obviously, balancing so many diverse objectives of development is an enormous challenge for any country. For instance, how would you compare the positive value of greater national security with the negative value of slower economic growth (loss of jobs and income) and some, possibly irreversible, environmental damage? There is no strictly scientific method of performing such valuations and comparisons. However, governments have to make these kinds of decisions on a regular basis. If such decisions are to reflect the interests of the majority, they must be taken in the most democratic and participatory way possible. But even in this case, there is a high risk that long-term interests of our children and grandchildren end up unaccounted for, because future generations cannot vote for themselves. Thus, to ensure that future generations inherit the necessary conditions to provide for their own welfare, our present-day values must be educated enough to reflect their interests as well.

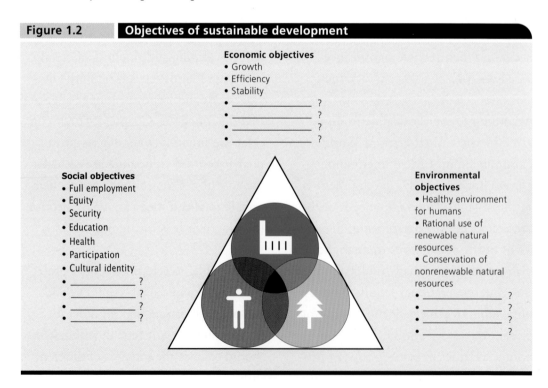

Figure 1.2 — Objectives of sustainable development

Economic objectives
- Growth
- Efficiency
- Stability
- _____ ?
- _____ ?
- _____ ?
- _____ ?

Social objectives
- Full employment
- Equity
- Security
- Education
- Health
- Participation
- Cultural identity
- _____ ?
- _____ ?
- _____ ?
- _____ ?

Environmental objectives
- Healthy environment for humans
- Rational use of renewable natural resources
- Conservation of nonrenewable natural resources
- _____ ?
- _____ ?
- _____ ?
- _____ ?

The challenge is further complicated by the fact that in today's interdependent world many aspects of sustainable development are in fact international or even global. On the one hand, many decisions taken at the national or even local level actually have international consequences–economic, social, environmental. When these consequences are negative, the situation is sometimes referred to as "exporting unsustainability." On the other hand, national policies are often inadequate to effectively deal with many challenges of sustainability. Thus international cooperation on the wide range of so-called transboundary and global problems of sustainable development becomes indispensable.

Arguably, the most critical problem of sustainable development—in each country as well as globally—is eradicating extreme poverty. That is because poverty is not only an evil in itself. It also stands in the way of achieving most other goals of development, from clean environment to personal freedom. Another, closely related, global problem is establishing and preserving peace in all regions and all countries. War, as well as poverty, is inherently destructive of all economic as well as social and environmental goals of development (see Fig. 1.2).

In the final analysis sustainable development is about long-term conditions for humanity's multidimensional well-being. For example, the famous Rio Declaration, adopted by the United Nations Conference on Environment and Development in 1992 (also called the Earth Summit, held in Rio de Janeiro, Brazil), puts it this way: "Human beings are at the center of concern for sustainable development. They are entitled to a healthy and productive life in harmony with nature."

What are the necessary conditions for sustainable development?

2

Comparing Levels of Development

Countries are unequally endowed with natural resources. For example, some countries benefit from fertile agricultural soils, while others have to put a lot of effort into artificial soil amelioration. Some countries have discovered rich oil and gas deposits within their territories, while others have to import most "fossil" fuels. In the past a lack or wealth of **natural resources** made a big difference in countries' development. But today a wealth of natural resources is not the most important determinant of development success. Consider such high-income countries as Japan or the Republic of Korea. Their high economic development allows them to use their limited natural wealth much more productively (efficiently) than would be possible in many less developed countries. The **productivity** with which countries use their productive resources—**physical capital, human capital,** and **natural capital**—is widely recognized as the main indicator of their level of **economic development.**

Theoretically, then, economists comparing the development of different countries should calculate how productively they are using their capital. But such calculations are extremely challenging, primarily because of the difficulty of putting values on elements of natural

and human capital. In practice economists use **gross national product (GNP) per capita** or **gross domestic product (GDP)** per capita for the same purpose. These statistical indicators are easier to calculate, provide a rough measure of the relative productivity with which different countries use their resources, and measure the relative material welfare in different countries, whether this welfare results from good fortune with respect to land and natural resources or from superior productivity in their use.

Gross Domestic Product and Gross National Product

GDP is calculated as the value of the total final output of all goods and services produced in a single year within a country's boundaries. GNP is GDP plus incomes received by residents from abroad minus incomes claimed by non-residents.

There are two ways of calculating GDP and GNP:

- By adding together all the incomes in the economy—wages, interest, profits, and rents.

- By adding together all the expenditures in the economy—consumption, investment, government purchases of goods and services, and net exports (exports minus imports).

In theory, the results of both calculations should be the same. Because one person's expenditure is always another person's income, the sum of expenditures must equal the sum of incomes. When the calculations include expenditures made or incomes received by a country's citizens in their transactions with foreign countries, the result is GNP. When the calculations are made exclusive of expenditures or incomes that originated beyond a country's boundaries, the result is GDP.

GNP may be much less than GDP if much of the income from a country's production flows to foreign persons or firms. For example, in 1994 Chile's GNP was 5 percent smaller than its GDP. If a country's citizens or firms hold large amounts of the stocks and bonds of other countries' firms or governments, and receive income from them, GNP may be greater than GDP. In Saudi Arabia, for instance, GNP exceeded GDP by 7 percent in 1994. For most countries, however, these statistical indicators differ insignificantly.

GDP and GNP can serve as indicators of the scale of a country's economy. But to judge a country's level of economic development, these indicators have to be divided by the country's population. GDP per capita and GNP per capita show the approximate amount of goods and services that each person in a country would be able to buy in a year if incomes were divided equally (Figure 2.1). That is

What are the main limitations of per capita income as a measure of development?

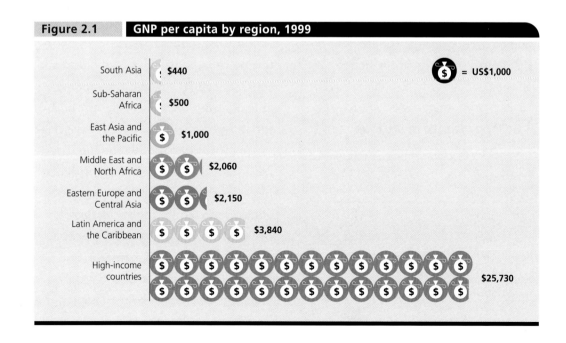

Figure 2.1 **GNP per capita by region, 1999**

Region	GNP per capita
South Asia	$440
Sub-Saharan Africa	$500
East Asia and the Pacific	$1,000
Middle East and North Africa	$2,060
Eastern Europe and Central Asia	$2,150
Latin America and the Caribbean	$3,840
High-income countries	$25,730

($) = US$1,000

why these measures are also often called "per capita incomes."

In the data tables at the end of this book GNP per capita is shown not only in U.S. dollars but also in PPP dollars—that is, adjusted with the help of a **purchasing power parity (PPP)** conversion factor. The PPP conversion factor shows the number of units of a country's currency required to buy the same amount of goods and services in the domestic market as one dollar would buy in the United States. By applying this conversion factor, one can, for example, convert a country's **nominal** GNP per capita (expressed in U.S. dollars in accordance with the market exchange rate of the national currency) into its **real** GNP per capita (an indicator adjusted for the difference in prices for the same goods and services between this country and the United States, and independent of the fluctuations of the national currency exchange rate). GNP in PPP terms thus provides a better

comparison of average income or consumption between economies.

In developing countries real GNP per capita is usually higher than nominal GNP per capita, while in developed countries it is often lower (Table 2.1). Thus the gap between real per capita incomes in developed and developing countries is smaller than the gap between nominal per capita incomes.

Although they reflect the average incomes in a country, GNP per capita and GDP per capita have numerous limitations when it comes to measuring people's actual well-being. They do not show how equitably a country's income is distributed. They do not account for pollution, environmental degradation, and resource depletion. They do not register unpaid work done within the family and community, or work done in the shadow (underground and informal) economy. And they attach equal importance to "goods" (such as medicines) and "bads" (cigarettes, chemical weapons) while ignoring the value of leisure and human freedom. Thus, to judge the relative quality of life in different countries, one should also take into account other indicators showing, for instance, the distribution of income and incidence of poverty (see Chapters 5 and 6), people's health and longevity (Chapter 8) and access to education (Chapter 7), the quality of the environment (Chapter 10), and more. Experts also use compos-

Table 2.1   Nominal and real GNP per capita in various countries, 1999

Country	GNP per capita (U.S. dollars)	GNP per capita (PPP dollars)
India	450	2,149
China	780	3,290
Russia	2,270	6,339
United States	30,600	30,600
Germany	25,350	22,404
Japan	32,230	24,041

ite statistical indicators of development (Chapter 15).

Grouping Countries by Their Level of Development

Different organizations use different criteria to group countries by their level of development. The World Bank, for instance, uses GNP per capita to classify countries as low-income (GNP per capita of $765 or less in 1995), middle-income (including lower-middle-

income, $766 to $3,035, and upper-middle-income, $3,036 to $9,385), or high-income ($9,386 or more; Map 2.1).

A more popular, though apparently more disputable, approach involves dividing all countries into "developing" and "developed"—despite the general understanding that even the most developed countries are still undergoing development. Dividing countries into "less developed" and "more developed" does not help much, because it is unclear where to

What problems are associated with dividing countries into "developed" and "developing"?

Map 2.1	Gross national product per capita, 1999

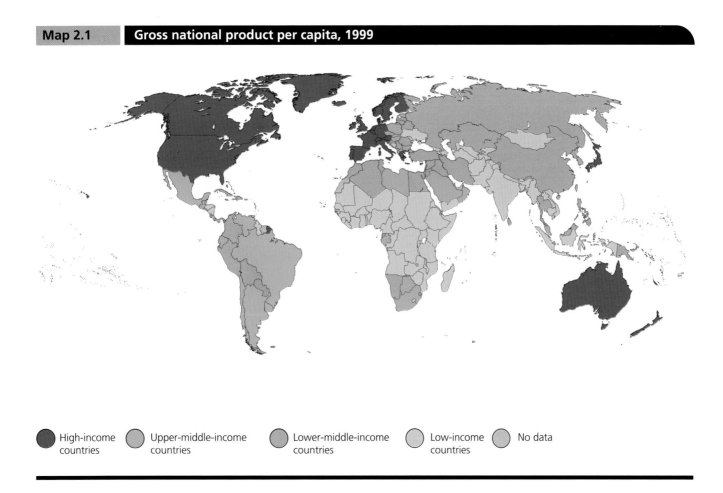

High-income countries   Upper-middle-income countries   Lower-middle-income countries   Low-income countries   No data

draw the line between the two groups. In the absence of a single criterion of a country's development, such divisions can only be based on convention among researchers. For example, it is conventional in the World Bank to refer to low-income and middle-income countries as "developing," and to refer to high-income countries as "industrial" or "developed."

The relatively accurate classification of countries into "developing" and "developed" based on their per capita income does not, however, work well in all cases. There is, for instance, a group of "high-income developing countries" that includes Israel, Kuwait, Singapore, and the United Arab Emirates. These countries are considered developing because of their economic structure or because of the official opinion of their govern-

ments, although their incomes formally place them among developed countries.

Another challenge is presented by many of the countries with "transition" or "formerly planned" economies—that is, countries undergoing a transition from centrally planned to market economies. On the one hand, none of these countries has achieved the established threshold of high per capita income. But on the other, many of them are highly industrialized. This is one reason their classification by the World Bank is currently "under review." Note that in the World Bank's *World Development Report 1982* these same countries were classified as "industrial nonmarket," and in current United Nations publications most of them are still grouped among "industrial" countries.

3

World Population Growth

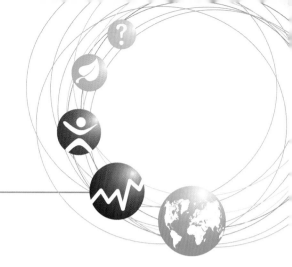

Population dynamics are one of the key factors to consider when thinking about development. In the past 50 years the world has experienced an unprecedented increase in population (see Fig. 3.1). Do you know why?

A "natural population increase" occurs when the **birth rate** is higher than the **death rate.** While a country's **population growth rate** depends on the natural increase *and* on migration, global population growth is determined exclusively by the natural increase.

Around the world, death rates gradually decreased in the late 19th and the 20th centuries, with death rates in **developing countries** plummeting after World War II thanks to the spread of modern medicine that allowed control of infectious diseases. In much of the developing world the decline in death rates preceded the decline in birth rates by 20 years or more (see Fig. 3.2), resulting in record-high rates of population growth of 3 percent or even 4 percent a year. Since the 1960s birth rates have also been declining rapidly in most developing countries except those in Sub-Saharan Africa and the Middle East. This decrease in birth rates in the developing world is even more rapid than that characteristic of Europe and the United States in the 19th century.

Why is world population growing faster than ever before? When will it stabilize?

| Figure 3.1 | World population, 1750–2050 |

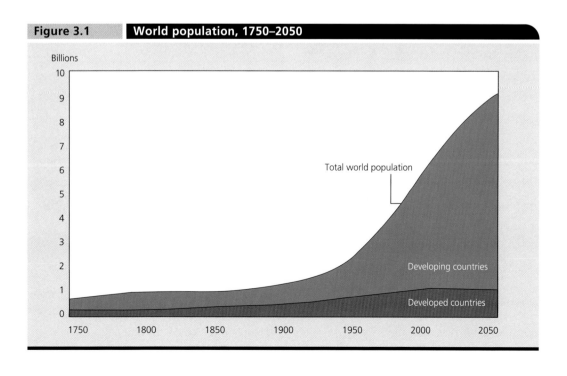

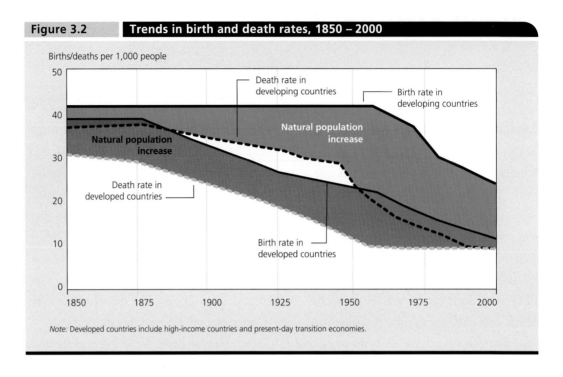

Figure 3.2   **Trends in birth and death rates, 1850 – 2000**

Births/deaths per 1,000 people

Death rate in developing countries

Birth rate in developing countries

Natural population increase

Natural population increase

Death rate in developed countries

Birth rate in developed countries

Note: Developed countries include high-income countries and present-day transition economies.

Today's low-income countries still have the world's highest birth rates (see Map 3.1), although women tend to have fewer children than before. The reasons for lower **fertility** are varied, but most are related to developing countries' **economic growth** and development (see Fig. 3.3; see also Chapters 4, 7, 8). Parents choose to have smaller families when health conditions improve because they no longer have to fear that many of their babies might die, and when they do not have to rely on their children to work on the family farm or business or to take care of them in their old age. In addition, more parents are sending their daughters to school, which is important because women with basic education tend to produce healthier children and smaller families. More women now have opportunities to work outside the home, so they are starting their families later and having fewer children. On top of all that, access to modern contraceptives for family planning is improving, making it easier for parents to control the number and spacing of their children.

Lower fertility rate does not immediately lead to lower birth rate and lower population growth rate if a country has a larger proportion of men and women in their reproductive years than before. Population growth caused by more women giving birth even though each has the same number of or fewer children is called "population momentum." Population momentum is particularly significant in developing countries that had the highest fertility rates 20 to 30 years ago.

Map 3.1 **Population growth rates, 1990–1999**

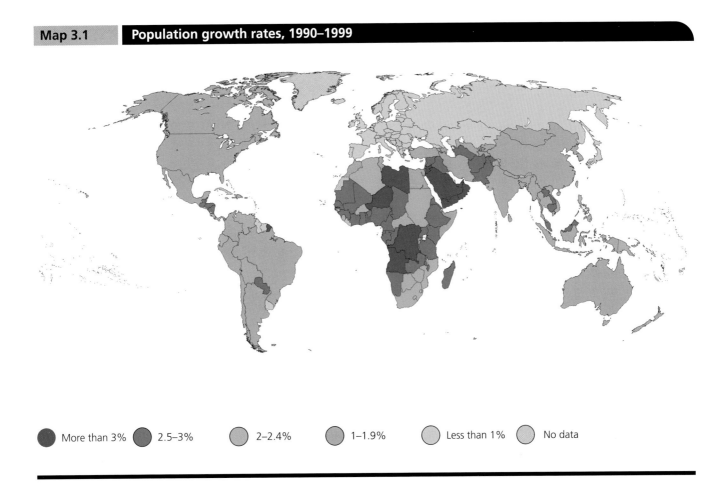

● More than 3%　● 2.5–3%　● 2–2.4%　● 1–1.9%　○ Less than 1%　○ No data

The decline in birth rates over the past few decades has lowered population growth rates in developing countries despite a continuing decline in death rates. Population growth is even slower in **developed countries** (see Fig. 3.4). Stabilizing birth rates and increasing death rates (the latter being a result of aging populations, see Chapter 8) have already led to a natural population decrease in Italy and Germany. Japan and Spain are expected to follow soon. (see birth rates and death rates in Data Table 1).

The formerly socialist countries of Central and Eastern Europe present a major exception to the broad similarity of demographic trends in developed and developing countries. The rapid decline in death rates that occurred in the 1950s and 1960s slowed down in the 1970s and 1980s. In the 1990s death rates actually increased in Russia and some other **transition countries,** including Belarus, Bulgaria, Estonia, Latvia, Lithuania, Moldova, Romania, and Ukraine. In the late 1990s death rates in these middle-income countries exceeded

Why are fertility and population growth rates different in different countries?

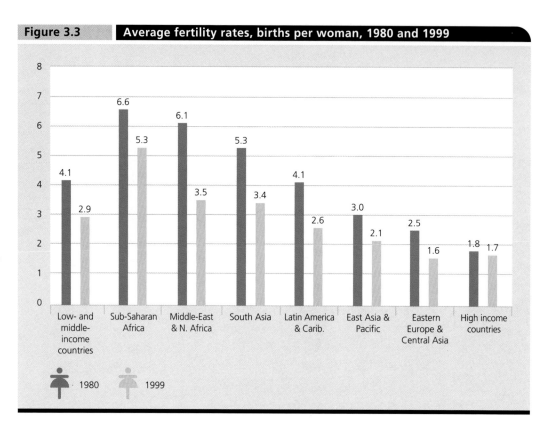

Figure 3.3 | **Average fertility rates, births per woman, 1980 and 1999**

🔴 1980   🔵 1999

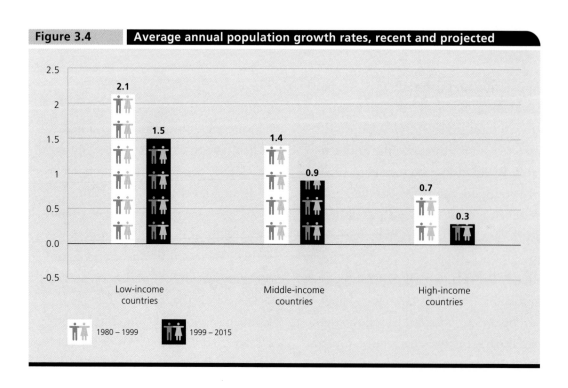

Figure 3.4 | **Average annual population growth rates, recent and projected**

1980 – 1999   1999 – 2015

the average death rate for low-income countries and approached the rates in Sub-Saharan Africa.

This dramatic and historically unprecedented reversal in mortality trends is primarily explained by higher adult male mortality: among older men mainly because of the increase in cardiovascular disease, among younger men because of more accidents, suicides, and murders. Many of these factors can be related to stress and substance abuse (heavy drinking and smoking), which in turn can be linked to the increased unemployment, worsening living conditions, and greater economic uncertainty that have accompanied the transition. But rapid economic reforms have not necessarily been detrimental to people's health in all tran-

sition countries. For example, in the Czech Republic the death rate has continued to decline (see Fig. 3.5), while in Hungary and Poland it has held steady.

Birth rates in the transition countries of Europe have dropped sharply in the past 5 to 10 years, just as the death rates were on the increase. The reasons for that drop are different from those in most developing countries: they are believed to be closely associated with a lower **quality of life** and the uncertainties caused by the social and economic crisis of transition. As a result fertility rates in these countries are now far below the "replacement level" (the level at which population size would become stable, considered to be slightly more than two children per family) and lower than

Why are demographic changes in transition countries of Europe different from those occurring in most developing countries?

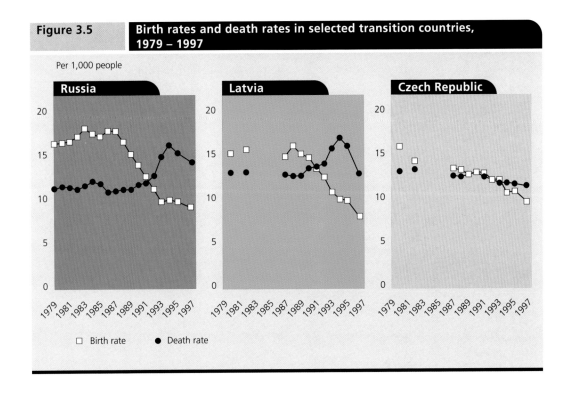

| Figure 3.5 | Birth rates and death rates in selected transition countries, 1979 – 1997 |

Per 1,000 people

Russia • Latvia • Czech Republic

☐ Birth rate   ● Death rate

those in most developed countries (see Fig. 3.3).

Because of these unusual demographic trends—increasing death rates combined with dropping birth rates—many of the transition countries of Europe have already experienced natural decreases in population.

* * *

On the global scale, falling fertility rates already have decreased the population growth rate—from more than 2.0 percent to 1.5 percent a year over the past 30 years. Experts expect this trend to continue, so that by the end of this century the world's population will stabilize at 9 to 10 billion people. But in the meantime, in absolute numbers it is still growing faster than ever before—by about 230,000 people a day. This is happening because of the larger-than-ever population base—in 2000 there were about 6 billion people on earth, about twice as many as in 1970.

The projected increase of the world's population from the current 6 billion to 9-10 billion at the end of the century will be attributable almost entirely to population growth in developing countries. Thus the share of developing countries in the world's population is expected to increase from the current 84 percent to 88 percent or more. Rapid growth of the developing countries' population, particularly in the next 50 years, poses many economic, social, and environmental challenges, not only for these countries but also for the entire global community. Whether these additional billions of people get access to adequate education and health services, are able to find gainful employment, and manage to avoid poverty and hunger will be critical for the possibility of global sustainable development.

4

Economic Growth Rates

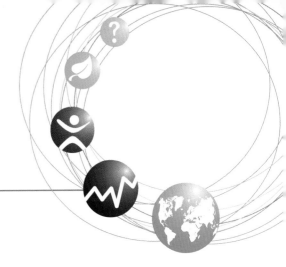

GDP growth rates in developing countries are on average higher than those in developed countries. Over the 1965-99 period, the average annual growth rate was 4.1 percent in low-income countries, 4.2 percent in middle-income countries, and 3.2 percent in high-income countries (see Fig. 4.1). So does this mean that the poor countries will soon catch up with the rich?

Unfortunately, the growth patterns described above do not mean that the world is on its way to "convergence"— that is, to the gradual elimination of the development gap between rich and poor

countries. Much faster population growth in most developing countries is offsetting comparatively faster GDP growth, causing GDP per capita growth rates in these countries to be relatively low or even negative (see Fig. 4.1; Map 4.1; Data Table 1).

As a result the gulf between the average GNP per capita in developing and developed countries continues to widen. In the last 40 years of the 20th century, the gap between the average income of the richest 20 countries and that of the poorest 20 countries doubled in size, with the wealthiest group reaching a level more than 30

Will the poor countries catch up with the rich?

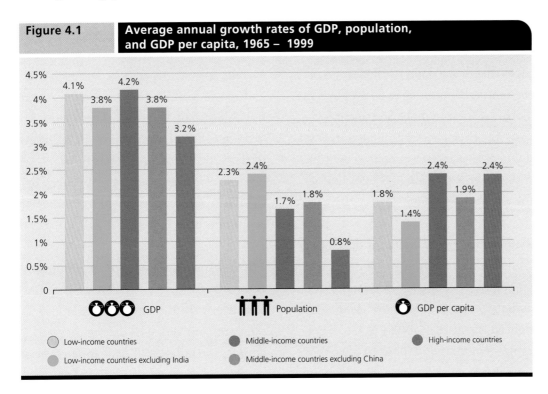

| Figure 4.1 | Average annual growth rates of GDP, population, and GDP per capita, 1965 – 1999 |

- ○ Low-income countries
- ○ Low-income countries excluding India
- ● Middle-income countries
- ● Middle-income countries excluding China
- ● High-income countries

| Map 4.1 | GDP per capita growth rates, 1990–1999 |

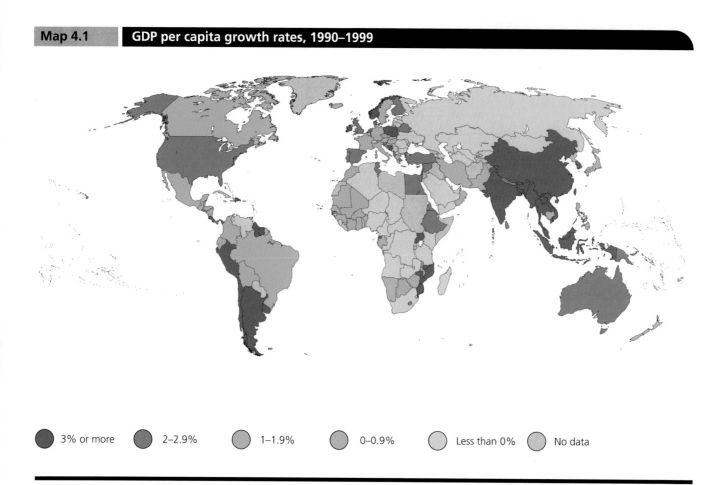

● 3% or more   ● 2–2.9%   ● 1–1.9%   ● 0–0.9%   ○ Less than 0%   ○ No data

times that of the poorest. By the end of the century, of more than $29 trillion in global GDP, only about $6 trillion—less than 22 percent—was generated in developing countries, even though these countries accounted for about 85 percent of the world's population.

The average growth data for developing countries also mask growing disparities among these countries. Between 1990 and 1999 East Asia and the Pacific experienced the fastest growth of GDP per capita—more than 6 percent a year. At the same time in Sub-Saharan Africa the average annual growth rate was negative, and in the Middle East and North Africa it was less than 1 percent. The biggest drop in GDP per capita growth occurred in Eastern Europe and Central Asia because of the economic crisis caused by the transition from planned to market economies (see Fig. 4.2).

The news is not all bad for developing countries, however. The two developing countries with the biggest populations did comparatively well during the past decade. In India GDP per capita grew by about 2.4 percent a year, and in

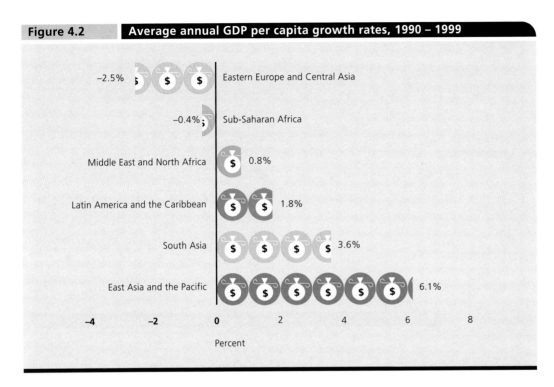

Figure 4.2 — **Average annual GDP per capita growth rates, 1990 – 1999**

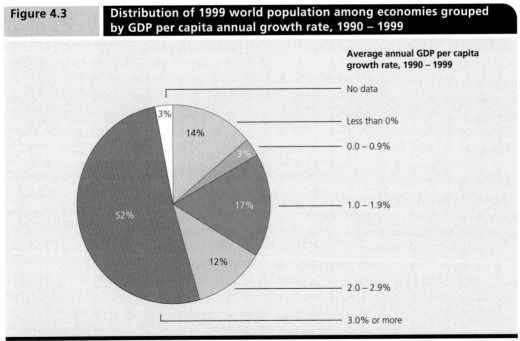

Figure 4.3 — **Distribution of 1999 world population among economies grouped by GDP per capita annual growth rate, 1990 – 1999**

China by an unprecedented 6.4 percent a year. Rapid growth rates in China and India explain why almost two-thirds of the world's population live in economies growing faster than 2 percent a year (see Fig. 4.3). But if India is excluded from the group of low-income countries and China is excluded from the group of

How has the economic gap between developed and developing countries changed over the past few decades?

middle-income countries, average annual growth rates in these groups become considerably lower than in high-income countries (see Fig. 4.1). During the last decade of the 20th century 54 developing countries had negative average growth rates, and most of those with positive growth rates were growing slower than high-income countries (see Map 4.1 and Data Table 1).

Between 1965 and 1995 the gap between developed countries and most

developing countries widened considerably (see Fig. 4.4). Asia was the only major region to achieve significant convergence toward the developed countries' level of GNP per capita. Per capita income in the newly industrialized economies of Asia—Hong Kong (China), the Republic of Korea, Singapore, and Taiwan (China)—increased from 18 percent of the developed country average in 1965 to 66 percent in 1995. At the same time Africa, for instance, became even poorer

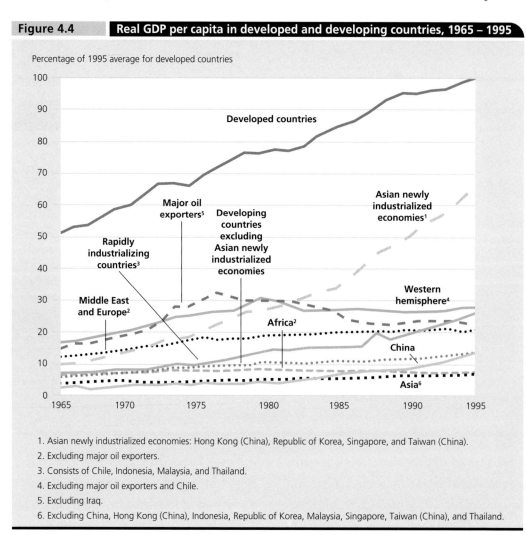

Figure 4.4   **Real GDP per capita in developed and developing countries, 1965 – 1995**

Percentage of 1995 average for developed countries

1. Asian newly industrialized economies: Hong Kong (China), Republic of Korea, Singapore, and Taiwan (China).
2. Excluding major oil exporters.
3. Consists of Chile, Indonesia, Malaysia, and Thailand.
4. Excluding major oil exporters and Chile.
5. Excluding Iraq.
6. Excluding China, Hong Kong (China), Indonesia, Republic of Korea, Malaysia, Singapore, Taiwan (China), and Thailand.

in relative terms. The average per capita income in African countries equaled 14 percent of the developed country level in 1965 and just 7 percent in 1995. Even though Figure 4.4 does not cover the second half of the 1990s, you can still find the approximate position of your country in it, using Data Table 1 in the back of this book (see the PPP estimate of GNP per capita in your country as of 1999 and use the average of $24,930 for GNP per capita in developed countries).

Based on existing trends, only about 10 developing countries—those with GNP per capita growth rates more than 1 percentage point higher than the average for developed countries—can look forward to catching up with developed countries within the next hundred years. And those 10 countries will catch up only if they can maintain their high growth rates. Doing so will be a challenge. In fact, the poorer a country is, the harder it is to maintain the high volume of investment needed for its economic growth (see Chapter 6).

Sustained economic growth in developing countries is a critical tool for reducing poverty and improving most people's **standard of living.** But economic growth alone is not enough. In some countries poverty worsened in spite of overall economic growth, owing to increased income inequality (see Chapter 5). Such economic growth can be socially unsustainable—leading to social stress and conflict, detrimental to further growth. In addition, fast economic growth can lead to fast environmental degradation, lowering people's **quality of life** and eventually reducing economic **productivity** (see Chapter 10 and Chapter 14). Consider the fact that, if the global economy continues to grow by 3 percent a year for the next 50 years, the total global GDP will more than quadruple. Whether such a drastic increase in human economic activity will be compatible with the requirements of environmental and social sustainability will depend on the "quality of growth," on the proper balancing of economic goals with environmental and social goals (see Fig.1.2 and Chapter 16).

Will further economic growth be environmentally and socially sustainable?

5

Income Inequality

How does income inequality affect poverty and quality of life in a country?

To begin to understand what life is like in a country—to know, for example, how many of its inhabitants are poor—it is not enough to know that country's per capita income. The number of poor people in a country and the average **quality of life** also depend on how equally—or unequally—income is distributed.

Cross-country Comparisons of Income Inequality

In Brazil and Hungary, for example, the GNP per capita levels are rather close, but the incidence of poverty in Brazil is higher. The reason for this difference can

be understood with the help of Figure 5.1, which shows the percentages of national income received by equal percentiles of individuals or households ranked by their income levels.

In Hungary the richest 20 percent (quintile) of the population received about 4.5 times more than the poorest quintile, while in Brazil the richest quintile received more than 30 times more than the poorest quintile. Compare these ratios with an average of about 6:1 in high-income countries. In the developing world income inequality, measured the same way, varies by region: 4:1 in South Asia, 6:1 in East Asia and the Middle East

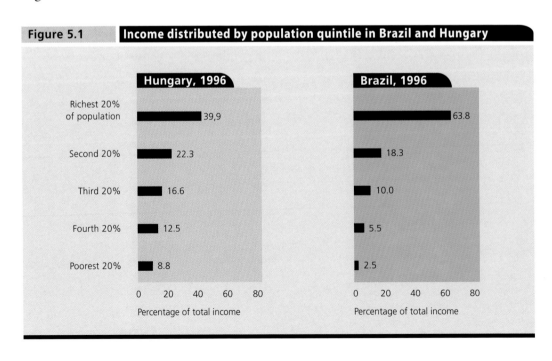

Figure 5.1 — Income distributed by population quintile in Brazil and Hungary

Hungary, 1996

Richest 20% of population	39,9
Second 20%	22.3
Third 20%	16.6
Fourth 20%	12.5
Poorest 20%	8.8

Percentage of total income

Brazil, 1996

Richest 20% of population	63.8
Second 20%	18.3
Third 20%	10.0
Fourth 20%	5.5
Poorest 20%	2.5

Percentage of total income

and North Africa, 10:1 in Sub-Saharan Africa, and 12:1 in Latin America.

Lorenz Curves and Gini Indexes

To measure income inequality in a country and compare this phenomenon among countries more accurately, economists use Lorenz curves and Gini indexes. A Lorenz curve plots the cumulative percentages of total income received against the cumulative percentages of recipients, starting with the poorest individual or household (see Fig. 5.2). How do they construct the curve?

First, economists rank all the individuals or households in a country by their income level, from the poorest to the richest. Then all these individuals or

households are divided into 5 groups, 20 percent in each, (or 10 groups, 10 percent in each) and the income of each group is calculated and expressed as a percentage of GDP (see Fig. 5.1). Next, economists plot the shares of GDP received by these groups cumulatively— that is, plotting the income share of the poorest quintile against 20 percent of the population, the income share of the poorest quintile and the next (fourth) quintile against 40 percent of the population, and so on, until they plot the aggregate share of all five quintiles (which equals 100 percent) against 100 percent of the population. After connecting all the points on the chart— starting with the 0 percent share of income received by 0 percent of the population—they get the Lorenz curve for this country.

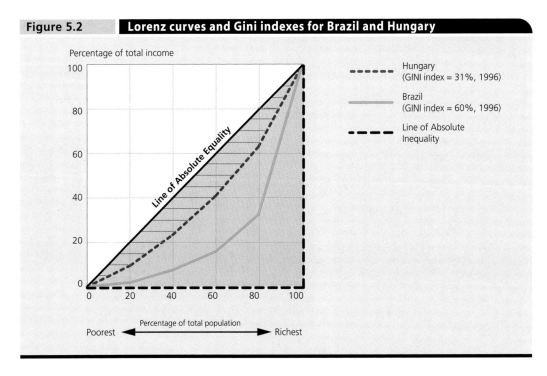

Figure 5.2   Lorenz curves and Gini indexes for Brazil and Hungary

Percentage of total income

Hungary
(GINI index = 31%, 1996)

Brazil
(GINI index = 60%, 1996)

Line of Absolute
Inequality

Line of Absolute Equality

Percentage of total population

Poorest ◄――――► Richest

Is a more equal distribution of income good or bad for a country's development?

The deeper a country's Lorenz curve, the less equal its income distribution. For comparison, see in Figure 5.2 the "curve" of absolutely equal income distribution. Under such a distribution pattern, the first 20 percent of the population would receive exactly 20 percent of the income, 40 percent of the population would receive 40 percent of the income, and so on. The corresponding Lorenz curve would therefore be a straight line going from the lower left corner of the figure (x = 0 percent, y = 0 percent) to the upper right corner (x = 100 percent, y = 100 percent). Figure 5.2 shows that Brazil's Lorenz curve deviates from the hypothetical line of absolute equality much further than that of Hungary. This means that of these two countries Brazil has the higher income inequality.

A Gini index is even more convenient than a Lorenz curve when the task is to compare income inequality among many countries. The index is calculated as the area between a Lorenz curve and the line of absolute equality, expressed as a percentage of the triangle under the line (see the two shaded areas in Fig. 5.2). Thus a Gini index of 0 percent represents perfect equality—the Lorenz curve coincides with the straight line of absolute equality. A Gini index of 100 implies perfect inequality—the Lorenz curve coincides with the x axis and goes straight upward against the last entry (that is, the richest individual or household; see the thick dotted line in Figure 5.2). In reality, neither perfect equality nor perfect inequality is possible. Thus Gini indexes are always greater than 0 percent but less than 100 percent (see Fig. 5.3 and Data Table 1).

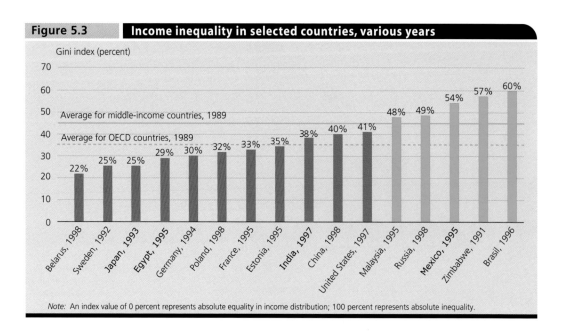

Figure 5.3 — **Income inequality in selected countries, various years**

Gini index (percent)

Average for middle-income countries, 1989

Average for OECD countries, 1989

Belarus, 1998 — 22%; Sweden, 1992 — 25%; Japan, 1993 — 25%; Egypt, 1995 — 29%; Germany, 1994 — 30%; Poland, 1998 — 32%; France, 1995 — 33%; Estonia, 1995 — 35%; India, 1997 — 38%; China, 1998 — 40%; United States, 1997 — 41%; Malaysia, 1995 — 48%; Russia, 1998 — 49%; Mexico, 1995 — 54%; Zimbabwe, 1991 — 57%; Brasil, 1996 — 60%

Note: An index value of 0 percent represents absolute equality in income distribution; 100 percent represents absolute inequality.

Costs and Benefits of Income Inequality

Is a less equal distribution of income good or bad for a country's development? There are different opinions about the best pattern of distribution—about whether, for example, the Gini index should be closer to 25 percent (as in Sweden) or to 40 percent (as in the United States). Consider the following arguments.

An excessively equal income distribution can be bad for economic efficiency. Take, for example, the experience of socialist countries, where deliberately low inequality (with no private profits and minimal differences in wages and salaries) deprived people of the incentives needed for their active participation in economic activities—for diligent work and vigorous entrepreneurship. Among the consequences of socialist equalization of incomes were poor discipline and low initiative among workers, poor quality and limited selection of goods and services, slow technical progress, and eventually, slower economic growth leading to more poverty.

In many high-income countries relatively low inequality of incomes is achieved with the help of considerable **transfer payments** from the government budget. However, economists often argue that mitigating inequality by increasing the burden of government taxes tends to discourage **investment,** slow **economic growth,** and undermine a country's international competitiveness.

On the other hand, excessive inequality adversely affects people's quality of life, leading to a higher incidence of poverty, impeding progress in health and education, and contributing to crime. Think also about the following effects of high income inequality on some major factors of economic growth and development:

- High inequality reduces the pool of people with access to the resources—such as land or education—needed to unleash their full productive potential. Thus a country deprives itself of the contributions the poor could make to its economic and social development.
- High inequality threatens a country's political stability because more people are dissatisfied with their economic status, which makes it harder to reach political consensus among population groups with higher and lower incomes. Political instability increases the risks of investing in a country and so significantly undermines its development potential (see Chapter 6).
- High inequality may discourage certain basic norms of behavior among economic agents (individuals or enterprises) such as trust and commitment. Higher business risks and higher costs of contract enforcement impede economic growth by slowing down all economic transactions.

- High inequality limits the use of important market instruments such as changes in prices and fines. For example, higher rates for electricity and hot water might promote energy **efficiency** (see Chapter 15), but in the face of serious inequality, governments introducing even slightly higher rates risk causing extreme deprivation among the poorest citizens.

These are among the reasons why some international experts recommend decreasing income inequality in developing countries to help accelerate economic and human development. But the simple fact that high levels of income inequality tend to strike many people as unfair, especially when they imply starkly different opportunities available to children born in the same country, also matters for sustainable development. After all, how can people care about the needs of future generations if they don't care about people living today?

6

Poverty and Hunger

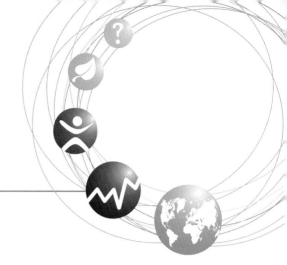

The Nature of Poverty

Poverty is pronounced deprivation of well-being. But what is "deprivation," and how can it be measured? Traditionally poverty was understood primarily as material deprivation, as living with low income and low consumption, characterized primarily by poor nutrition and poor living conditions. However, it is easy to observe that income poverty in most cases is associated with so-called human poverty—the low health and education levels that are either the cause or the result of low income. Income and human poverty also tend to be accompanied by such social deprivations as high vulnerability to adverse events (for example, disease, economic crisis, or natural disaster), voicelessness in most of society's institutions, and powerlessness to improve one's living circumstances. This multidimensional nature of poverty is revealed by interviews with the poor themselves and confirmed by special sociological studies.

The broader definition of poverty as a multidimensional phenomenon leads to a clearer understanding of its causes and to a more comprehensive policy aimed at poverty reduction. For example, in addition to the issues of **economic growth** and income distribution, it brings to the fore equitable access to health and education services and development of social security systems. Poverty reduction strategies also must allow for the fact that different aspects of poverty interact and reinforce each other. For example, improving social security not only makes poor people feel less vulnerable, but also allows them to take advantage of higher-risk opportunities, such as moving to another location or changing qualifications. And increasing poor people's representation and participation not only helps them overcome the feeling of being excluded from society, but also contributes to better targeting of public health and education services.

Note that this chapter is devoted only to income poverty and hunger while the other dimensions of poverty are discussed, in more or less detail, in some of the following chapters.

Measures of income poverty are different in different countries. Generally speaking, the richer a country is, the higher its national poverty line. To allow for international comparisons, the World Bank has established an international poverty line of $1 a day per person in 1985 **purchasing power parity** (PPP) prices, which is equivalent to $1.08 a day per person in

What is poverty? How can poverty in different countries be compared?

1993 PPP prices. According to this measure, the portion of extremely poor people in the world's population—those living on less than $1 a day—fell between 1990 and 1999, from 29 percent to 23 percent. But, owing to the fast growth of the world's population, the absolute number of people living in extreme poverty decreased by only 123 million in that time period. For **middle-income countries,** an international poverty line of $2 a day, $2.15 in 1993 PPP prices, is closer to a practical minimum. Of the 6 billion people living on Earth at the end of the 20th century, almost half—about 2.8 billion—lived on less than $2 a day, and about one-fifth—1.2 billion—lived on less than $1.

The Geography of Poverty

Most of the world's poor live in South Asia (over 40 percent), Sub-Saharan Africa (almost 25 percent), and East Asia (about 23 percent). Almost half of the world's poor live in just two large countries—China and India.

The highest incidence of poverty is observed in Sub-Saharan Africa, with almost half of its population living below the $1 poverty line (see Data Table 2). Sub-Saharan Africa is followed by South Asia, where over the 1990s the incidence of poverty went down from about 41 percent to about 32 percent (see Fig. 6.1), although the absolute

number of poor people decreased very modestly. Using Map 6.1 and Data Table 2, you can identify the **developing countries** with the highest percentages of their population living below the international poverty line.

Analysts have found a strong positive relationship between economic growth and poverty reduction. For example, East Asia (including China), which contains the world's fastest-growing economies, reduced the share of its population living below the international poverty line from about 29 percent in 1990 to about 15 percent in 2000. In China alone, nearly 150 million people were lifted out of

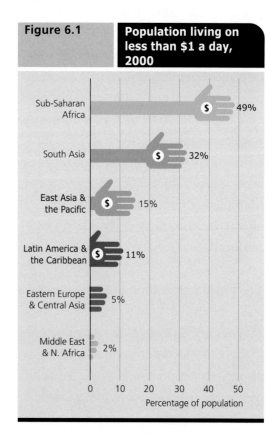

Figure 6.1 Population living on less than $1 a day, 2000

Sub-Saharan Africa — 49%
South Asia — 32%
East Asia & the Pacific — 15%
Latin America & the Caribbean — 11%
Eastern Europe & Central Asia — 5%
Middle East & N. Africa — 2%

Percentage of population

Map 6.1 | **Percentage of population living on less than US$1 a day, 1985–1998**

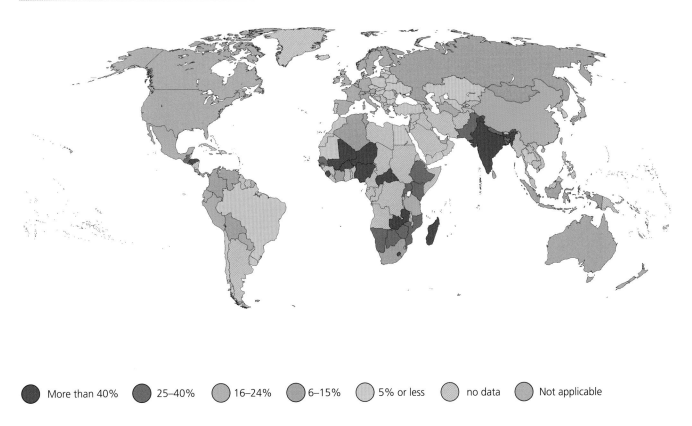

More than 40%　　25–40%　　16–24%　　6–15%　　5% or less　　no data　　Not applicable

poverty. But in Sub-Saharan Africa, where negative growth of **GNP per capita** predominated during that period, both the incidence of poverty and the absolute number of poor people increased—from 47 percent to 49 percent and by 74 million. In relative terms, the fastest growth of poverty took place in the region of Eastern Europe and Central Asia that lived through the acute economic recession associated with market-oriented reforms. Between 1987 and 1998, the incidence of poverty in this region increased from 0.2 percent to 5.1 percent and the number of poor people from about 1 million to 24 million.

The Vicious Circle of Poverty

Economists generally assume that people's willingness to save for future consumption grows with their incomes. It seems natural that the poorer people are, the less they can afford to plan for the future and save. Thus in poor countries, where most incomes have to be spent to meet current—often urgent—needs, national **saving** rates tend to be lower. In combination with the small size of poor countries' economies, lower saving rates account for a much smaller pool of savings available for desperately needed domestic **investment** in both

Can poor countries break the vicious circle of poverty?

physical capital and **human capital.** For example, Sub-Saharan Africa consistently has the lowest saving rate and the smallest pool of savings. By contrast, high-income countries in 1996–2000 saved a smaller share of their GDP than some developing countries, but their pool of savings was about three times as large as all the savings of developing countries combined (see Fig. 6.2). But without new investment, an economy's **productivity** cannot be increased and incomes cannot be raised. That closes the vicious circle of poverty (see Fig. 6.3). So are poor countries doomed to remain poor?

The data on saving and investment in East Asia over the past two decades suggest that the answer is no. Despite low initial GNP per capita, the rates of **gross domestic saving** and **gross domestic investment** in the region were higher than in any other region and resulted in some of the highest economic growth rates (see Fig. 6.2 and Fig. 4.4). Experts are still trying to explain this phenomenon. Generally speaking, however, many of the factors that encourage people to save and invest are well known. They include political and economic stability, a reliable banking system, and favorable government policy.

In addition to domestic investment, foreign investment can help developing countries break out of the vicious circle of poverty, particularly if such investment is accompanied by transfers of

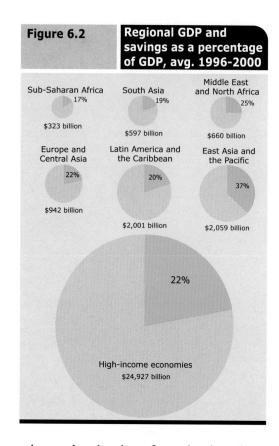

Figure 6.2 — Regional GDP and savings as a percentage of GDP, avg. 1996-2000

Sub-Saharan Africa 17% — $323 billion

South Asia 19% — $597 billion

Middle East and North Africa 25% — $660 billion

Europe and Central Asia 22% — $942 billion

Latin America and the Caribbean 20% — $2,001 billion

East Asia and the Pacific 37% — $2,059 billion

High-income economies 22% — $24,927 billion

advanced technology from developed countries. The opportunity to benefit from foreign investment and technology is sometimes referred to as the "advantage of backwardness," which should (at least theoretically) enable poor countries to develop faster than did today's rich countries. However, many of the conditions needed to attract foreign investment to a country are the same as those needed to stimulate domestic investment.

A favorable *investment climate* includes many factors that make investing in one country more profitable and less risky than in another country. Political stability is one of the most important of these factors. Both domestic and foreign

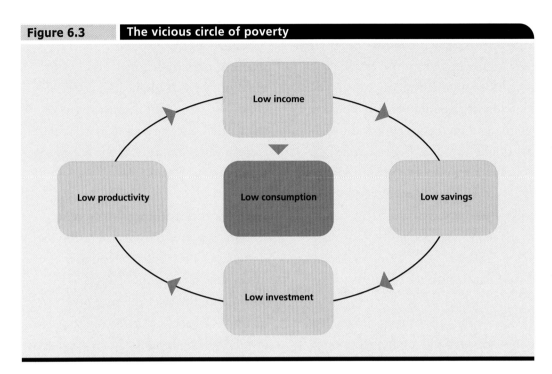

Figure 6.3 — The vicious circle of poverty

What is the relationship between poverty and political instability?

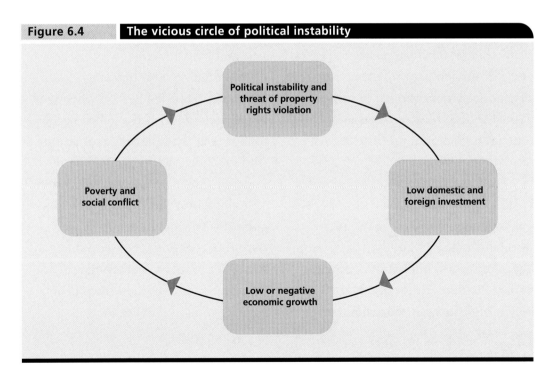

Figure 6.4 — The vicious circle of political instability

investors are discouraged by the threat of political upheaval and by the prospect of a new regime that might impose punitive taxes or expropriate capital assets. As a result a country can fall into another vicious circle, one seen historically in many African and some Latin American countries (see Fig. 6.4).

Political instability scares away new investments, which prevents faster economic growth and improvements in people's economic welfare, causing even more dissatisfaction with the political regime and increasing political instability. Falling into this vicious circle of political instability can seriously impede efforts to boost economic development and reduce poverty.

The Challenge of Hunger

Hunger is the most extreme manifestation of poverty and arguably the most morally unacceptable. In the globalized world of the 21st century, with more than enough food produced to feed all of its 6 billion inhabitants, there are still over 800 million poor suffering from chronic undernourishment (which is more than the entire population of Latin America or Sub-Saharan Africa). According to the recent estimate of the UN Food and Agriculture Organization (FAO), in 1999-2001 there were 842 million undernourished people in the world, including 798 million in developing countries, 34 million in **countries with transition economies,** and 10 million in **high-income countries.** See

Figure 6.5 for the regional distribution of hunger and Data Table 2 for the shares of undernourished adults[1] and malnourished children[2] in individual countries. Note that three-quarters of the world's hungry people live in rural areas and the majority of the hungry are women.

Particularly disturbing is the recent dynamics of world hunger. During the first half of the 1990s the number of undernourished people decreased by 37 million, but over the next 5 years it increased by more than 18 million. The numbers of undernourished have fallen in East Asia and Pacific, but remain high in South Asia and continue to rise in Sub-Saharan Africa and in the Middle East and North Africa. In India, after a decline of 20 million between 1990–1992 and 1995–1997, the number of undernourished climbed by 19 million over the following four years. And in China, where the number of undernourished people was reduced by 58 million over the 1990s, progress is gradually slowing. In countries with transition economies the second half of the 1990s brought another increase in the number of undernourished people, from 25 million to 34 million.

---

[1]Undernourishment means consuming too little food to maintain a normal level of activity. The Food and Agriculture Organization (FAO) sets the average requirement at 1,900 calories a day, although the needs of individuals vary with age, sex, and height. In the FAO's estimation, extreme hunger occurs with a shortfall of more than 300 calories.

[2]Child malnutrition is measured by comparing these children's weight and height with those of well-nourished children of the same age.

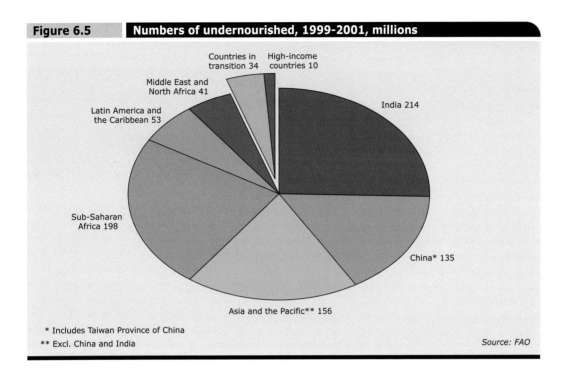

Figure 6.5 — Numbers of undernourished, 1999-2001, millions

Countries in transition 34
High-income countries 10
Middle East and North Africa 41
Latin America and the Caribbean 53
India 214
Sub-Saharan Africa 198
China* 135
Asia and the Pacific** 156

* Includes Taiwan Province of China
** Excl. China and India

Source: FAO

On the surface, the causes of hunger appear to be multiple and to differ among countries. Many hungry people live in countries that lack sufficient arable land or water to feed their growing populations. But there are also many hungry people in other countries, with plentiful **natural capital.** Some of these latter countries specialize in producing and exporting a single agricultural commodity, such as cacao, coffee, or cotton, and suffer from declining prices in the world markets. It is arguable that these same land and water resources could be better used for growing food and making it available to these countries' populations. But still other countries, like Brazil, specialize in exporting those same food products that are desperately needed by their own poor and malnourished.

Statistics show that in the world as a whole there is more than enough food produced to feed all the hungry. Moreover, they also show that countries with smaller proportions of undernourished people tend to be more dependent on food imports than countries with more widespread undernourishment (even though they spend smaller shares of their export earnings on food imports). The conclusion appears to be that persistent hunger is an issue not of insufficient global food production but of extremely unequal distribution among countries as well as within countries. The low export earnings of the poorest countries prevent them from buying enough food in the world markets, but even where food is available inside a country, the poorest of its citizens are often unable to pay for it.

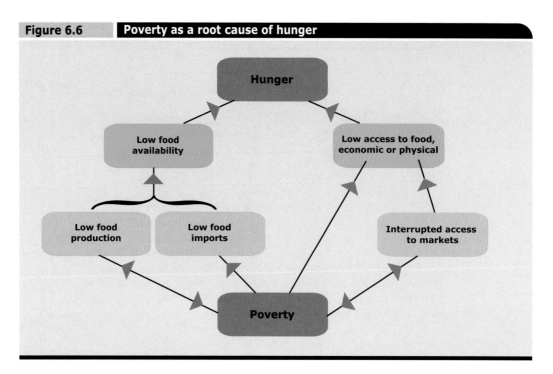

Figure 6.6   **Poverty as a root cause of hunger**

Poverty of countries and extreme poverty of households are the most undisputable causes of hunger.

According to FAO observations, most food emergencies across the world are directly caused by natural disasters (droughts and floods), conflicts, refugees, and economic crises. But is it not poverty that makes people so vulnerable to natural as well as man-made disasters? And is it not poverty that lies at the root of many of these disasters? For example, poverty impedes investment in irrigation that could prevent the disastrous consequences of droughts in many countries. And poverty (low export earnings) hinders the food imports that could compensate for unpredictable nat-

ural emergencies. Poverty breeds conflicts, and many refugees are trying to escape not only violence but also economic deprivation.

But seeing poverty only as a root cause of hunger (see Fig. 6.6) actually oversimplifies the real picture. In fact, poverty is both a cause and a consequence of hunger. Undernourishment is a critical link in the vicious circle of poverty, leading to poor health, lower learning capacity and diminished physical activity, and thus to lower productivity and poverty (see Fig. 6.7).[3] Nearly one-third of poor health outcomes in developing countries are associated with hunger and malnutrition. Malnourishment negatively affects children's school attendance and their educational attain-

---

[3]Think also about other vicious circles of poverty, linked through other aspects of human poverty, such as poor education (Chapter 7) or serious disease (Chapter 8).

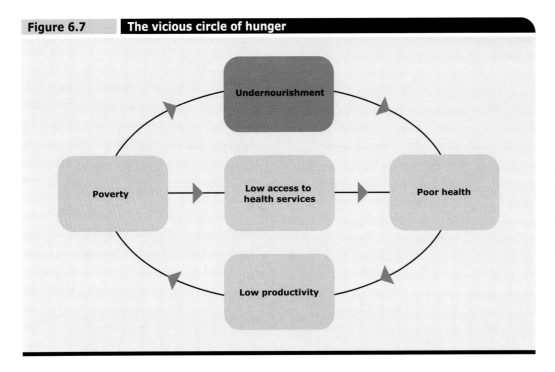

Figure 6.7   The vicious circle of hunger

How can global
hunger be
eliminated
for good?

ment, and the legacy of malnourishment in childhood, combined with insufficient food intake in adulthood, manifests itself in lower wages and reduced earning capacity for adults, who will be unable to support their own families. In addition, malnourished mothers are more likely to give birth to underweight babies. Thus closes an intergenerational vicious circle of malnourishment and poverty, particularly threatening to the social sustainability of national and global development.

So, given the close and complex interaction between hunger and poverty, is there a hope of doing away with hunger—as the most demeaning of human deprivations—any time soon?

Obviously, a lot will depend on the political will and responsibility of

national governments. For example, in Brazil, President Luiz Inácio Lula da Silva has pledged to eradicate hunger by the end of his four-year term and has launched the comprehensive Fome Zero (Zero Hunger) Project. Note that Brazil is one of the major exporters of crops and meat, but over 40 million of its 170 million people live on less than $1 a day.

However, many developing countries may fail to meet the enormous twin challenges of hunger and poverty on their own. The role of the international community is therefore indispensable too. As a practical step, the World Summit on Sustainable Development in Johannesburg (South Africa, August–September 2002) and the United Nations General Assembly (December 2002) called for immediate implementation of the World Solidarity Fund to reinforce the global fight against extreme poverty and hunger. However, perhaps even more important for improving the lot of developing countries' poor and hungry might be pro-poor reforms in international trade, such as those discussed during the Doha round of world trade negotiations (see Chapter 12).

Finally, identifying and committing to the most effective policy measures will be of crucial importance. In the short term, even emergency measures aimed at giving hungry people direct access to the food they need (such as public food distribution or food-for-work programs) may hold important keys to breaking the persistent vicious circle of undernourishment and poverty. But most experts agree that any longer-term and more sustainable solutions should address hunger and poverty simultaneously. For example, environmentally sound irrigation in drought-prone areas can raise the productivity of local agriculture, simultaneously improving the local availability of food and increasing local farmers' incomes (see food availability and economic access to food in Fig. 6.6). Public investment in construction of rural roads can simultaneously improve the physical access of the rural poor to markets (for buying food as well as for selling their outputs, see Fig. 6.6) and create additional jobs outside of agriculture. Government strategies directly attacking such root causes of poverty as unemploy-

ment and landlessness can be most effective in ensuring the sustainable eradication of hunger.

Vietnam appears to be a good example. Economic reforms started in 1986 gave farmers control over land, allowed them to increase sales to the market, reduced agricultural taxation, and increased public investments in rural infrastructure. That allowed Vietnamese farmers to take advantage of improved access to global markets and resulted in the doubling of per capita food production and in even faster growth of agricultural exports. Over the 1990s, agricultural growth helped boost overall economic growth to an average of 7 percent a year and helped reduce the proportion of undernourished people from 27 percent to 19 percent. This shows how rapid economic growth and trade can result in sustainable reductions of poverty and hunger thanks to pro-poor policies and investments.

* * *

FAO Director-General Jaques Diouf appealed to national governments and the international community to create an international Alliance against Hunger that would be based "not on a plea for charity but on . . . recognizing that the suffering of 800 million hungry people represents . . . a threat to economic growth and political stability on a global scale." Would you agree with the logic of this appeal?

7
Education

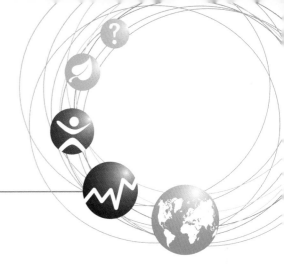

Capital is a stock of wealth used to produce goods and **services.** Most often, by capital people mean physical capital: buildings, machines, technical equipment, stocks of raw materials and goods. But "human capital"—people's abilities, knowledge, and skills—is at least as important for production, and at least as valuable to people who have it. The importance of the "human factor" in modern production is reflected in the distribution of income among people who own physical capital and people who "own" knowledge and skills. For example, in the United States in the 1980s the income received on knowledge and skills (through wages and salaries) was about 14 times that received on physical capital (through dividends and undistributed corporate profits). This phenomenon led economists to acknowledge the existence of **human capital.**

Next, in the 1990s, came the recognition of a new stage in global economic development: the "knowledge economy," knowledge-based and knowledge-driven.[1] This recognition stemmed from the fact that the countries that invested most actively in knowledge creation and adaptation (through investing in research and development activities, R&D) as well as in knowledge dissemination (through investing in education as well as in information and communication technologies, ICT) tended to become most successful in solving their development problems (see Data Table 2). Moreover, it is now widely believed that even poor countries, with insufficient resources to invest in creating new knowledge, can "leapfrog" in their development provided that they succeed in absorbing advanced global knowledge and adapting it for the needs of their developing economies. A well-educated and adaptive population is seen as central to this task.

Education and Human Capital

Most human capital is built up through education or training that increases a person's economic productivity—that is, enables him or her to produce more or more valuable goods and services and thus to earn a higher income. Governments, workers, and employers invest in human capital by devoting money and time to education and training (to accumulating knowledge and skills). Like any other investment, these

How are human capital and physical capital similar? How are they different?

[1] These terms are relatively new and are not yet strictly defined, although many researchers and journalists use them, often interchangeably.

investments in human capital require sacrifices. People agree to make these sacrifices if they expect to be rewarded with additional income in the future.

What are the best ways to build a country's human capital?

Governments spend public funds on education because they believe that a better-educated population will contribute to faster and more sustainable development. Employers pay for employee training because they expect to cover their costs and gain additional profits from increased **productivity.** And individuals are often prepared to spend time and money to get education and training, since in most countries people with better education and skills earn more. Educated and skilled people are usually able to deliver more output or output that is more valuable in the marketplace, and their employers tend to recognize that fact with higher wages.

Economic returns to education are not always the same, however. Returns to education may be lower if:

- The quality of education is low or knowledge and skills acquired at school do not match market demand. In this case investments in human capital were not efficient enough, resulting in less human capital and lower returns to individuals and society.
- There is insufficient demand for human capital because of slow economic growth. In this case workers' human capital may be underused and underrewarded.

- Workers with lower and higher education and skills are deliberately paid similar wages to preserve a relative equality of earnings—as used to happen in centrally planned economies. These distortions in relative wages are being eliminated as part of these countries' transition to market economies.

The national stock of human capital and its rate of increase are critical to a country's level and rate of economic development, primarily because these are important determinants of a country's ability to produce and adopt technological innovations. But investing in human capital, although extremely important, is not sufficient for rapid economic growth. Such investment must be accompanied by the right development strategy.

Consider the Philippines and Vietnam. In both countries adult literacy is higher than in most other Southeast Asian countries (see Data Table 2). Nevertheless, until recently both countries were growing relatively slowly, largely because of development strategies that prevented them from taking full advantage of their stock of human capital. In Vietnam central planning stood in the way, and in the Philippines economic isolation from the global market was to blame. In recent years, however, both countries have realized a return on their investments in human capital—Vietnam by adopting a more market-based approach to development and radically improving its growth rate, and the Philippines by "exporting" many of its educated workers and "importing" their foreign exchange earnings.

Most governments are playing an increasingly active role in providing education (see Map 7.1 and Data Table 2). Differences in public spending on education (relative to GDP) across countries reflect differences in government efforts to increase national stocks of human capital. Governments of developing countries devote a larger share of their

GDP to education today than they did in 1980. But this share is still smaller than that in developed countries: 3.3 percent of GDP in low-income countries and 4.8 percent in middle-income counties compared with 5.4 percent in high-income countries. Using Data Tables 1 and 2, you can calculate the absolute gap between per capita public spending on education in developed and developing countries. This gap is an important manifestation of the vicious circle of poverty described in Chapter 6: low per capita income inhibits investment in human (as well as physical)

Map 7.1 **Public expenditure on education, percent of GNP, 1997**

More than 8%   6–8%   4–5.9%   2–3.9%   Less than 2%   No data

capital, slows productivity growth, and so prevents per capita income from increasing significantly.

Data on public education spending do not, however, paint a complete picture of investment in human capital because in many countries private spending on education is considerable. Around the world, the difference between public and private spending on education varies enormously and does not seem to be correlated with a country's average income. Among low-income countries, for example, the share of private spending on education ranges from about 20 percent in Sri Lanka to 60 percent in Uganda and Vietnam, while among high-income countries it ranges from 5 percent in Austria to 50 percent in Switzerland.

There are, however, certain patterns in the balance between public and private spending on different levels of education. Most governments are committed to providing free primary and often secondary education because it is believed that not just individuals but the entire country benefits significantly when most of its citizens can read, write, and fully participate in social and economic life. At the same time, tertiary education institutions, both private and public, usually charge tuition, because more of the benefits from this level of education are believed to accrue to graduates (in the form of much higher future earnings) rather than to society at large.

In vocational education, employers often play an important role in providing on-the-job training for employees and in financing training in vocational schools. Governments try to encourage employers' involvement in order to save public funds and to link vocational education to the needs of the labor market. Specific work skills are best developed through training during employment, especially in jobs involving substantial technological change.

Public financing of vocational training is generally considered justified when employer training capacity is weak (as in small and medium-size firms) or absent (as with retraining for unemployed workers). High-quality general pre-employment education is the best guarantee of an individual's ability to learn new skills throughout a career and of employers' willingness to invest in that individual's professional training. Most importantly, employees must be able to communicate clearly in writing and to use mathematics and science skills to diagnose and solve problems.

Primary Education and Literacy

Attending primary school helps children acquire basic literacy and numeracy as well as other knowledge and skills needed for their future education. In low-income countries primary education in itself often improves the welfare of the poor by making them more productive workers, enabling them to learn new skills throughout their working lives, and reducing the risk of unemployment. In addition, primary education—especially for girls and women—leads to healthier and smaller families and fewer infant deaths.

Despite rapid growth in the number of children of primary school age, since 1970 developing countries have succeeded in considerably increasing the percentage of children enrolled in primary school (see Fig. 7.1). But universal primary education, a goal being pursued by most governments of developing countries, is still far from being achieved in many of them (see Data Table 2). Low enrollments in many low-income countries may signal inadequacies in education system capacity as well as social conditions that prevent children from enrolling.

Because economic and social returns to society are known to be higher for primary education than for other levels of study, most governments are committed to providing free access to primary school to all children. But in low-income countries the public funds available for this purpose are often insufficient to meet the increasing demand of rapidly growing populations. These funds also tend to be allocated inequitably, with better education opportunities often provided to urban children relative to rural children, to well-off children relative to poor children, and to boys relative to girls.

Even when primary education is accessible, poor children may be unable to benefit from it. Many of these children must work rather than attend school. Premature and extensive involvement in work damages their health and impedes development of their social skills, decreasing their

For low-income countries, what are the main obstacles to universal primary education?

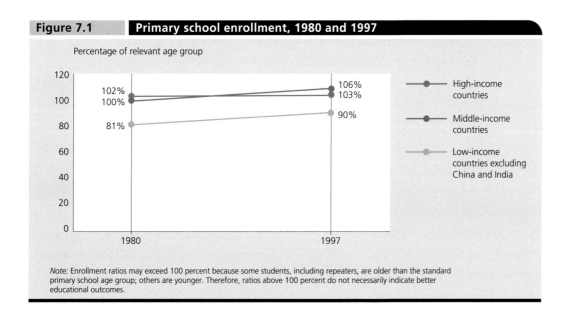

Figure 7.1   **Primary school enrollment, 1980 and 1997**

Percentage of relevant age group

High-income countries

Middle-income countries

Low-income countries excluding China and India

Note: Enrollment ratios may exceed 100 percent because some students, including repeaters, are older than the standard primary school age group; others are younger. Therefore, ratios above 100 percent do not necessarily indicate better educational outcomes.

future earning power as adults and perpetuating the vicious circle of poverty.

In addition, primary school enrollments are generally lower for girls than for boys. This gender gap is widest in South Asia, Sub-Saharan Africa, and the Middle East. The only developing region that has already managed to do away with the gender gap in primary (and even secondary) education is Latin America and the Caribbean (see Data Table 2). The persistent gender gap in education reflects cultural norms, early childbearing, and limited employment opportunities for women, as well as traditional expectations of girls' larger contribution to household work. As a result, of the 900 million adults in developing countries who are illiterate (nearly one in three), almost two-thirds are women (see Fig. 7.2).

Note that child labor is known to be a poverty issue—that is, its incidence declines as per capita income rises. That means that further economic growth will tend to remove this obstacle to universal primary education. By contrast, gender disparities in school enrollments are not correlated with overall living standards, so countries do not just "grow out of them." Narrowing the gender gap requires supportive national policies, such as reducing the direct and indirect costs of girls' schooling for their parents and building more schools for girls in education systems that are segregated by sex.

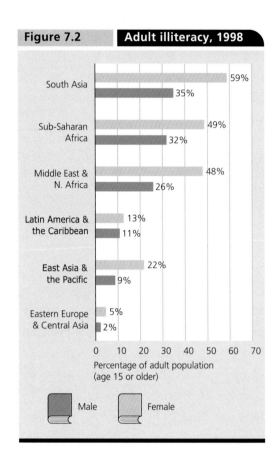

Figure 7.2 **Adult illiteracy, 1998**

Percentage of adult population (age 15 or older)

Male   Female

Issues in Secondary and Tertiary Education

In most developing countries enrollment in secondary schools is much lower than in primary schools (see Data Table 2). Although the situation has been improving over the past few decades, on average less than 60 percent of children of secondary school age in low- and middle-income countries are enrolled, while in high-income countries secondary education has become almost universal (see Fig. 7.3). Among the world's regions, Sub-Saharan Africa has the largest share of children not enrolled in secondary school. Check Data Table 2 for the indi-

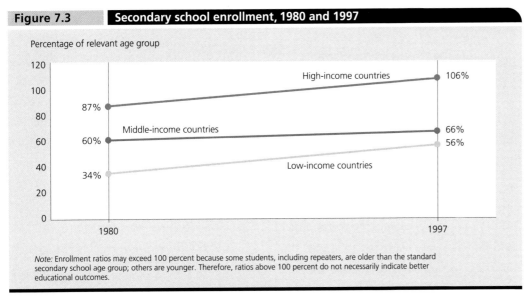

Figure 7.3 — Secondary school enrollment, 1980 and 1997

Percentage of relevant age group

High-income countries: 87% (1980) → 106% (1997)
Middle-income countries: 60% (1980) → 66% (1997)
Low-income countries: 34% (1980) → 56% (1997)

Note: Enrollment ratios may exceed 100 percent because some students, including repeaters, are older than the standard secondary school age group; others are younger. Therefore, ratios above 100 percent do not necessarily indicate better educational outcomes.

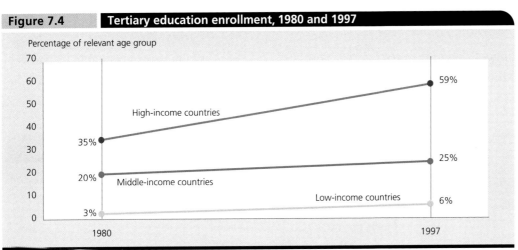

Figure 7.4 — Tertiary education enrollment, 1980 and 1997

Percentage of relevant age group

High-income countries: 35% (1980) → 59% (1997)
Middle-income countries: 20% (1980) → 25% (1997)
Low-income countries: 3% (1980) → 6% (1997)

How does a country's economic position affect its education needs?

cator of child labor incidence—that is, the percentage of children in the 10–14 age range who work. Note that this indicator too is highest in Sub-Saharan Africa. Child labor remains the most formidable obstacle to education for children in low-income countries. According to available data, almost one-third of children in the 10–14 age range are in the labor force in low-income countries (excluding China and India), while in

many Sub-Saharan countries this proportion is one-half. In fact, the situation may be even worse: in many countries data on child labor are underreported or not reported at all because officially the problem is presumed not to exist.

The gap between developed and developing countries is particularly wide in tertiary education (see Fig. 7.4 and Data Table 2). In high-income countries tertiary enrollments have increased rapidly since 1980, but in low- and middle-income countries they have improved only slightly.

Note that neither the number of students enrolled at a level of study nor the amount of resources invested in education can indicate the quality of education and thus provides only a rough idea of a country's educational achievements. For example, Figure 7.5 shows that across the countries, secondary students' performance in math and science appears to be unrelated to per student real educational expenditure, so that the best international test scores were received by students from the countries with relatively modest cost of a student's education

(Singapore and Republic of Korea), while the most "expensive" students (those from Denmark and Switzerland) showed relatively modest results. Thus increased expenditure on education may not always be the answer—improving the quality of curriculum and pedagogy and the quality of management in education may be more effective.

Vast opportunities for improving the quality of education in the lagging developing countries are offered by modern information and communication technologies (ICT). Computers with Internet access can be used by teachers and students as an invaluable source of up-to-date information and cutting-edge knowledge, particularly precious in

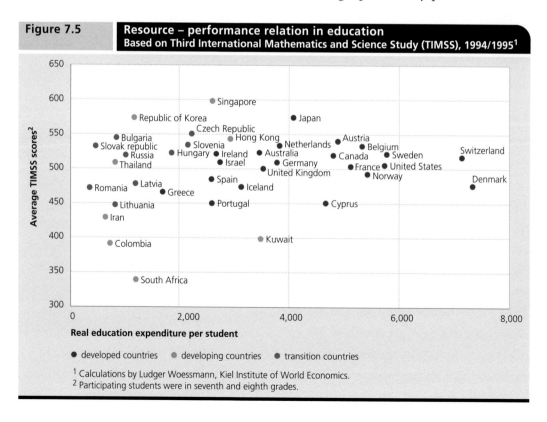

Figure 7.5 | **Resource – performance relation in education**
Based on Third International Mathematics and Science Study (TIMSS), 1994/1995[1]

[1] Calculations by Ludger Woessmann, Kiel Institute of World Economics.
[2] Participating students were in seventh and eighth grades.

places with limited access to other teaching and learning resources. Potentially, ICT in education could be instrumental in bridging the knowledge gap between developed and developing countries (see also Chapter 9). But this potential can materialize only if the so-called digital divide–the gap in access to ICT dividing these countries—is bridged first. In fact, as of 2000 even Eastern Europe and Central Asia, leading other developing regions in access to ICT, had about 50 computers per 1,000 people compared with almost 400 in high-income countries. At the same time South Asia and Sub-Saharan Africa had just 4 and 10 computers per 1,000 people respectively. The gap in access to the Internet is even wider (see Data Table 2).

Given the high cost and limited availability of computers and Internet connectivity in low- and middle-income countries, their benefits can be maximized by installing computers first in schools, libraries, and community centers. For example, when the government of the Republic of Korea decided to eliminate the digital divide (in April 2000), it engaged in distributing personal computers to school teachers, providing free-of-charge high-speed Internet access to schools, and organizing computer training for educators (as well as the wider public). Note that the Republic of Korea—one of the most successful developing countries—has recently crossed the boundary of high

per capita income largely thanks to its successes in education and technological innovation and in spite of its insufficient natural resource base.

To see which countries appear to provide the best-quality math and science education to their secondary students, examine the recent outcomes of the **OECD** Program for International Student Assessment (PISA). Among the 32 countries that participated in PISA 2000 (29 OECD countries plus Brazil, Latvia, and the Russian Federation), the highest rankings were received by Korea, Japan, Finland, New Zealand, the United Kingdom, Canada, and Australia (see Fig. 7.6). Brazil and Mexico were at the bottom of the list. This cross-country comparison is particularly important because PISA's methodology was aimed at testing students' ability to use their knowledge rather than to just present it—to recognize scientific and mathematical problems in real-life situations, identify the relevant facts and methods involved, develop chains of reasoning, and support their conclusions.

To generate economic returns, education and training have to meet the ever-changing demands of the labor market— that is, they have to equip graduates with the knowledge and skills needed at each stage of a country's economic development. For example, countries moving from planned to market economies usually need more people trained in

Is there any hope of bridging the digital divide?

Figure 7.6

Mean Mathematical Literacy			Mean Scientific Literacy		
Range of rank order positions for each country based on sample (with 95% confidence)			Range of rank order positions for each country based on sample (with 95% confidence)		
Country	Rank		Country	Rank	
	Highest possible	Lowest possible		Highest possible	Lowest possible
Japan	1	3	Korea	1	2
Korea	2	3	Japan	1	2
New Zealand	4	8	Finland	3	4
Finland	4	7	United Kingdom	3	7
Australia	4	9	Canada	4	8
Canada	5	8	New Zealand	4	8
Switzerland	4	10	Australia	4	8
United Kingdom	6	10	Austria	8	10
Belgium	9	15	Ireland	9	12
France	10	15	Sweden	9	13
Austria	10	16	Czech Republic	10	13
Denmark	10	16	France	13	18
Iceland	11	16	Norway	13	18
Liechtenstein	9	18	United States	11	21
Sweden	13	17	Hungary	13	21
Ireland	16	19	Iceland	14	20
Norway	17	20	Belgium	13	21
Czech Republic	17	20	Switzerland	13	21
United States	16	23	Spain	16	22
Germany	20	22	Germany	19	23
Hungary	20	23	Poland	19	25
Russian Fed.	21	25	Denmark	21	25
Spain	23	25	Italy	22	25
Poland	23	26	Liechtenstein	20	26
Latvia	25	28	Greece	25	29
Italy	26	28	Russian Fed.	25	29
Portugal	26	29	Latvia	25	29
Greece	27	30	Portugal	26	29
Luxembourg	29	30	Luxembourg	30	30
Mexico	31	31	Mexico	31	31
Brazil	32	32	Brazil	32	32

economics and business management to work in emerging private sectors as well as in reformed public sectors. Today's ICT revolution requires more people with computer skills, and globalization (see Chapters 12 and 13) has increased the demand for foreign language skills.

But perhaps most importantly, flexible workers who are ready to learn are needed everywhere, and an education system that fails to develop these qualities in its graduates can hardly be considered fully effective. Given the accelerating rate of technological and economic change, today's students should be morally and intellectually prepared for several career changes over their working lifetime. The ability for lifelong learning is becoming a major requirement of the new job market, characteristic of the knowledge economy.

* * *

Investing in education is not only an important way to build a country's human capital and move it closer to the knowledge economy, thus improving its prospects for economic growth and higher **living standards.** For every individual, education also has a value in its own right because education broadens people's horizons and helps them to live healthier, more financially secure, and more fulfilling lives. This is why experts use data on literacy, for example, as important indicators of the **quality of life** in a country.

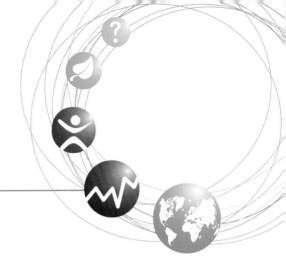

8

Health and Longevity

The health of a country's population is often monitored using two statistical indicators: life expectancy at birth and the under-5 mortality rate. These indicators are also often cited among broader measures of a population's **quality of life** because they indirectly reflect many aspects of people's welfare, including their levels of income and nutrition, the quality of their environment, and their access to health care, safe water, and sanitation.

Life expectancy at birth indicates the number of years a newborn baby would live if health conditions prevailing at the time of its birth were to stay the same throughout its life. This indicator does not predict how long a baby will actually live, but rather reflects the overall health conditions characteristic of this particular country in this particular year. The **under-5 mortality rate** indicates the number of newborn babies who are likely to die before reaching age 5 per 1,000 live births. Because infants and children are most vulnerable to malnutrition and poor hygienic living conditions, they account for the largest portion of deaths in most developing countries. Therefore, decreasing under-5 mortality is usually seen as the most effective way of increasing life expectancy at birth in the developing world.

Global Trends

During the second half of the 20th century health conditions around the world improved more than in all previous human history. Average life expectancy at birth in **low-** and **middle-income countries** increased from 40 years in 1950 to 65 years in 1998. Over the same period the average under-5 mortality rate for this group of countries fell from 280 to 79 per 1,000. But these achievements are still considerably below those in **high-income countries,** where average life expectancy at birth is 78 years and the average under-5 mortality rate is 6 per 1,000.

Throughout the 20th century, national indicators of life expectancy were closely associated with **GNP per capita.** If you compare Figure 8.1 (Life expectancy at birth, 1998) with Figure 2.1 (GNP per capita, 1999), you will find that in general the higher a country's income per capita, the higher is its life expectancy—although this relationship does not explain all the differences among regions and countries. (See Data Tables 1 and 3 for country-specific data.) The two other factors believed to be the most important for increasing national and regional life expectancies are improvements in medical technology (with some countries clearly making better use of it than others) and

Which factors account for most of the health improvements in the 20th century?

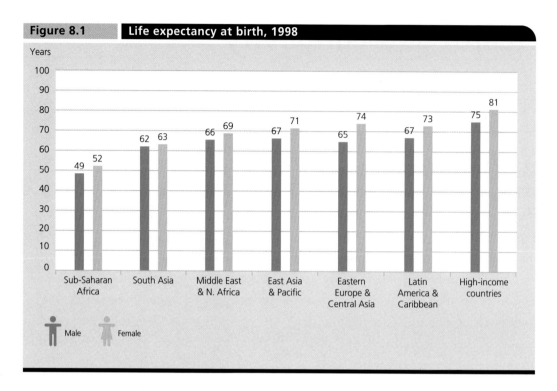

Figure 8.1 | **Life expectancy at birth, 1998**

Years

Sub-Saharan Africa: 49 (Male), 52 (Female)
South Asia: 62 (Male), 63 (Female)
Middle East & N. Africa: 66 (Male), 69 (Female)
East Asia & Pacific: 67 (Male), 71 (Female)
Eastern Europe & Central Asia: 65 (Male), 74 (Female)
Latin America & Caribbean: 67 (Male), 73 (Female)
High-income countries: 75 (Male), 81 (Female)

Male   Female

development of and better access to public health services (particularly clean water, sanitation, and food safety control). Education, especially of girls and women, makes a big difference too, because wives and mothers who are knowledgeable about healthier lifestyles play a crucial role in reducing risks to their families' health.

These other factors help explain how most **developing countries** are catching up with **developed countries** in terms of people's health even though they are generally not catching up in terms of per capita income (see Chapter 4). Progress in medical technology, public health services, and education allows countries to realize "more health" for a given income than before. For example, in 1900 life expectancy in the United States was about 49 years and income per capita was more than $4,000. In today's Sub-Saharan Africa life expectancy is about 50 years even though GNP per capita is still less than $500.

In general, for nearly all countries, life expectancy at birth continued to grow in recent years (see Data Table 3). In developing countries this growth was largely due to much lower under-5 mortality (see Fig. 8.2). Better control of communicable diseases that are particularly dangerous for children, such as diarrhea and worm infections, accounts for most of the gains. In many countries higher per capita incomes (see Chapter 4 and Data Table 1) also contributed to better nutrition and housing for most families.

Governments of developing countries have invested in improving public health measures (safe drinking water, sanitation, mass immunizations), training medical personnel, and building clinics and hospitals. But much remains to be done.

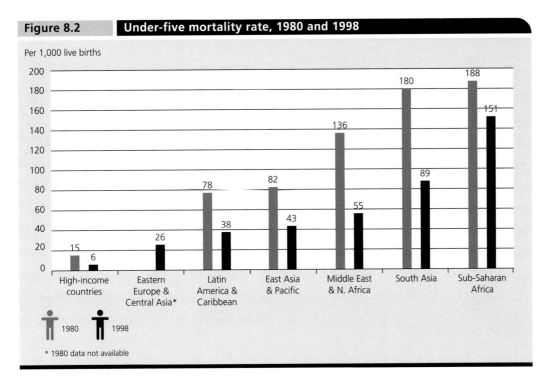

Figure 8.2 Under-five mortality rate, 1980 and 1998

Per 1,000 live births

1980

1998

* 1980 data not available

How are major health risks changing for different groups of countries?

The average level of public health expenditures in low-income countries is still only 1 percent of GDP compared with 6 percent in high-income countries. Malnutrition, especially among women and children, is still a big problem (see Chapter 6). Communicable, largely preventable diseases still claim millions of lives (see below in this chapter). And little progress has been made in reducing **maternal mortality** rates. Over half a million women die every year in pregnancy or childbirth, most often in low-income countries (see Data Table 3). The main reasons are low access of poor women to trained health personnel and emergency care combined with high **fertility rates.** Whereas in Europe 1 in 2,400 women dies in pregnancy or childbirth, in Africa this figure is as high as 1 in every 20 women. Initiatives aimed at helping women prevent unwanted pregnancies and at getting personnel trained in midwifery to attend all deliveries could make a big difference.

In those countries where the total burden of disease has declined, the structure of disease has shifted from a preponderance of communicable disease (diarrhea, worm infections, measles) to a preponderance of non-communicable disease (heart and circulatory disease, cancer). However, this shift is particularly obvious in industrialized countries (including European transitional countries), while in developing countries infectious diseases are responsible on average for almost half of mortality.

Population Age Structures

The health and the longevity of a country's people are reflected in its population age structure—that is, the percentages of

What are the social and economic challenges that result from different population age structures?

total population in different age groups. A population age structure can be illustrated using a "population pyramid," also known as an age-sex pyramid. In such pyramids a country's population is divided into males and females as well as age groups (for example, five-year age groups, as in Figure 8.3). Figure 8.3 shows population pyramids typical of low- and high-income countries in 1995 and those expected to be typical in 2025 if current population trends continue. Note how these shapes represent higher **birth rates,** higher death rates (particularly among children), and lower life expectancies in low-income countries. Think about why in poor countries the base of the pyramid is broader and the pyramid is basically triangular rather than pear-shaped or rectangular as in rich countries. Explain also the changes

expected to happen to both pyramids by 2025.

As seen in Figure 8.3, in low-income countries more than one-third of the population is under 15, compared with less than one-fifth in high-income countries. From a social and economic perspective, a high percentage of children in a population means that a large portion is too young to work and, in the short run, is dependent on those who do. This is the main reason for the relatively high **age dependency ratio** in most developing countries. While in high-income countries there are roughly 2 people of working age to support each person who is too young or too old to work, in low-income countries this number is around 1.0–1.5. The good news is that declining fertility

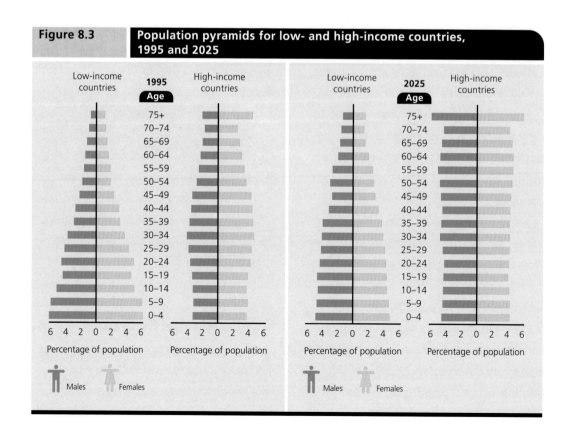

Figure 8.3   **Population pyramids for low- and high-income countries, 1995 and 2025**

in developing countries (see Chapter 3) is expected to result in declining dependency ratios for the next few decades, before the enormous army of today's and tomorrow's young workers become too old to work, and dependency ratios rise again. Experts point out that this opens a "window of opportunity" for developing countries to spend relatively less on supporting the nonworking, economically dependent population and to invest more of their **savings** in improving **productivity** and reducing poverty (see Chapter 6). However, this window of opportunity can be used only if almost all the members of the working-age population are gainfully employed and able to save and to invest in their children's future. High unemployment would not allow these benefits to materialize.

High-income countries currently face the problem of an aging population—that is, a growing percentage of elderly nonworking people. In 1997 people 65 and above made up 13.6 percent of the population in these countries, and this portion is expected to grow to almost 17.4 percent by 2015. In several of these countries (Belgium, Germany, Greece, Italy, Japan, Sweden) the share of elderly people has already reached or surpassed 15 percent. An aging population puts greater pressure on a country's pension, health care, and social security systems. As life expectancy continues to increase in developing countries, they too will face the problem of an aging population (see Fig. 8.3). In fact, developing countries are expected to be hit even harder because they are financially

less prepared to deal with it and because the rate of growth in life expectancy and therefore population aging is much faster there than in developed countries.

The Burden of Infectious Disease

In sharp contrast to successes in controlling some of the most dangerous killers of children such as diarrhea and worm infections, other infectious diseases persist into the 21st century. For example, the average rate of measles immunization worldwide is only about 80 percent, and every year more than 1 million children die of the disease. Many of those children are in Sub-Saharan Africa, where the rate of measles immunization is the lowest—under 60 percent.

About half of all infectious disease mortality in developing countries—more than 5 million deaths a year—can be attributed to just three diseases: HIV/AIDS, tuberculosis (TB), and malaria. None of the three has an effective vaccine, but there are proven and cost-effective ways to prevent these diseases. Prevention, however, is complicated by the fact that infections occur primarily in the poorest countries and among the poorest people, perpetuating their poverty even further.

HIV/AIDS, according to United Nations Secretary General Kofi Annan, "has become a major development crisis." Despite recent medical advances

Can the spread of HIV in developing countries be curbed?

there is still no cure available, while the total number of people living with HIV/AIDS has reached 40 million. In the hardest-hit low-income countries AIDS has already lowered the average life expectancy by a decade or more. Since the disease first surfaced in the late 1970s-early 1980s, about 22 million people have died from it (including 3 million in the year 2000 alone), and 13 million children have lost one or both parents. About three-quarters of these deaths occurred in Africa, where AIDS is now the primary cause of death. In many African countries 10 to20 percent of all adults are infected with HIV. The Caribbean has the highest prevalence of HIV infection outside of Sub-Saharan Africa (in percentage terms), while in other regions HIV prevalence is considerably lower (see Data Table 3).

An extremely steep increase in the number of new HIV infections is currently being seen in the countries of Eastern Europe and Central Asia, where the epidemic arrived only in the early 1990s. Between the end of 1999 and that of 2000, the number of people living with HIV/AIDS in this region almost doubled, rising from 420,000 to more than 700,000. This is already more than in Western Europe both in absolute terms (compare with 540,000 in Western Europe) and in percentage of the total adult population (0.35 percent versus 0.24 percent). Particularly alarming is the number of new infections in this region and in Asia, although nowhere else is HIV spreading on a scale comparable with that in Sub-Saharan

Africa (see Map 8.1). Note that about half of all new infections are estimated to occur in the age group 15–24.

In high-income countries, the number of AIDS-related deaths considerably decreased in the late 1990s thanks to effective therapy that is keeping infected people alive longer. However, this newly developed therapy is very expensive—from US$10,000 to US$20,000 per year—so for most people in developing countries it is utterly out of reach. *Preventing* new HIV infections is much more affordable, particularly in the early stage of an epidemic. Raising awareness about AIDS and simple ways of personal protection can go a long way in forestalling a full-blown national epidemic. At the same time the African countries hardest hit by HIV/AIDS cannot be expected to cope with this crisis without substantial support from the international community. According to some estimates, effectively fighting the epidemic in low- and middle-income countries would require US$10.5 billion annually, while in reality the total amount of international assistance for this purpose reached US$2.5 billion in 2003 (after increasing eight-fold since 1996).

Tuberculosis—another global epidemic—threatens to get out of control as a result of combination with HIV/AIDS and the emergence of multi-drug-resistant TB strains. HIV radically weakens a person's immune system, and TB becomes the first manifestation of AIDS in over 50 percent of all cases in developing coun-

Map 8.1 | **Estimated number of adults and children newly infected with HIV during 2000**

North
America
45 000

Caribbean
60 000

Latin
America
150 000

Western
Europe
30 000

Eastern Europe
& Central Asia
250 000

North Africa &
Middle East
80 000

Sub-Saharan
Africa
3.8 million

East Asia & Pacific
130 000

South &
South-East Asia
780 000

Australia &
New Zealand
500

Total: 5.3 million

UNAIDS
Joint United Nations Programme on HIV/AIDS
UNICEF • UNDP • UNFPA • UNDCP
UNESCO • WHO • WORLD BANK

World Health
Organisation

tries. In addition, multi-drug-resistant TB develops, caused by inconsistent and partial TB treatment. And poverty remains the main factor of TB epidemics because the probability of becoming infected and that of developing active TB are both associated with homelessness, crowded living conditions, poor air circulation and sanitation, malnutrition, psychological stress, and substance abuse. Thus TB thrives on the most vulnerable such as refugees, seasonal migrant workers, and prison inmates.

Tuberculosis kills about 2 million people a year worldwide even though modern, low-cost anti-TB drugs can cure at least 85 percent of all cases. In fact, according to World Health Organization (WHO) estimates, only 19 percent of all TB cases in 20 high TB burden countries[1] are currently cured. Tragically, there are more TB deaths today than at any other point in history. The main burden of TB is carried by Southeast Asia and Sub-Saharan Africa, where most of the world's poor reside (see Chapter 6). In

[1]The 20 high TB burden countries, which in March 2000 adopted the Amsterdam Declaration to Stop TB, are Bangladesh, Brazil, Cambodia, China, Democratic Republic of Congo, Ethiopia, India, Indonesia, Kenya, Nigeria, Pakistan, Peru, Philippines, Russian Federation, South Africa, Tanzania, Thailand, Uganda, Vietnam, and Zimbabwe.

addition, new outbreaks of TB have recently occurred in a number of countries of Eastern Europe and the former Soviet Union, fueled by socioeconomic crises and growing poverty.

Malaria, a largely preventable and treatable infectious disease, nevertheless kills almost as many people as TB each year. Its spread is limited to countries with tropical climates and has shrunk considerably over the past 50 years. Former gains are being eroded, however, because of global climate warming (see Chapter 14), poorly designed irrigation projects, and multiple social crises including armed conflicts, mass movements of refugees, and disintegration of health services. As with TB, the situation is exacerbated by the emergence of multi-drug-resistant strains of the parasite. And like TB, malaria hits the poor hardest of all, because they are the least able to afford treatment as well as preventive measures: moving out of malaria-affected areas, using sprays to control mosquito nuisance, buying mosquito repellents and special bed-nets.

The total number of people suffering from malaria worldwide is estimated to be 300-500 million each year, with 90 percent of them living in Sub-Saharan Africa. Malaria exacts a particularly high toll on the poorest countries of Africa through work loss, school drop-out, cost of treatment and prevention, decreased

investment, and increased social instability. According to the WHO, African countries lose 1 to 5 percent of their GDP because of malaria. By reducing the accumulation of both **physical** and **human capital** in malaria-affected countries, the disease undermines their long-term development prospects.

The most radical solution to the problem of hard-to-treat infectious diseases like HIV/TB or hard-to-prevent diseases like malaria would come from development of effective vaccines that are affordable for poor countries. But the search for low-cost vaccines to prevent diseases that affect largely the poor is generally slowed down by the highly unequal distribution of global income among countries. Pharmaceutical companies find it more profitable to invest in research and development (R&D) devoted to issues of concern primarily to developed countries, where customers are able to pay higher prices. The WHO estimates that in the early 1990s only 5 percent of all health-related R&D in the world was devoted to the health concerns of the much more populous developing world. Many experts believe that the failure of the market to provide sufficient incentives for production of such global **public goods** as anti-AIDS vaccine calls for action on the part of donor governments and international development institutions such as the United Nations and the **World Bank** (see also Chapter 13).

Lifestyle Challenges

In most middle- and high-income countries noncommunicable diseases affecting mostly people in their middle and older years are the leading cause of death. These diseases are expensive and difficult to treat, so prevention should be the main focus of public health measures. But prevention will require changing people's behaviors and lifestyles.

The importance of lifestyle choices can be illustrated by the health gap between Eastern and Western Europe. The largest contributors to this health gap are heart attacks and strokes, for which the main risk factors include unhealthy diet, lack of exercise, excessive consumption of alcohol, and smoking. All these factors, particularly smoking, are more prevalent in Eastern Europe (see Fig. 8.4 and Data Table 3).

Cigarette smoke does more damage to human health than all air pollutants combined. Smoking is hazardous not only to smokers, about half of whom die prematurely from tobacco-related diseases including cancer, heart disease, and respiratory conditions, but also to "passive" smokers (those inhaling second-hand smoke). According to some estimates, passive smokers increase their risk of cancer by 30 percent and their risk of heart disease by 34 percent.

Why is the incidence of smoking higher in poorer countries?

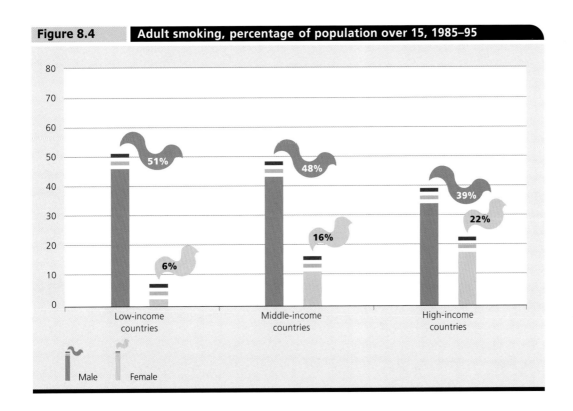

Figure 8.4 **Adult smoking, percentage of population over 15, 1985–95**

Male Female

The governments of most developed countries have made efforts to reduce smoking and so lower its costs to society by introducing tobacco taxes, limiting tobacco advertising, and educating people about the risks of smoking. Cigarette taxes are highest in Western Europe. According to a 1998 report by the Worldwatch Institute, smokers in Norway pay $5.23 in taxes per pack of cigarettes, which is 74 percent of the total price. And in the United Kingdom smokers pay $4.30 in taxes, which is 82 percent of the total price. Experience in many countries has shown that tobacco taxes are effective in discouraging smoking: a 10 percent increase in cigarette prices leads to a 5 percent decrease in smoking among adults and a 6-8 percent decrease among young adults (age 15 to 21), who usually have less disposable income.

According to the same report, while in Western Europe and the United States the number of smokers is declining, in most developing countries smoking is on the rise, particularly among women and young people. European and U.S. tobacco firms, facing declining demand in their home countries, have managed to increase sales by entering underregulated and underinformed overseas markets. In the past 10 years exports of cigarettes as a share of production have doubled to 60 percent in the United Kingdom and 30 percent in the United States, the two largest exporters. If current smoking trends persist, the number of tobacco-related deaths worldwide will soar from 3 million a year today to 10 million a year in 2020, with 70 percent of the deaths occurring in the developing world.

9

Industrialization and Postindustrialization

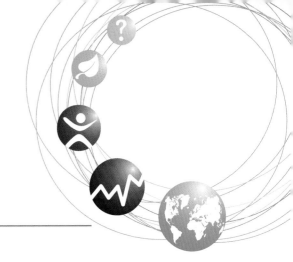

Everything that grows also changes its structure. Just as a growing tree constantly changes the shape, size, and configuration of its branches, a growing economy changes the proportions and interrelations among its basic sectors—**agriculture, industry,** and **services**—and between other sectors—rural and urban, public and private, domestic- and export-oriented (see Chapters 10, 11, and 12). Are there any common patterns in how all growing economies change? Which changes should be promoted and which should be prevented from occurring? Think of these questions while reading this chapter and the three that follow it.

Major Structural Shifts

One way to look at the structure of an economy is to compare the shares of its three major sectors—agriculture, industry, and services[1]—in the country's total output (see Fig. 9.1) and employment

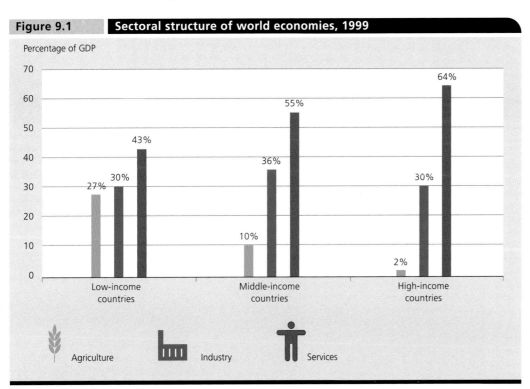

| Figure 9.1 | Sectoral structure of world economies, 1999 |

Percentage of GDP

Low-income countries: Agriculture 27%, Industry 30%, Services 43%
Middle-income countries: Agriculture 10%, Industry 36%, Services 55%
High-income countries: Agriculture 2%, Industry 30%, Services 64%

Agriculture   Industry   Services

[1]Agriculture here refers to crop cultivation, livestock production, forestry, fishing, and hunting. Industry includes manufacturing, mining, construction, electricity, water, and gas. Services cover all other economic activities, including trade, transport, and communications; government, financial, and business services; and personal, social, and community services.

What are the economic reasons behind industrialization and postindustrial- ization?

(see Fig. 9.2). Initially, agriculture is a developing economy's most important sector. But as **income per capita** rises, agriculture loses its primacy, giving way first to a rise in the industrial sector, then to a rise in the service sector. These two consecutive shifts are called indus- trialization and postindustrialization (or "deindustrialization"). All growing economies are likely to go through these stages, which can be explained by struc- tural changes in consumer demand and in the relative labor **productivity** of the three major economic sectors.

Industrialization. As people's incomes increase, their demand for food—the main product of agriculture—meets its natural limit, and they begin to demand relatively more industrial goods. At the

same time, because of new farm tech- niques and machinery, labor productiv- ity increases faster in agriculture than in industry, making agricultural products relatively less expensive and further diminishing their share in **gross domes- tic product** (GDP). The same trend in relative labor productivity also dimin- ishes the need for agricultural workers, while employment opportunities in industry grow. As a result, industrial out- put takes over a larger share of GDP than agriculture and employment in industry becomes predominant.

Postindustrialization. As incomes con- tinue to rise, people's needs become less "material" and they begin to demand more services—in health, education, information, entertainment, tourism,

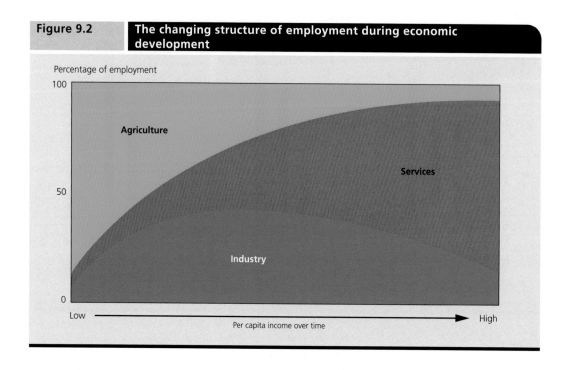

Figure 9.2 — **The changing structure of employment during economic development**

Percentage of employment

100

Agriculture

50

Services

Industry

0

Low → High

Per capita income over time

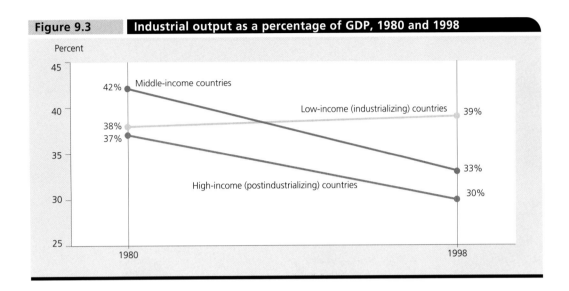

Figure 9.3 Industrial output as a percentage of GDP, 1980 and 1998

Percent

- Middle-income countries: 42% (1980)
- Low-income (industrializing) countries: 38% (1980), 39% (1998)
- High-income (postindustrializing) countries: 37% (1980), 33%, 30% (1998)

and many other areas. Meanwhile, labor productivity in services does not grow as fast as it does in agriculture and industry because most service jobs cannot be filled by machines. This makes services more expensive relative to agricultural and industrial goods, further increasing their share of GDP. Lower mechanization of services also explains why employment in the service sector continues to grow while employment in industry and agriculture declines because of technological progress that increases labor productivity and eliminates jobs (see Fig. 9.2). Eventually, the service sector replaces the industrial sector as the leading sector of the economy.

Most **high-income** and **middle-income countries** today are postindustrializing—becoming less reliant on industry—while many **low-income countries** are still industrializing—becoming more

reliant on industry (see Fig. 9.3 and Map 9.1). But even in countries still industrializing, the service sector is growing relative to the economy taken as a whole. By the end of the 1990s services made up almost two-thirds of world GDP (see Data Table 3), whereas they had only been about half of world GDP in the early 1980s.

Knowledge Revolution

The fastest-growing part of the service sector consists of knowledge- and information-related services such as education, research and development (R&D), modern communications (telephones and Internet), and business services. This is the result of the so-called *knowledge revolution* that started in the second half of the 20th century—a radical speeding up of scientific advances and their eco-

| Map 9.1 | The share of services in GDP, 1999 |

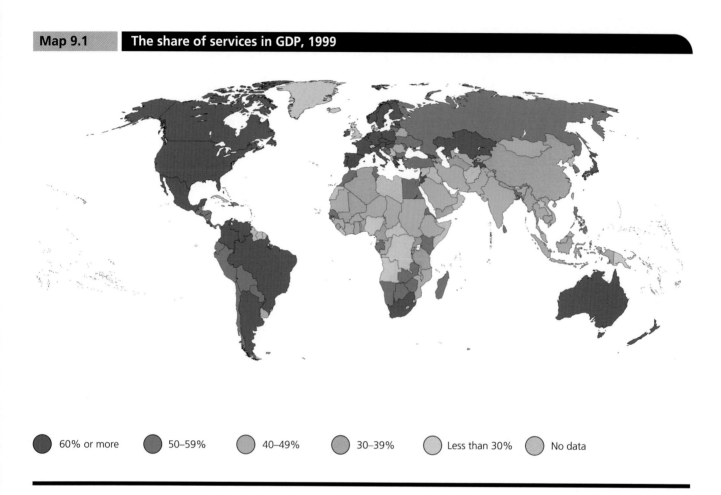

● 60% or more   ● 50–59%   ● 40–49%   ● 30–39%   ○ Less than 30%   ○ No data

nomic applications in the form of new technologies as well as new consumer products. Technological innovation rather than investment per se became the main source of increased productivity, the major tool of economic competition in the world market, and the most important driver of **economic growth** (see Table 9.1). So developing countries striving to improve their economic prospects today should aim at investing not only in their **physical capital** (see Chapter 6), but also directly in their "knowledge base"—in their capacity to create, absorb, adapt, disseminate, and

use new knowledge for their economic and social development.

However, the majority of developing countries face considerable difficulties in joining the global knowledge revolution because of the wide knowledge, education, and information and communication technology (ICT) gaps dividing them from the most knowledge-based economies of the world. Consider the fact that about 85 percent of global R&D expenditure is concentrated in high-income countries. Clearly, this is where most new knowledge is created.

Table 9.1 Stages of Economic Development

Characteristics	Stages		
	Preindustrial, agrarian	*Industrial*	*Postindustrial, knowledge-based*
Leading economic sector	Agriculture	Industry	Services
Nature of dominant technologies	Labor- and natural resource-intensive	Capital-intensive	Knowledge-intensive
Major type of consumer products	Food and hand-made clothes	Industrial goods	Information and knowledge services
Nature of most production processes	Human-nature interaction	Human-machine interaction	Human-human interaction
Major factor of economic wealth/growth	Nature's productivity (soil fertility, climate, biological resources)	Labor productivity	Innovation/intellectual productivity

How can poor countries benefit from the ongoing knowledge revolution?

Moreover, developing countries' capacity to tap the internationally available flows of knowledge and adapt them for their specific needs is impeded by the relatively small number of scientists and engineers working in these countries (see Data Table 3) and the relatively low level of their populations' education. Consider that the average number of years of schooling received by adults in low- and middle-income countries is only about 5.5 years, compared with 10 years in high-income countries. Add to that the so-called *digital divide*—the fact that about 80 percent of the world's personal computers and almost 90 percent of its Internet users are also found in high-income countries (see Data Table 3). And you will understand that although the global knowledge revolution has the potential to solve many development problems, it is also fraught with the danger of dramatically aggravating global inequality.

In the interests of sustainable global development, the international community should help developing countries bridge the widest knowledge and information gaps by increasing official development aid and private capital flows (see Chapter 13) as well as by directly facilitating the transfer of modern technologies from developed countries, including technologies for improved agricultural productivity (see Chapter 6), education (Chapter 7), control of infectious diseases (Chapter 8), and environmental protection (Chapter 10 and Chapter14).

Implications for Development Sustainability

The service sector produces "intangible" goods, some traditional—government, health, education—and some quite new, central for transition to a knowledge economy—modern communication,

Is "over-consumption" a threat to sustainable development?

information, and business services. Producing services tends to require relatively less **natural capital** and more **human capital** than producing agricultural or industrial goods. As a result, demand is growing for more educated workers, prompting countries to invest more in education—an overall benefit to their people. Another benefit of the growing service sector is that by using fewer **natural resources** than other sectors, it puts less pressure on the local, regional, and global environment.[2]

Conserving natural capital and building up human capital may help national and global development become more environmentally and socially sustainable. But growth of the service sector will not be a miracle solution to the problem of sustainability, since agricultural and industrial growth are still going to be necessary to meet the material needs of the fast-growing population of developing countries and the consumption preferences of the relatively affluent population of developed countries (such as personal cars or fashion-driven remodeling). There is an ongoing

discussion about what part of today's developed countries' consumption should be seen as *overconsumption,* as meeting people's competitive wants rather than their real needs. For example, is air-conditioning a need or just a want? Do people really need so many cars or could they benefit from better-developed public transport in combination with cleaner urban air? Should rich countries attempt to limit their consumption so as to enable increased consumption in poor countries? Or should they at least try to modify the composition of their growing consumption so as to minimize its unsustainable environmental and social impacts? Anyway, there are reasons to believe that if people's needs (and wants) across the world are met by making greater use of knowledge—embodied in better-educated workers and more productive, more socially and environmentally appropriate technologies—rather than by using more of the same kinds of machines, equipment, and processes, the damage to the natural environment and the potential for social conflict can be lessened.

---

[2] Note that the pressure put by high-income countries on the global environment is in fact much heavier than might be suggested by the postindustrial-appearing structure of their economies. This is because in today's globalized world many natural resources extracted and industrial products manufactured in developing countries are actually consumed by the "golden billion" of people living in rich countries.

10
Urban Air Pollution

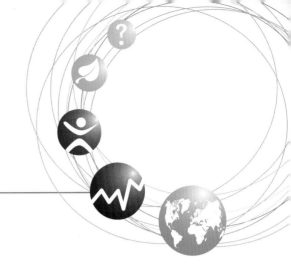

Urbanization is a process of relative growth in a country's urban population accompanied by an even faster increase in the economic, political, and cultural importance of cities relative to rural areas. There is a worldwide trend toward urbanization. In most countries it is a natural consequence and stimulus of **economic development** based on **industrialization** and **postindustrialization** (see Chapter 9). Thus the level of urbanization, as measured by the share of a country's urban population in its total population, is highest in the most developed, **high-income countries** and lowest in the least developed, **low-income countries** (see Data Table 4).

However, because the population of **developing countries** is larger, percent-

ages of this population represent more people. In addition, urbanization in the developing world is progressing much faster than in **developed countries** (see Fig. 10.1). As a result, by the late 1990s about three-quarters of the world's 2.5 billion urban residents lived in developing countries. The share of the urban population in the total population of low- and middle-income countries increased from less than 22 percent in 1960 to 41 percent in 1998 and is expected to exceed 50 percent by 2015.

A rough indication of the urban contribution to GDP is the combined share of GDP produced in the industry and service sectors relative to agriculture. Judging by this indicator, cities in developing countries are already more economically

Figure 10.1   Urban population, 1980 and 1998

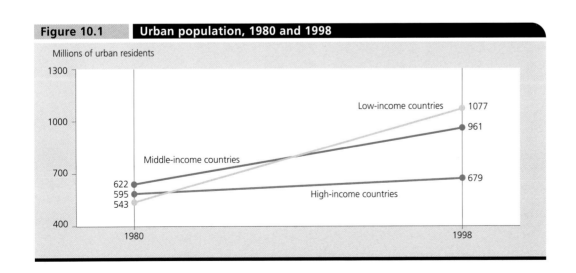

Why is urban air pollution often higher in developing countries?

important than rural, primarily agricultural areas, because more than half of the developing world's GDP originates in cities. (This is not yet true for every country, as you can see in Data Table 4.)

While urbanization is characteristic of nearly all developing countries, levels of urbanization vary quite significantly by region. Most Latin American countries are as urbanized as Europe, with about three-quarters of the population living in urban areas. At the same time, South Asia, East Asia, and Sub-Saharan Africa remain predominantly rural, though they are urbanizing rapidly (see Fig. 10.2).

Most of the world's most populous cities are in developing countries. Many of

these cities are in Asian countries with low per capita incomes but big populations, such as China, India, and Indonesia. These cities have high concentrations of poor residents and suffer from social and environmental problems including severe air pollution.

Particulate Air Pollution

Suspended particulate matter is made up of airborne smoke, soot, dust, and liquid droplets from fuel combustion. The amount of suspended particulate matter, usually measured in micrograms per cubic meter of air, is one of the most important indicators of the quality of the air that people breathe. According to

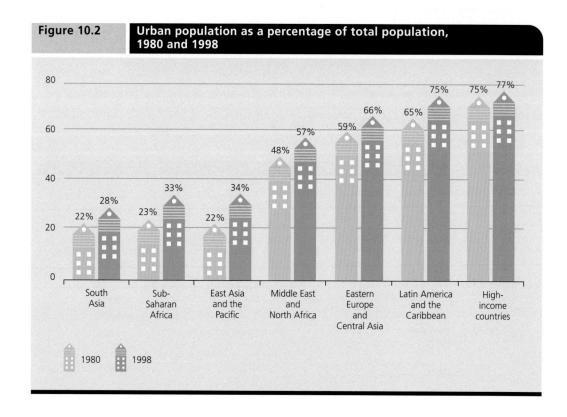

Figure 10.2 — Urban population as a percentage of total population, 1980 and 1998

Region	1980	1998
South Asia	22%	28%
Sub-Saharan Africa	23%	33%
East Asia and the Pacific	22%	34%
Middle East and North Africa	48%	57%
Eastern Europe and Central Asia	59%	66%
Latin America and the Caribbean	65%	75%
High-income countries	75%	77%

the World Health Organization's air quality standards, the concentration of suspended particulates should be less than 90 micrograms per cubic meter. In many cities, however, this number is several times higher (see Table 10.1 and Map 10.1).

High concentrations of suspended particulates adversely affect human health, provoking a wide range of respiratory diseases and exacerbating heart disease and other conditions. Worldwide, in 1995 the ill health caused by such pollution resulted in at least 500,000 premature deaths and 4–5 million new cases of chronic bronchitis. Most of the people at risk are urban dwellers in developing countries, especially China and India. In many Chinese cities air quality is so poor that nationwide, economic losses caused by excess illness and mortality of urban residents are estimated at 5 percent of GDP. According to estimates for 18 cities in Central and Eastern Europe, 18,000 premature deaths a year could be prevented and $1.2 billion a year in working time lost to illness could be regained by achieving European Union pollution standards for dust and soot.

The level of air pollution depends on a country's technologies and pollution control, particularly in energy production. Using cleaner **fossil fuels** (such as natural gas and higher-grade coal), burning these fuels more efficiently, and increasing reliance on even cleaner,

Table 10.1   Particulate air pollution in the largest cities, 1995

Country	City	City population (thousands)	SPM (micrograms per m³)
Brazil	São Paulo	16,533	86
Australia	Sydney	3,590	54
Austria	Vienna	2,060	47
Belgium	Brussels	1,122	78
Brazil	São Paulo	16,533	86
	Rio de Janeiro	10,187	139
Bulgaria	Sofia	1,188	195
Canada	Toronto	4,319	36
	Montreal	3,320	34
China	Shanghai	13,584	246
	Beijing	11,299	377
	Taiwan	2,502	568
	Lanzhou	1,747	732
Czech Republic	Prague	1,225	59
Finland	Helsinki	1,059	40
France	Paris	9,523	14
Germany	Berlin	3,317	50
India	Bombay	15,138	240
	Calcutta	11,923	375
	Delhi	9,948	415
Indonesia	Jakarta	8,621	271
Italy	Rome	2,931	73
Japan	Tokyo	26,959	49
	Osaka	10,609	43
Korea, Rep.	Seoul	11,609	84
Mexico	Mexico City	16,562	279
Philippines	Manila	9,286	200
Russian Federation	Moscow	9,269	100
	Nizhny Novgorod	1,456	170
Sweden	Stockholm	1,545	9
Ukraine	Kiev	2,809	100
United States	New York (1987-90)	16,332	61

| Map 10.1 | Particulate air pollution in selected cities, 1990–1995 |

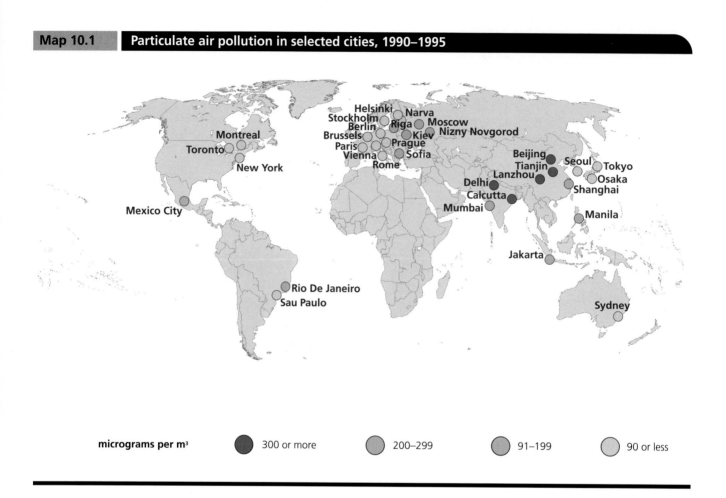

| microgatms per m³ | ● 300 or more | ● 200–299 | ○ 91–199 | ○ 90 or less |

renewable sources of energy (hydro, solar, geothermal, wind) are some of the best ways to control and reduce air pollution without limiting **economic growth.** See Figure 10.3 for the main sources of electricity in China, the United States, and Russia. Judge these data against the concentrations of suspended particulates in the biggest cities of these three countries as shown in Table 10.1. Note that coal and oil are considered to be the "dirtiest" of the sources shown, although a lot depends on their quality and methods of combustion. In many ways nuclear energy is

one of the "cleanest" sources of electricity, but safe disposal of nuclear waste and the risks of radioactive pollution in case of a serious accident are of major concern. Sources with the least environmental impact, such as solar and wind energy, are not shown because they account for only a small fraction of generated electricity in these countries.

Fuel combustion by motor vehicles is another major source of suspended particulate emissions in urban areas. These emissions are particularly detrimental to human health because pollutants are

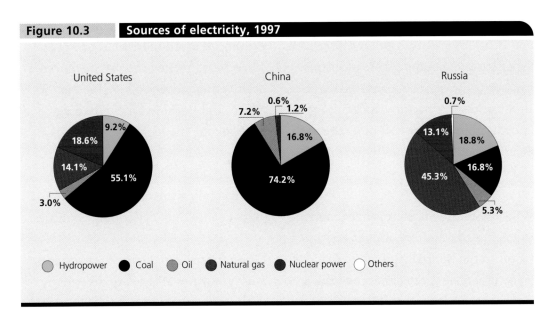

Figure 10.3 | **Sources of electricity, 1997**

United States

9.2%
18.6%
14.1%
55.1%
3.0%

China

7.2%
0.6%
1.2%
16.8%
74.2%

Russia

0.7%
13.1%
18.8%
45.3%
16.8%
5.3%

○ Hydropower ● Coal ● Oil ● Natural gas ● Nuclear power ○ Others

Is it possible to reduce air pollution without slowing economic growth?

emitted at ground level. Motor vehicles are much more common in developed countries: in 1998 there were 585 of them per 1,000 people in high-income countries compared with just 9 per 1,000 people in low-income countries and 104 in middle-income countries. (See Data Table 4 for the number of motor vehicles in individual countries.) But motor vehicles in developing countries still cause serious air pollution because they are concentrated in a few large cities, many are in poor mechanical condition, and few emission standards exist.

According to World Bank estimates, demand for gasoline in developing countries tends to grow 1.2–1.9 times faster than **GNP per capita.** Then, with per capita income growth rates of 6–8 percent a year observed in some fast-growing developing countries, growth

rates in motive fuel consumption of 10–15 percent a year are possible. And in many transition countries, the number of cars in use grew rapidly despite the contraction in economic activity and reduced per capita incomes in the late 1980s and early 1990s. For example, in Moscow (Russian Federation) the passenger car fleet grew 10 percent a year during 1984-94 and 17.5 percent a year during 1990-94. Without effective policies to curb motor vehicle emissions, the growing number of cars can have grave consequences for urban residents' health.

Airborne Lead Pollution

Airborne lead is one of the most harmful particulate pollutants. Young children are especially vulnerable: lead poisoning of children leads to permanent brain damage, causing learning disabilities, hearing loss, and behavioral abnormalities. In adults lead absorption causes hypertension, blood pressure problems, and heart disease. The main sources of airborne lead are motor vehicles using leaded gasoline, industrial processes such as ferrous and nonferrous metallurgy, and coal combustion.

While governments increasingly control large industrial sources of pollution, motor traffic is rapidly growing. In many urban areas vehicles using leaded gasoline cause more than 80 percent of lead pollution. Therefore, since the 1970s—when medical evidence on the adverse health impacts of lead became available—many countries have reduced or eliminated lead additives in gasoline. The elimination of leaded gasoline has been achieved, for example, in Austria, Japan, and Sweden. But in much of the developing world lead additives are still widely used, especially in Africa. Experts suspect that in developing countries all children under 2 and more than 80 percent of those between 3 and 5 have blood lead levels exceeding World Health Organization standards. Economists have calculated that, with the technological options available today, phasing out leaded gasoline is highly cost-effective. Shifting production from leaded to unleaded gasoline rarely costs more than 2 cents a liter, and countries can save 5 to 10 times as much as that, mostly in health savings from reduced illness and mortality. When the

United States converted to unleaded gasoline, it saved more than $10 for every $1 it invested thanks to reduced health costs, savings on engine maintenance, and improved fuel **efficiency.** Recognizing the high costs of the damage to human health caused by lead emissions and adopting appropriate national policy are matters of high urgency for many developing countries.

International experience shows that in most countries air quality deteriorates in the early stages of industrialization and urbanization. But as countries become richer their priorities shift— they recognize the value of their **natural resources** (clean air, safe water, fertile topsoil, abundant forests), enact and enforce laws to protect those resources, and have the money to tackle environmental problems. As a result air quality and other environmental conditions start to improve. Certain experts have even calculated the average levels of per capita income at which levels of various pollutants peaked for a panel of countries between 1977 and 1988. Smoke, for example, tended to peak in the urban air when a country reached a per capita income of about $6,000, after which this kind of air pollution tended to decrease. For airborne lead, peak concentrations in urban air were registered at considerably lower levels of per capita income—about $1,900. However, these past observations should not be interpreted as comforting and automatic "laws of nature." An improved quality of air does not result directly from economic growth. Any environmental benefits are usually achieved only as a result of political pressures from environmentally concerned population groups, and only through democratic mechanisms can these pressures translate into regulatory and technological changes.

11

Public and Private Enterprises: Finding the Right Mix

Is a growing share of government spending a reliable indicator of development?

During the 20th century the economic importance of the state grew all over the world. In **developed countries** central government spending accounted for less than 10 percent of **gross domestic product (GDP)** in the early 1900s, but by the 1990s that share had grown to nearly 50 percent in many of those countries (see Fig. 11.1, Data Table 4). Historians point out that the Great Depression of the 1930s and economic competition with socialist countries contributed to this government expansion. But the data suggest that this expansion probably continues. Over the past 35 years the share of government spending in the GDP of developed countries roughly doubled.

In **developing countries** the economic role of government grew dramatically in the second half of the 20th century, after the end of colonialism and in pursuit of such development goals as **industrialization** and social equity. In many of these countries the state was striving to mobilize resources and direct them toward accelerated economic **growth,** rather than just to stabilize the economy, as in most developed countries. Until

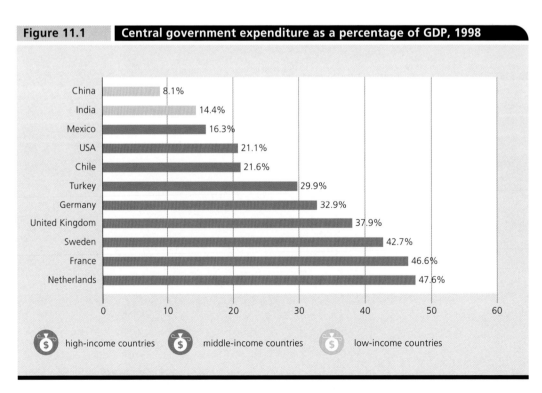

| Figure 11.1 | Central government expenditure as a percentage of GDP, 1998 |

the 1980s the pattern of state-dominated development—which included central-ized planning and state control of the economy—was widely followed. Still, the share of government spending in the GDP of developing countries is less than half that in developed countries (see Fig. 11.1 and Data Table 4). Does this mean that a growing share of government spending in GDP should be seen as a sign of development?

The Dilemma of Public-Private Ownership

Government budgets in developing countries are not only proportionately smaller, but they are also structured dif-ferently. In developed countries more than half of government spending is devoted to social services, including pen-sions, unemployment insurance, social security, and other **transfer payments.** In developing countries much less government spending goes for social services and much more is used to sub-sidize commercial (that is, selling goods and services) state-owned enterprises. Unlike other state-owned enterprises that provide free public services (for example, schools and health clinics), these state-owned enterprises could also be run for profit by private firms. Governments, however, sometimes pre-fer to keep them under their direct con-trol. The share of commercial state enterprises in GDP and in **gross**

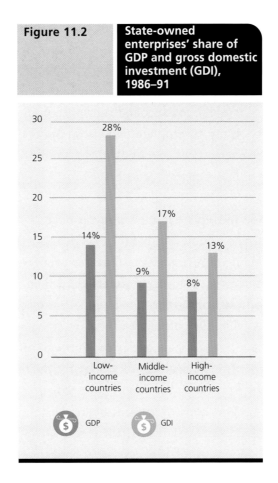

Figure 11.2 State-owned enterprises' share of GDP and gross domestic investment (GDI), 1986–91

domestic investment tends to be higher in poorer countries (see Fig. 11.2).

Is a high share of state enterprises a problem? Is it good or bad for the eco-nomic growth and development of developing countries?

Those who want to preserve extensive state enterprises argue that:

• Only government is capable of pro-viding sufficient investment for tech-nical modernization of major national industries.

When should governments intervene in economic activities?

- Only direct government control over certain enterprises can prevent socially unacceptable high prices for basic goods and services such as energy, housing, and transportation.
- Only government ownership of the biggest enterprises can help avoid mass unemployment.

On the other hand, proponents of privatization point out that the experience of many countries demonstrates that state enterprises are usually less **efficient** than private firms as measured by their profitability. One of the main reasons is that state enterprise managers have little or no incentive to pursue profitability for their enterprises. Easy access to government subsidies and government-guaranteed loans effectively remove the threat of bankruptcy. Besides, it is often hard to run state enterprises at a profit because governments tend to keep state enterprises' selling prices artificially low, and because rules often do not allow these enterprises to lay off excess employees. In countries where the share of state enterprises is high, their typically low efficiency can hinder economic growth. In addition, governments have to cover the financial losses of these unprofitable enterprises. To meet the resulting budget deficits, governments often have to either print more money and thus cause inflation, or borrow and build up their domestic or foreign debt. In both cases national economies are destabilized and growth opportunities are lost.

Note that this argumentation focuses on profitability as the main indicator of economic efficiency. Indeed, an enterprise's profitability summarizes all the indicators of economic efficiency as seen from the viewpoint of its private owners. But from the point of view of national economic growth and development, social costs and benefits, which are not reflected in profitability, can be no less important. For example, when a privatized enterprise achieves profitability by dismissing its excess workers, the economy as a whole does not necessarily become more efficient. If economic conditions prevent the fired workers from finding other employment or starting their own business, this downsizing might lead to an overall economic loss for the country because people were moved from low-productivity jobs to zero-productivity unemployment. Additional social costs might include increased child labor/lower educational achievement, a heavier load on the government budget for providing social services, higher crime, and greater social and political instability (see Fig. 6.4).

Given all that, when is it preferable to keep enterprises under government ownership? What is the ideal size and composition of a country's public sector? And can there be any general answers to these questions independent of ideological beliefs?

In fact, it is increasingly recognized that, generally speaking, state intervention in economic activities is justified only where the market system (based on private ownership) fails. But market systems are not the same in different countries. In particular, in developing countries markets are underdeveloped and in some sectors even nonexistent. For example, there are often no private enterprises interested in purchasing agricultural produce from small farmers and marketing it domestically or internationally. So governments have to fill this gap by creating state-owned marketing boards, engaged in business activities which, in more developed countries, are carried out by private firms.

Furthermore, even in well-established market economies there are five basic situations, called **market failures,** where the private sector tends to underproduce or overproduce certain goods and services:

- underproduction of **public goods** such as defense, law and order, roads, and environmental protection;
- underproduction of goods and services with positive **externalities** (for example, public health and education) and overproduction of goods and services with negative externalities (for example, cigarettes, see Chapter 8);
- overpricing and underproduction by **natural monopolies,** for example, by electric and water utilities;

- insufficient supply of social services such as pensions or medical and unemployment insurance;
- insufficient information available to some parties affected by market processes (for example, information about the quality of food products and medicines available to consumers whose health is at risk).

These five situations call for some kind of government intervention. But even where markets clearly fail, government provision of undersupplied goods and services is not necessarily the best option. We have already discussed the reasons for the typically low profitability of state enterprise management. Add to that the possibility of corruption among government bureaucrats (see Chapter 16) and you get what came to be called "government failure." Increased awareness of this problem is among the reasons explaining why some governments of developed countries are searching for alternatives to state ownership, such as new models of public-private partnership, based on privatization plus close government regulation or government funding for private provision of public goods. An extraordinary example of such an alternative solution to both market and government failures is provided by the new phenomenon of public funding for private prisons in the United States.[1] But particularly important for sustainable development of

[1] Prisons were traditionally state-owned "enterprises" because they "produce" such public goods as obedience to the law and public safety.

When is privatization economically warranted? When can it be detrimental?

most countries is the ongoing debate about the optimal public-private interaction in providing water and sanitation services.

As of 2000, about 2 of every 10 people in developing countries were without access to safe water; 5 of 10 lived without adequate sanitation; and 9 of 10 lived without their waste-water being treated in any way. As a result water-related diseases rank among the top reasons for child mortality (see Chapter 8) and adult illness. Moreover, in Africa and Asia—where the world's poor are concentrated—the overall trends in the 1990s showed little or no progress. The main argument in favor of private companies' involvement is that it will help mobilize the additional investment needed for bringing water and sanitation services to a greater number of people. On the other hand, experience shows that privatization often leads to increased tariffs unaffordable to poor households and sometimes to outright exclusion of poor rural areas viewed as unprofitable by private providers. Only pro-poor government regulation, including subsidies for the poor and special economic incentives for private companies to work for the poor, can neutralize these drawbacks of private service delivery. Overall, the experience of various countries appears to present a mixed picture of success and failure both in mostly public and in mostly private service delivery, and the conclu-

sion may be that no single solution fits all countries. However, there is general agreement that the final responsibility for providing such vital services as water and sanitation (as well as basic health and education services) lies with governments.

Is There a Trend toward Privatization?

By privatizing all the enterprises that can be successfully run by private firms, governments can often make national economies more efficient, on the one hand, and free their budgets from the burden of subsidizing loss-making enterprises, on the other. As a result they are able to focus on tasks that cannot be handed over to markets, such as building **human capital** and providing for human development (see Chapter 1) or developing and implementing national development strategies (see Chapter 17). For example, according to some estimates, shifting budget funds from state enterprise subsidies to public health care would have allowed central governments to increase their health spending by about four times in Mexico and five times in India. Alternatively, Mexico's central government could have increased its education spending by 50 percent, and India's by 550 percent.

But if governments are to shift away from supplying marketable goods and services, there must be active private sectors that are ready to take up their activities. In some cases reducing the economic prominence of state enterprises is even possible without extensive privatization, mainly by means of market **liberalization** that leads to accelerated growth of the private sector. That was the case in the Republic of Korea in the 1970s and 1980s, and in China in the 1980s and 1990s. But more often, particularly where public sectors are much larger than private sectors and so absorb a lot of scarce national resources, special privatization programs are needed.

Since the 1980s many developing and some developed countries have adopted privatization programs. You can attempt to judge their scale by examining data on government proceeds from privatization in Data Table 4. Note that this indicator depends not only on the scale of privatization but also on its methods. Selling state enterprises to outside owners normally brings more revenue than selling them to enterprise managers and employees, while voucher privatization (such as in Russia in 1991–93) brings no revenue at all. The most impressive privatization took place in former socialist countries over the 1990s. Their transition to market-oriented economies required unprecedented mass privatization of formerly dominant state enterprises. For the different starting points and speeds of privatization in this group of countries, see Figure 11.3. Among

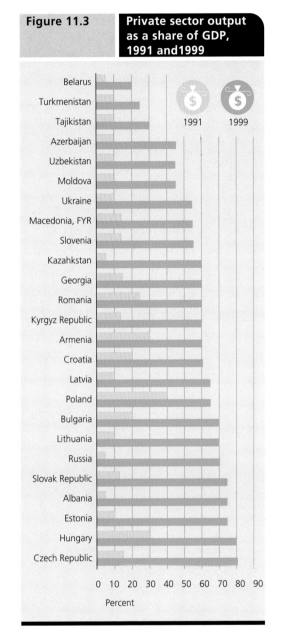

Figure 11.3

Private sector output as a share of GDP, 1991 and1999

1991   1999

other regions of the developing world, privatization programs were implemented in Latin America and Southeast Asia, while in Sub-Saharan Africa the process was less pronounced.

Unfortunately, in some transition countries radical market reforms have resulted in neglect of the state's vital functions, such as law and order or critical social services. Important programs in education and health, for instance, have been cut along with or even instead of cutting subsidies to money-losing enterprises. Such policies have not only damaged people's welfare, they have also eroded the foundations of these countries' further national development. Another case of the government's questionable priorities involved an African country, where local authorities attempted to improve the economic efficiency of their water services by cutting water supplies to a settlement whose residents were unable to afford increased user fees. Shortly after that a cholera epidemic broke out in that province and nearly 14,000 people became infected.

* * *

Many experts argue that, although state-dominated development has failed, so would "stateless" development. Think about it: why are an effective state and a viable private sector both important for development?

12

Globalization: International Trade and Migration

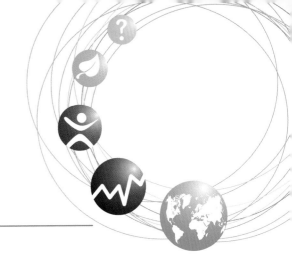

"Globalization" refers to the growing interdependence of countries resulting from their increased economic integration via trade, **foreign investment,** foreign aid, and international migration of people and ideas. Is globalization an inevitable phenomenon of human history? Can all countries benefit from it? Or does it bring about new forms of inequality and exploitation? The balance of globalization's costs and benefits for different groups of countries and different groups of people within these countries is one of the hottest topics in development. It inspires not only academic and public debates but also violent clashes in the streets of many capital cities.

Most activists of various antiglobalization movements would probably agree that they are not against the idea of closer international trade ties and cooperation per se. What really concerns them is the practice of globalization driven by narrow economic interests of large transnational corporations (TNCs). They argue that the interests of poorer countries and the interests of the less privileged in developed countries are often not taken into account. Or that the environmental and social costs of economic development tend to be underestimated. And the economic ben-

efits of globalization are distributed too unfairly. In short, they see the ongoing globalization process as unsustainable (see Chapter 1). Is it the only kind of globalization possible? Is deglobalization the only alternative? Or can a more democratic, more inclusive management of globalization turn it into the most effective tool for dealing with the pressing problems of our time?

Waves of Modern Globalization

Globalization is not altogether new. Researchers point out three waves of modern globalization, the first of which started more than 100 years ago and took place between 1870 and 1914. Over this period, exports nearly doubled relative to world **GDP** (to about 8 percent) and foreign investment nearly tripled relative to the GDP of developing countries in Africa, Asia, and Latin America. International migration was particularly dramatic, with about 10 percent of the world's population moving from Europe to the New World and from China and India to the less populated neighboring countries. However, this impressive wave of globalization was virtually reversed during the First World War, the Great Depression, and the

Can globalization serve the interests of sustainable development?

Second World War. By the end of the 1940s foreign trade as a share of GDP was at about the same level as in 1870.

The second wave of globalization lasted from the 1950s to the 1980s and involved mostly **developed countries.** Trade and investment flows were growing among the countries of Europe, North America, and Japan, aided by a series of multilateral agreements on trade **liberalization** under the auspices of the **General Agreement on Tariffs and Trade (GATT).** At the same time most **developing countries** were stuck in the role of **primary goods** exporters and were largely isolated from international capital flows. Researchers also noticed that while there was a trend toward convergence of per capita incomes between the richer and poorer members of the **Organization for Economic Cooperation and Development (OECD)**, the gap between the developed and the developing countries widened (see also Fig. 4.4).

The third, current wave of globalization started in the 1980s and continues today, driven by two main factors. One involves technological advances that have radically lowered the costs of transportation, communication, and computation to the extent that it is often economically feasible for a firm to locate different phases of production in different and far-away countries. The other factor has to do with the increasing lib-

eralization of trade and capital markets: more and more governments of developing countries choose to reduce **protection** of their economies from foreign competition and influence by lowering **import tariffs** and minimizing nontariff barriers such as **import quotas,** export restraints, and legal prohibitions. A number of international institutions established in the wake of the Second World War—including the **World Bank,** the **International Monetary Fund (IMF) ,** and the **World Trade Organization (WTO,** preceded by the GATT until 1995)—play an important role in promoting global free trade in place of protectionism.

Over the past two decades some 24 developing countries have approximately doubled their ratio of trade (exports plus imports) to GDP. This group of "new globalizers" includes the countries with the largest populations–China and India–and is home to about 3 billion people overall. On the other hand, about 2 billion people live in developing countries that are trading less today than they did 20 years ago.

Statistical data suggest that the most globalized developing economies enjoyed the highest GNP per capita growth rates and were gradually catching up with the group of developed countries (see Asian newly industrialized economies and China in Fig. 4.4). But much of the rest of the developing world, including most of Sub-Saharan Africa, failed to participate in globalization processes and faced negative income growth rates (see Chapter 4). There are good reasons to believe that international trade and foreign investment do explain much of the difference in economic growth between the more and the less globalized developing countries (see below in this chapter and Chapter 13). However, some may argue that the cause-and-effect connection can also work in the opposite direction: those countries that are most successful in economic development and growth can afford to be more open to foreign trade (and thus to foreign competition) and also tend to be more attractive for foreign investors (see also Chapter 13). Moreover, for countries that are actively engaged in globalization, the benefits come with new risks and challenges.

Costs and Benefits of Free Trade

For participating countries the main benefits of **free foreign trade** (unrestricted, liberalized trade) stem from the increased access of their producers to larger, international markets. For a national economy that access means an opportunity to benefit from the international division of labor by moving its resources to the most productive uses—by specializing in producing and exporting what it can produce best, while importing all the rest. Overall, domestic

producers utilizing their country's **comparative advantages** in the global markets produce more efficiently, and consumers enjoy a wider variety of domestic and imported goods at lower prices.

In addition, an actively trading country benefits from the new technologies that "spill over" to it from its trading partners, such as through the knowledge embedded in imported production equipment. These technological spillovers are particularly important for developing countries because they give them a chance to catch up more quickly with the developed countries in terms of **productivity.** Former centrally planned economies, which missed out on many of the benefits of global trade because of their politically imposed isolation from market economies, today aspire to tap into these benefits by reintegrating with the global trading system.

But a country opening to international trade (undertaking trade liberalization) also faces considerable risk associated with the strong competition in international markets. On the one hand, it can be argued that international competition creates the necessary pressures to prevent economic and technological stagnation, to stimulate domestic producers to produce better goods, and to lower the costs of production. But on the other hand, there is a high risk that many national enterprises and even entire industries—

Should all countries be equally open to foreign trade?

those that are less competitive and adaptable—will be forced out of business. Unfortunately, in real life, the **physical** and **human capital** previously employed in these industries is not easily transferable to other, more productive uses for many reasons—the lack of additional investment, shortage of information on markets and new technologies, and others. Meanwhile, closing of enterprises and higher unemployment impoverish people and slow national economic growth. That explains why trade liberalization is so often opposed even in high-income, better prepared countries.

Not surprisingly, governments of developing countries often argue that many of their national industries require temporary protection until they become better established and less vulnerable to foreign competition. To protect domestic producers, governments seek to weaken competition from foreign-produced goods by introducing import quotas or, more often, by imposing import tariffs to make foreign goods more expensive and less attractive to consumers. Economists justify protectionist policies—used by developed countries too—mostly as temporary measures. In the long run, such policies can be economically dangerous because

they allow domestic producers to continue producing less efficiently and eventually lead to economic stagnation. Wherever possible, investing in increased international competitiveness of key industries should be considered as an alternative to protectionist policies.[1]

But "free global trade" is still more of an ideal to be reached than a present-day reality. Although developing countries have cut their average import tariffs by half over the past 20 years (from 15 percent to 7 percent), the remaining tariffs still constitute a serious obstacle to expanding trade relationships within the developing world.[2] In developed countries, the average import tariffs are considerably lower (about 2–2.5 percent), but they are much higher for exactly those goods in which developing countries are most competitive—for agricultural products (frequently higher than 100 percent) and labor-intensive manufactures, such as textiles and clothing. As a result, according to the World Bank estimate, developing countries on average face tariffs twice as high as those faced by developed countries. The situation is additionally aggravated by the non-tariff barriers (sanitary, environmental, and others) extensively used by developed countries and often seen as

[1]Some development experts argue that the most successful, newly industrialized developing countries of East Asia succeeded in maximizing their benefits from globalization by lowering their protective barriers very carefully, after they considerably expanded their exports, accelerated economic growth, and made sure that enough new enterprises and jobs would be created in place of those that would have to be closed as internationally uncompetitive.
[2]In some developing regions and countries tariffs remain much higher than average—20 percent in South Asia, 13 percent in Latin America, 31 percent in India, and 15 percent in China (all as of 2001).

unjustifiable by developing countries. The World Bank has estimated that lowering tariff barriers to trade in textiles and agricultural products by developed countries could boost annual economic growth in developing countries by an extra 0.5 percent in the long run and by 2015 could lift an additional 300 million people out of poverty.

The issues of trade and development interrelationships are at the center of attention during the current round of global trade negotiations launched by the World Trade Organization (WTO) in 2001 in Doha, the capital of Qatar. The previous Uruguay round of the WTO negotiations ended in outcomes that were, according to its many critics, more favorable for developed countries, because trade in industrial goods and services exported by advanced economies—from automobiles and machinery to information technology and financial services—was liberalized first. So in the next round developing countries signaled their determination to push for more balanced liberalization with priority given to the interests of the poorest countries.

During the WTO ministerial meeting in Cancún (Mexico, September 2003) a new block of 21 developing countries emerged (the so-called G-21), led by Brazil, China, and India and representing half the world's population and two-thirds of its farmers. The major unifying theme was indignation over the destructive impact that enormous government subsidies paid to developed countries' farmers have on global agricultural trade. These subsidies amount to $300 billion a year (compared with about $50 billion given to all developing countries as official development assistance) and result in much lower world prices for the agricultural exports of developing countries. But the initial Doha declarations about the need to contribute to development by reducing "trade-distorting" farm subsidies and cutting import tariffs on agricultural goods and textiles did not meet with sufficient support from the rich countries in Cancún. The talks were closed with no agreement achieved and with unclear prospects for further global trade negotiations.

Geography and Composition of Global Trade

The costs and benefits of participating in international trade also depend on such country-specific factors as the size of a country's domestic market, its natural resource endowment, and its geographic location. For instance, countries with large domestic markets generally trade less. Countries that are well endowed with a few natural resources, such as oil, tend to trade more. And the so-called land-locked countries—with no easy access to sea port—face particular difficulties in developing foreign

How is the role of developing countries in global trade changing?

trade because of much higher transportation costs. (Think of examples of countries whose geographic location is particularly favorable or unfavorable for their participation in global trade.)

Despite the many risks of economic globalization, most countries have been choosing to globalize their economies to a greater extent. One way to measure the extent of this process is by the ratio of a country's trade (exports plus imports) to its GDP or GNP. By this measure, globalization has roughly doubled on average since 1950. Over the last 35 years of the 20th century world exports increased about twice as fast as GNP (see Fig. 12.1). As a result, by the end of the 20th

century the ratio of world trade to world GDP (in **purchasing power parity** terms) had reached almost 30 percent— on average about 40 percent in developed countries and about 15 percent in developing countries (see Map 12.1 and Data Table 4).

The growing role of international trade in the economies of most developing countries (see Fig. 12.1) has not yet resulted in a considerably increased share of developing countries in total global trade as compared with what this share was in the 1980s. Developed countries still trade mostly among themselves. In 1999 only 23 percent of world imports went to low- and middle-income coun-

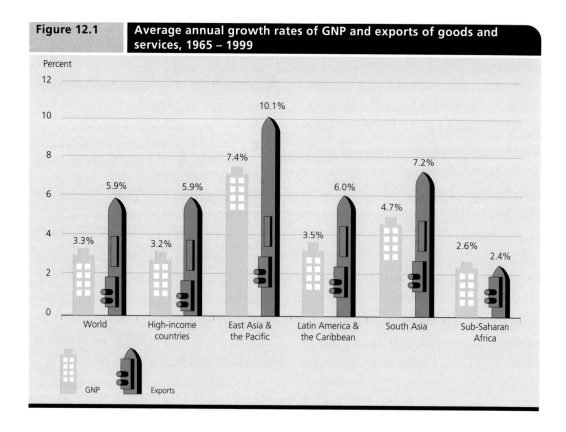

Figure 12.1   **Average annual growth rates of GNP and exports of goods and services, 1965 – 1999**

Percent

World: GNP 3.3%, Exports 5.9%
High-income countries: GNP 3.2%, Exports 5.9%
East Asia & the Pacific: GNP 7.4%, Exports 10.1%
Latin America & the Caribbean: GNP 3.5%, Exports 6.0%
South Asia: GNP 4.7%, Exports 7.2%
Sub-Saharan Africa: GNP 2.6%, Exports 2.4%

GNP   Exports

| Map 12.1 | **Trade as a percentage of real GDP, 1998** |

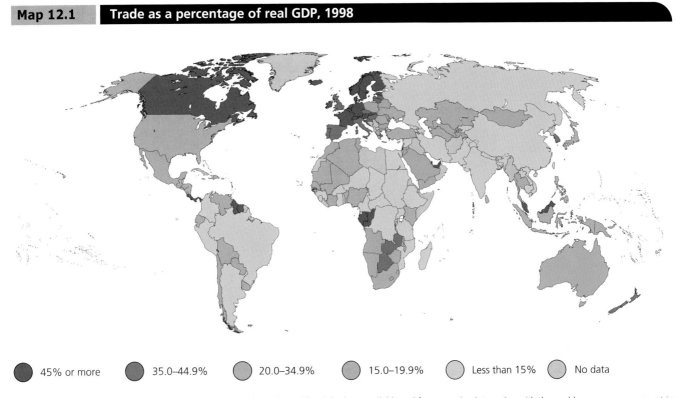

● 45% or more ● 35.0–44.9% ● 20.0–34.9% ● 15.0–19.9% ○ Less than 15% ○ No data

Note: The ratio of trade to purchasing power parity – adjusted GDP is considered the best available tool for comparing integration with the world economy across countries. But the use of this tool is complicated by the different shares of the service sector in the economies of different countries. For example, developed countries appear to be less integrated because a larger share of their output consists of services, a large portion of which are by their nature nontradable.

tries, of which 9 percent went to East Asia and the Pacific and only 1 percent to Sub-Saharan Africa and 1 percent to South Asia. The Middle East and North Africa received about 2 percent of world imports, while Europe and Central Asia and Latin America and the Caribbean received 5 percent each. Even though developing countries have increased trade among themselves, developed countries still remain their main trading partners, the best markets for their exports, and the main source of their imports.

Most developing countries' **terms of trade** deteriorated in the 1980s and

1990s because prices of **primary goods**—which used to make up the largest share of developing country exports—have fallen relative to prices of **manufactured goods.** For example, between 1980 and 2000 **real prices** of wheat and rice dropped about twofold, prices of cocoa more than threefold, and sugar about fivefold. Even petroleum prices went down fourfold between 1980 and 1998 (although by 2000 they grew about twofold). There is still debate about whether this relative decline in commodity prices is permanent or transitory, but developing countries that depend on these exports have already suffered heavy economic losses that have slowed their economic growth and development.

Generally speaking, a country that would attempt to produce almost everything it needs domestically would deprive itself of the enormous economic benefits of international specialization. On the other hand, narrow international specialization, which makes a country overly dependent on exports of one or a few goods, is too risky because unfavorable changes in global demand can significantly worsen such a country's terms of trade. Thus a certain diversification of production and exports is considered to be desirable. Every country should con-

stantly search for its own best place in the international division of labor based on its dynamic comparative advantages and on considerations of economic risk minimization.

In response to the recent unfavorable changes in their terms of trade, many developing countries are increasing the share of manufactured goods in their exports, including exports to developed countries (see Fig. 12.2). The most dynamic categories of their manufactured exports are labor-intensive, low-knowledge products (clothes, carpets, some manually assembled products) that allow these countries to create more jobs and

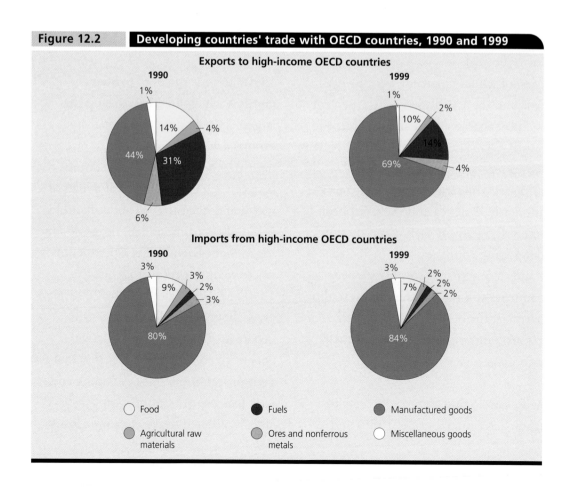

Figure 12.2 — Developing countries' trade with OECD countries, 1990 and 1999

make better use of their abundant labor resources. By contrast, developing country imports from developed countries are mostly capital- and knowledge-intensive manufactured goods—primarily machinery and transport equipment—in which developed countries retain their comparative advantage.

A popular debate in many developed countries asks whether the growing competitive pressure of low-cost, labor-intensive imports from developing countries pushes down the wages of unskilled workers in developed countries (thus increasing the wage gap between skilled and unskilled workers, as in the United Kingdom and United States) and pushes up unemployment, especially among low-skill workers (as in Western Europe). But empirical studies appear to suggest that although trade with developing countries affects the structure of industry and the demand for industrial labor in developed countries, the main reasons for the wage and unemployment problems are internal and stem from labor-saving technological progress and postindustrial economic restructuring (see Chapters 7 and 9).

International Migration

The increased international mobility of people is an important aspect of globalization. In 1985–1990 the annual rate of growth of the world's migrant population was 2.6 percent, more than twice the level recorded in the 1960s. There was a certain slowing of migration in the first half of the 1990s as the result of restrictions introduced by many high-income countries, but beginning in 1997–98 the flows of migrants accelerated again.[3] The major destination countries, rated by the size of migrant inflows in 2000, are the USA, Germany, Japan, Australia, Canada, the United Kingdom, and Italy. Rated by the share of the foreign and foreign-born population in the total population, the leaders are such traditional immigration countries as Luxembourg, Australia, Switzerland, Canada, the USA, Austria, and Germany, while in Japan and Italy, the new immigration countries, the proportions of foreigners are still relatively low (see Table 12.1).

Over 60 percent of the world's migrants moved from developing to developed countries, and this South-North migration is expected to grow in the future owing to economic as well as demographic reasons. The enormous and still growing gap between per capita incomes in developed and developing countries (see Chapter 4), the rapid population growth in developing countries (see Chapter 3) with job creation failing to keep pace, the aging of developed countries' populations (see Chapter 8) with a resultant reduction in the size of their

[3]According to some estimates, there are currently about 150–160 million migrants in the world, if "migrants" are defined as people residing in foreign countries for more than one year.

Table 12.1 Foreign population and labor in selected OECD countries

	Inflows of foreign population (thousands)		Foreign or foreign-born population (% of total population)		Foreign or foreign-born labor force (% of total labor force)	
	1990	2000	1990	2000	1990	2000
Australia	121	316	22.8	23.6	25.7	24.5
Austria	..	66	5.9	9.3	7.4	10.5
Belgium	50	69	9.1	8.4	7.1	8.9
Canada	214	313	16.1	..	18.5	..
Denmark	15	20	3.1	4.8	2.4	3.4
Finland	6	9	0.5	1.8	..	1.5
France	102	119	6.3	5.6	6.2	6.0
Germany	842	649	8.4	8.9	..	8.8*
Ireland	..	24	2.3	3.3	2.6	3.7
Italy	..	272	1.4	2.4	1.3	3.6
Japan	224	346	0.9	1.3	0.1	0.2
Luxembourg	9	11	29.4	37.3	45.2*	57.3*
Netherlands	81	91	4.6	4.2	3.1*	3.4*
Norway	16	28	3.4	4.1	2.3	4.9
Portugal	14	16	1.1	2.1	1.0	2.0
Spain	..	..	0.7	2.2	0.6	1.2
Sweden	53	34	5.6	5.4	5.4	5.0
Switzerland	101	87	16.3	19.3	18.9	18.3
United Kingdom	204	289	3.2	4.0	3.3	4.4
United States	1,536	3,590	7.9	10.4	9.4	12.4

Includes cross-border workers

labor force, and the declining costs of migration (information and transportation costs)–all these factors are likely to contribute to a drastically greater supply of, and demand for, international migrants over the next several decades.

Employment-related migration is on the rise relative to other types of migration, such as migration of refugees or people seeking political asylum. And workers moving from developing to developed countries tend to be clustered at the extremes of the skills and education ladder—either more or less qualified than most residents of the host countries. A significant feature of recent years has been the particularly rapid rise in migration of qualified and highly qualified workers, most notably in response to labor shortages in the information and communications sectors of developed countries, but also in the research and development, health, and education sectors. For example, according to some estimates, there is a shortfall of some 850,000 IT technicians in the USA and nearly 2 million in Western Europe. Against this background, many high-income countries are competing to attract the needed human capital and adjusting their immigration rules to facilitate the entry of ICT specialists, scientists, medical doctors, and nurses. At the other extreme, demand is also high for low-skilled foreign labor for tasks resistant to automation, such as care of the elderly, house cleaning, agriculture, and construction.

There are reasons to believe that international migration of labor can be beneficial to both the receiving and the sending countries. While in the receiving countries migrants help meet labor shortages in certain industries, the sending countries benefit from easing of unemployment pressures and increased financial flows in the form of remittances from migrant workers to their families staying behind. Remittances to developing countries increased by more than 20 percent during 2001–03 and reached $93 billion, which was about one-third more than the total sum of official aid received from developed countries (see Chapter 13).

However, concerns are growing about the damage done to the development aspirations of the poorer countries by emigration of the most qualified professionals—the so-called "brain drain." Professionals from the developing world contribute to expanding knowledge-based industries in high-income countries, while their countries of origin struggle with a shortage of qualified staff to provide basic health and education services and find themselves unable to reach the critical threshold levels of research and development staff needed to succeed in the most productive, high-technology industries. At the same time, increased immigration from developing countries remains a politically sensitive issue in receiving countries, with some real issues related to cultural assimilation of foreigners as well as some exaggerated fears and misconceptions.

Dealing with all the stresses of increased international migration is a global challenge, requiring closer cooperation between sending and receiving countries. Solutions should take into account the interests of all the countries involved as well as those of the migrants themselves. For example, tighter controls on labor migration introduced in one receiving country will affect not only the sending countries but also other potentially receiving countries. In many cases it can also lead to higher illegal migration, most often associated with discriminatory and exploitative treatment of migrant workers.

The advice currently offered to developed and developing countries on managing international migration flows is incomplete and sometimes disputable.

For example, developing countries are advised to develop mechanisms for encouraging retention and return migration of their qualified workers. Returning migrants bring back foreign knowledge and experience (converting "brain drain" into "brain circulation") and can play an important role by facilitating the transfer of foreign technologies or by helping the development of cultural and economic ties with other countries.[4] Further, developing countries are advised to facilitate and reduce the cost of remittance of funds by their migrant workers.

How would you make South-North migration more beneficial to both sides?

[4]China is known to have some success in stimulating the return of former migrant engineers and researchers educated abroad.

As for developed countries, they are counseled to improve their immigration laws, policies, and practices for ensuring orderly migration and to strengthen enforcement of minimum labor and workplace standards so as to discourage illegal migration and employment. To ease the political tensions and to facilitate the integration of immigrants, governments are advised to assist the latter in learning the language of the host country and to fight all forms of racism and discrimination (in employment, housing, schooling, and all other areas).

Sometimes it is also suggested that both developing and developed countries should encourage temporary rather than permanent migration, so as to allow sending countries to benefit from the new knowledge and skills of returning migrants and simultaneously reduce some existing anxiety in receiving countries.

Are you personally concerned with international migration in any way? In your opinion, what should governments do to better manage this process?

13

Globalization: Foreign Investment and Foreign Aid

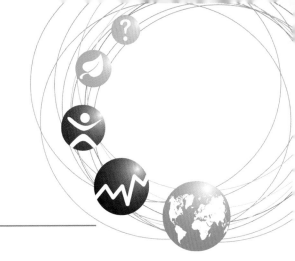

Financial flows to **developing countries** take three main forms—investment from foreign private companies, known as private capital flows, remittances from migrant workers, and aid from foreign governments, often called official development assistance (ODA).

After World War II and until the early 1990s, the main source of external financing for developing countries was official development assistance provided by the governments of high-income countries in the form of food aid, emergency relief, technical assistance, peace-keeping efforts, and financing for construction projects. Donor countries were motivated by the desire to support their political allies and trade partners,

to expand the markets for their exports, and to reduce poverty and military conflicts threatening international security. After the end of the Cold War and upon the start of market-oriented reforms in Eastern Europe and Central Asia, former centrally planned economies also started to receive official assistance, aimed primarily at supporting market reforms. However, the fast growth of private capital flows to developing countries and the declining total amount of ODA have shifted the latter into third place as a source of external financing for developing countries—after foreign direct investment (see Fig. 13.1) and even after remittances from migrant workers (see Chapter 12). Table 13.1 shows the 1999 amounts of net official assistance and

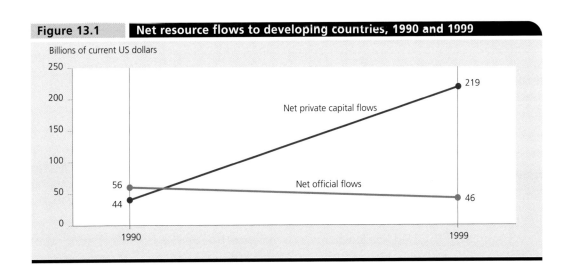

Figure 13.1 Net resource flows to developing countries, 1990 and 1999

Billions of current US dollars

Table 13.1   Net capital flows from high-income OECD countries, 1999
(millions of U.S. dollars)

| | Official assistance | | Private capital flows | | | | | |
| | | | Total | | Foreign direct investment | | Portfolio investment | |
	Total to developing countries	Total to transition countries	Total to developing countries	Total to transition countries	Total to developing countries	Total to transition countries	Total to developing countries	Total to transition countries
Australia	982	3	..	..	..	..	..	..
Austria	527	184	1,334	512	831	512	..	..
Belgium	760	82	4,765	17,604	277	1,825	4,636	15,691
Canada	1,699	165	4,484	-21	4,052	..	460	..
Denmark	1,733	128	410	..	344	..	..	..
Finland	416	74	313	378	145	225	70	167
France	5,637	550	3,524	8,229	5,517	3,953	-1,388	4,058
Germany	5,515	729	13,853	14,007	5,871	4,946	7,075	8,700
Greece	194	11	..	..	..	..	..	..
Ireland	245	..	..	..	..	..	..	..
Italy	1,806	92	9,484	6,137	1,655	-209	8,335	6,831
Japan	15,323	67	-4,297	1,018	5,277	2,624	-3,149	-1,656
Luxembourg	119	3	..	..	..	..	..	..
Netherlands	3,134	22	4,581	2,299	4,103	3,247	-327	..
New Zealand	134	0	16	..	16	..	..	..
Norway	1,370	28	522	556	340	548	..	0
Portugal	276	28	1,953	2,782	1,650	2,779	..	..
Spain	1,363	13	27,655	57	27,710	57	..	..
Sweden	1,630	99	1,192	1,215	665	1,133	..	0
Switzerland	969	70	2,236	6,899	1,834	6,894	..	0
United Kingdom	3,401	326	6,160	-6,446	6,361	-1,734	-98	-4,877
United States	9,145	3,521	32,218	16,221	22,724	15,693	9,319	3
Total	56,378	6,193	110,404	71,446	89,373	42,490	24,934	28,917

Note: Negative figures in the table indicate net outflow of capital to respective OECD countries. Total private capital flows in the table can be greater or smaller than the sum of foreign direct and portfolio investments because they also include smaller flows of capital such as private export credits and grants by nongovernmental institutions.

private capital flows to developing and **transition countries** from the member countries of the **Organization for Economic Co-operation and Development (OECD)** Development Assistance Committee.

Private Capital Flows

In 1997 the growing **net private capital flows** to developing countries reached their peak at about 7 times the **net official assistance** (see Fig. 13.2).

The structure of private flows also changed notably, shifting from a predominance of bank loans to **foreign direct investment** (FDI) and **portfolio investment** (see Table 13.1). The share of foreign direct investment going to developing countries has increased to 38 percent of global foreign direct investment, driven by rapid growth of transnational corporations and encouraged by **liberalization** of markets and better prospects for **economic growth** in a number of developing countries. However, following the East Asian financial crisis of 1997, net private capital flows to developing countries decreased to the level of the early 1990s (see Fig. 13.2) and the share of FDI to developing countries in global FDI fell to about 20 percent.

The distribution of FDI among developing countries remains extremely

unequal. In the second half of the 1990s, more than half of FDI went to just 4 countries and over one-third to just 2 big countries—China and Brazil (see Fig. 13.3). At the end of the 1990s the share of the top 10 developing countries receiving the largest amounts of FDI amounted to 78 percent (see Data Table 4). Note that about half of all developing countries receive little or no foreign direct investment. For example, Sub-Saharan Africa as a whole receives about 5 percent of all FDI and most is concentrated in countries rich in petroleum and minerals. The bulk of FDI flows tends to go to middle-income countries, so the exclusion of the poorest countries may have contributed to further widening of global income disparities.

The developing countries that attract the most private capital flows do so thanks

Can increased private capital flows to developing countries make up for reduced official assistance?

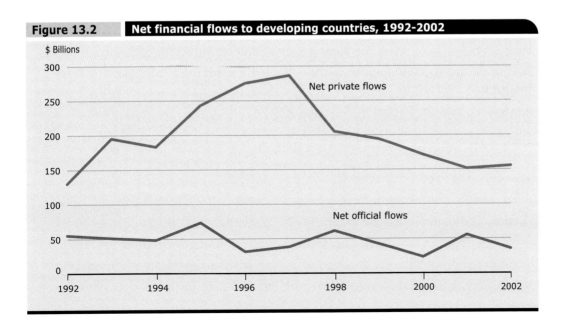

Figure 13.2 **Net financial flows to developing countries, 1992-2002**

Should developing and transition countries strive to attract more foreign investment?

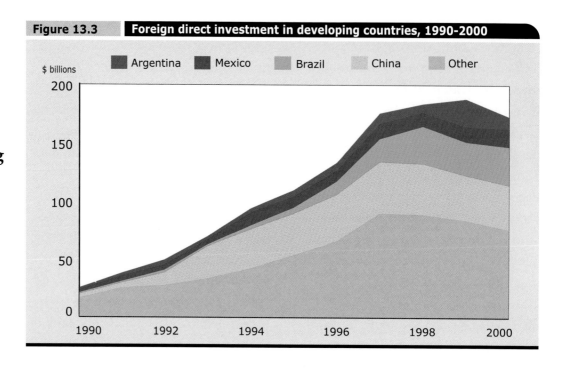

Figure 13.3 | **Foreign direct investment in developing countries, 1990-2000**

to their favorable investment climate, which includes such elements as a stable political regime, good prospects for economic growth, liberal and predictable government regulation, and easy convertibility of the national currency. Higher foreign investment in these countries helps them break the vicious circle of poverty (see Chapter 6) without adding to their foreign debt. In addition, foreign direct investment may bring with it advanced technologies, managerial and marketing skills, and easier access to export markets. The added competition between foreign and domestic companies may also make national economies more efficient. On the other hand, foreign investors can be less sensitive to social and economic needs of receiving countries. It is the

responsibility of national governments to protect their citizens from the possible negative consequences of foreign direct investments and to use these investments in the interests of national economic development. Unfortunately, in some cases competition among developing countries for attracting FDI prevents them from fully meeting this responsibility.

Furthermore, the increased international mobility of capital is associated with considerable economic risks. If private investors (foreign and domestic alike) suddenly lose confidence in a country's stability and growth prospects, they can move their capital out of the country much faster. In that respect portfolio investment is much more dangerous than foreign direct investment, because portfolio investors—who own only a small percentage of shares in a company and have little or no influence on its management—are much more likely to try to get rid of these shares at the first sign or suspicion of falling profits. The East Asian financial crisis of 1997 is seen by some experts as an example of the negative implications of excessive capital mobility.

Another example of excessive capital mobility can be found in Russia, where liberalization of capital markets was carried out in the midst of the transition crisis with high inflation, characteristic uncertainties about property rights and government regulations, and a generally negative investment climate. As a result, while some transition countries have managed to rely on foreign investment to alleviate the difficulties of their transition to market economies, Russia (as well as some other former Soviet Union countries) has suffered from significant capital outflows, legal and illegal. According to some estimates, about $20 billion in capital flowed out of Russia annually throughout most of the 1990s, making "capital flight" the biggest obstacle to Russia's economic development.[1] This situation underscores the importance of creating a favorable investment climate, which is critical not only for attracting foreign investors but, even

more important, for preventing and reversing domestic capital flight.

Official Development Assistance

For most low-income countries, unable to attract private investors, official development assistance (ODA) remains the most important source of foreign financial flows. However, the share of ODA in their economies is not as high as many people in developed countries tend to think—less than 3 percent of low-income countries' GDP and only 0.5 percent of GDP in middle-income countries. Most high-income donor countries decreased the share of their **gross domestic product (GDP)** spent for ODA from the average of 0.5 percent in the early 1960s to 0.3 percent in 1990 and 0.2 percent at the turn of the century. Many of the 22 members of the OECD Development Assistance Committee have pledged to provide 0.7 percent of their GDP for aid to developing countries, but only 4 of them—Denmark, the Netherlands, Norway, and Sweden—have met this target.

Even in absolute numbers, ODA expressed in **real** terms dropped by about 20 percent over the 1990s (see Fig. 13.2). In 2002 it increased to $58 billion, but remained more than 10

Should your country spend more on development assistance?

[1] If the illegal outflows of the 1990s were reflected in statistics (for example, see Table 13.1), the numbers for net capital flows to Russia and some other countries with unfavorable investment climate would turn negative.

times smaller than the sum of defense expenditure by high-income countries (about $600 billion). At the UN Conference on Financing for Development in Monterrey (Mexico, March 2002) a number of high-income countries made new commitments on aid that, if realized, would raise ODA's total in real terms by about $15 billion by 2006 (see Chapter 17).

Use Table 13.1 and Data Table 1 to calculate which donor countries spent the largest and the smallest shares of their GDP on official development assistance. Do you think that your country should spend a larger share of its GDP to aid developing countries in their fight against poverty?

Official assistance to developing and transition countries has three main components:

- Grants, which do not have to be repaid.
- Concessional loans, which have to be repaid but at lower interest rates and over longer periods than commercial bank loans.
- Contributions to multilateral institutions promoting development, such as the **United Nations, International Monetary Fund, World Bank,** and regional development banks (Asian Development Bank, African Development Bank, Inter-American Development Bank).

Grants account for 95–100 percent of the official assistance of most donor countries. A significant part of the official assistance, however, comes in the form of "tied" aid, which requires recipients to purchase goods and **services** from the donor country or from a specified group of countries. Tying arrangements may prevent a recipient from misappropriating or mismanaging aid receipts, but they may also reduce the value of aid if the arrangements are motivated by a desire to benefit suppliers of certain countries, and that may prevent recipients from buying at the lowest price.

Official assistance can also be "tied up" by conditionalities—can depend on the enactment of certain policy reforms that donors see as beneficial for recipient countries' economic growth and poverty reduction. For example, aid to transition countries is often tied to the speed of market reforms. That partially explains why such rapidly reforming countries as the Czech Republic and Poland received more official assistance (relative to their population and GDP) than other transition countries that were slower to reform (see Data Table 4).

The main problem with conditionalities is that, even if the donors' concept of beneficial reforms is fundamentally correct, the recipient government may not accept these reforms as its own priority. Conditionalities imposed on developing countries can weaken their governments' "ownership" of reforms and make these reforms' implementation but formal, superficial, and unsustainable. On the other hand, donors are legitimately concerned that their aid may not be used efficiently enough in the countries with poor policy environments and particularly in those suffering from high levels of corruption among government officials. Large amounts of development aid can be wasted in such countries, while they could have brought considerable improvements to people's lives in other countries.

An important example of policy-based development assistance is the program launched by the International Monetary Fund and the World Bank in 1996 and aiming to reduce the unsustainable burden of foreign debt of the "heavily indebted poor countries," the HIPCs. In order to qualify for assistance under this program, countries must be not only poor (**low-income countries,** by World Bank criteria), and not only severely indebted (with the sum of foreign debt exceeding 150 percent of their export returns). They must also be able to show their ability to develop and implement their own poverty reduction strategies. The goal is to make sure that the budget funds that will be freed up from servicing those countries' foreign debt will indeed be used in the interests of their development rather than diverted to other uses (such as military).[2]

Would you agree that the quality of national policies aimed at economic growth and poverty reduction should as a rule govern donors' decisions to provide aid to this or that country? Which other ways of improving ODA's effectiveness would you suggest?

[2]Developing countries spend on military purposes about $200 billion annually.

14

The Risk of Global Climate Change

Since the beginning of **industrialization, economic development** in most countries has been accompanied by growth in the consumption of **fossil fuels,** with more and more coal, oil, and natural gas being burned by factories, electric power plants, motor vehicles, and households. The resulting carbon dioxide (CO_2) emissions have turned into the largest source of **greenhouse gases**—gases that trap the infrared radiation from the earth within its atmosphere and create the risk of global warming. Because the earth's environmental systems are so complex, the exact timing and extent to which human economic activities will change the planet's climate are still unclear. But many scientists believe that the changes are already observable.

According to the 1995 report of the Intergovernmental Panel on Climate Change, by 2100 the mean global temperature could increase by 1.0–3.5 degrees Celsius and the global sea level could rise by 15–95 centimeters if current trends in greenhouse gas emissions continue. The 2001 report of the same Intergovernmental Panel has corrected the range of predicted temperature increase to 1.4–5.8 degrees Celsius.

Though these may still seem like minor increases, they could have multiple adverse consequences (along with some uncertain benefits). Forests, coral reefs, and other **ecological systems,** unable to adapt to changing temperatures and precipitation patterns, will be damaged and irreversible losses for biological diversity will result. People will also suffer—and those in poor countries are likely to suffer the most, being less prepared to cope with the changes.

Many developing countries in arid and semiarid regions may see their access to safe water worsen. (As things stand today, more than one billion people lack access to safe water.) Tropical diseases may spread farther to the north. Droughts will become more frequent and intense in Asia and Africa, and flooding will likely become a bigger problem in temperate and humid regions. While food production could become easier in middle and high latitudes (in areas that tend to have higher per capita incomes), in the tropics and subtropics yields will likely fall. Large numbers of people could be displaced by a rise in the sea level—including tens of millions in Bangladesh alone, as well as entire nations inhabiting low-lying islands such as those in the Caribbean Sea and the Pacific Ocean.

Most threatening is the fact that, according to current understanding, the global climate is a finely tuned mechanism that can be pushed out of balance and irreversibly set on a course toward catastrophic consequences that scientists can't even fully predict. These risks are hard to evaluate, but they appear credible enough to demand urgent attention.

Whose Responsibility Is It?

The amount of carbon dioxide a country emits into the atmosphere depends mainly on the size of its economy, the level of its **industrialization,** and the **efficiency** of its energy use. Even though **developing countries** contain most of the world's population, their industrial production and energy consumption per capita are relatively low. Thus at this point there seems to be little doubt that the primary responsibility for creating the risk of global warming lies with **developed countries** (see Map 14.1; Figs. 14.1 and 14.2).

The United States is the largest contributor to global greenhouse gas emissions. Although it contains just 4 percent of the world's population, it produces almost 25 percent of global carbon dioxide emissions. Russia was recently replaced

by China as the second largest emitter, but on a per capita basis it is still far ahead of China (see Figs. 14.1 and 14.2).

Traditionally, increased energy consumption—accompanied by increased carbon dioxide emissions—was directly linked to **economic growth** (so that the greater a country's GDP, the higher its energy consumption and pollutant emissions). However, in the 1980s and 1990s carbon dioxide emissions per dollar of GDP declined substantially across developed and developing countries (see Data Table 5). This occurred because environmentally cleaner technologies were introduced, and energy use became more efficient. In addition, the share of the service sector—which requires proportionately less energy than industry—increased in many countries (see Chapter 9). Unfortunately, these changes were not sufficient to stop the growth of global carbon dioxide emissions. To eliminate the risk of global climate change, concerted efforts are needed from the governments of most countries to further increase energy efficiency and move away from today's heavy reliance on fossil fuels.

At the 1992 Earth Summit in Rio de Janeiro (Brazil), developed and **transition countries** agreed to work toward stabilizing their greenhouse gas emissions at 1990 levels by 2000 (in the Framework Convention on Climate Change). However, by 1997, when

Who is primarily responsible for creating the risk of global climate change?

Map 14.1 **Carbon dioxide emissions per capita, 1996 (metric tons)**

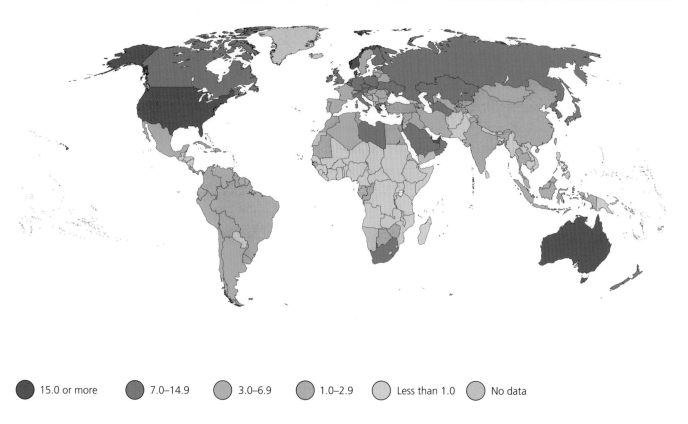

● 15.0 or more   ● 7.0–14.9   ● 3.0–6.9   ● 1.0–2.9   ○ Less than 1.0   ○ No data

representatives of 165 countries gathered in Kyoto (Japan) for the United Nations Conference on Climate Change, it was clear that most countries—including the United States—were falling far short of that target. The Kyoto Protocol, adopted at the conference, was for the first time meant to become legally binding and called on all wealthy nations to reduce greenhouse gas emissions by 6–8 percent below 1990 levels by 2008–12.

This agreement is still considered the most ambitious global environmental undertaking in history, given the high

cost of reducing global greenhouse gas emissions, the broad range of economic activities that will have to be affected by climate-friendly technological change, and the long-term nature of the environmental risks under consideration. Thus it is no wonder that achieving a broad international consensus on the ways of implementing the Kyoto Protocol proved extremely difficult. Developing countries' participation in it was postponed and concrete mechanisms of implementation remained to be further negotiated. At the next global conference in The Hague (Netherlands) in 2000,

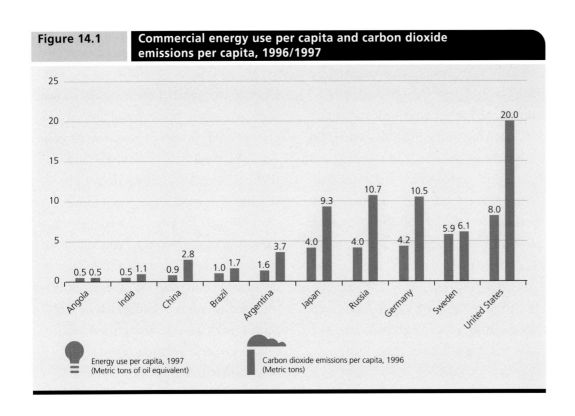

Figure 14.1 Commercial energy use per capita and carbon dioxide emissions per capita, 1996/1997

Energy use per capita, 1997
(Metric tons of oil equivalent)

Carbon dioxide emissions per capita, 1996
(Metric tons)

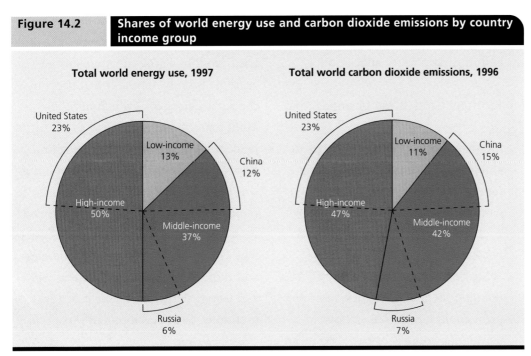

Figure 14.2 Shares of world energy use and carbon dioxide emissions by country income group

Total world energy use, 1997

Total world carbon dioxide emissions, 1996

representatives of 184 states still failed to agree on specific mechanisms for Kyoto Protocol implementation. Moreover, in 2001 US President George Bush officially refused to proceed with its ratification, referring to the possible damage to US economic interests and asserting that the scientific proof of the risk of global climate change was, in his opinion, still not sufficiently valid and that too many countries were not prepared to share in the global efforts.

True, most developing countries refuse to commit to reducing greenhouse gas emissions, arguing that

- the problem was created mostly by developed countries, and
- such commitments would undermine their economic development and impede poverty alleviation.

On the other hand, it can be argued that

- the share of developing countries in global carbon dioxide emissions is rapidly increasing, and
- without developing countries' cooperation any progress achieved in developed countries could be offset by "leakages" beyond their borders. For example, an energy-inefficient steel plant could move its operations to a developing country not covered by an agreement instead of switching to a more energy-efficient technology. As a result, the global greenhouse gas

output could rise in spite of the Kyoto Protocol implementation.

Developed countries are expected to take the lead in preventing global climate change even though in less than 20 years developing countries will likely surpass them as the main emitters of carbon dioxide. But it will take much longer than 20 years for per capita energy consumption in developing countries to become comparable to that in today's developed countries. So, in terms of fairness, today's poor countries have every right to continue polluting the atmosphere. The real question is whether it would be wise for them to follow a model of development that has already proven unsustainable? And is it true that environmental concerns cannot be addressed without impeding poor countries' economic growth? An inspiring example is set by China (not a party to the Kyoto Protocol), which in 1996-2000 managed to increase its GDP by 36 percent while still reducing its carbon dioxide emissions, largely through industrial restructuring and fuel improvements. Many analysts believe that the sooner developing countries take advantage of cleaner production technologies and more efficient ways of generating and using energy, the better it will be for their long-term development prospects.

Assume, for the sake of fairness, that every person on earth has an equal right to the atmosphere as a resource. In that

| **Figure 14.3** | **What if the countries' rights to emit carbon dioxide were proportional to their population?** |

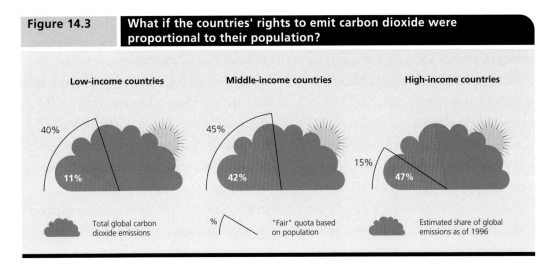

Should all developing countries join in international efforts to reduce carbon dioxide emissions?

case carbon dioxide emission quotas for countries would be determined by population size. Low-income countries would not yet have reached their quota and would have the right to continue emitting carbon dioxide. Middle-income countries would have almost reached their quota (if China with its 21 percent of the world's population is included among them) or already exceeded it (if China is counted among low-income countries, as it was till the end of the 1990s). Most important, high-income countries would have exceeded their quotas almost by a factor of three (compare Figs. 2.2 and 14.3).

Will the North-South cooperation work?

The challenge of agreeing on concerted global action in response to the risk of global climate change is complicated by the fact that the costs and benefits of such

action are distributed unevenly among countries. For example, the Alliance of Small Island States (AOSIS), whose members are directly threatened by the prospect of the rising sea level, has already adopted unilateral carbon abatement measures. But to most other developing countries, with much higher greenhouse gas emissions, increased burning of fossil fuels in the course of their industrialization and continued burning of forests for agriculture appear to be much higher economic and social priorities.

The potential benefits of preventing the global climate change are estimated to be several times greater for the group of developing countries—avoiding the loss of up to 9 percent of their GDP compared with 1.0–1.5 percent in developed countries. At the same time the costs of prevention of greenhouse gas emissions are considerably lower in developing countries as compared with developed, where energy production and consumption are already relatively efficient and simple improvements are harder to make. According to some estimates, reducing carbon dioxide emissions by 1 ton can cost over US$12 in developed countries, but only US$2-3 in many developing countries, where introducing modern, energy-efficient technologies (already widely used in high-income economies) can make a big and quick difference. Does not this mean that developing countries should be more interested in taking action against the global climate change?

In fact, low-income countries can rarely afford any long-term planning, and the cost of US$2–3 per ton of carbon dioxide emissions prevented is still too high for them in the presence of many other urgent socioeconomic needs. Is there a way to further increase the benefits of climate-friendly programs for developing countries and to further reduce their costs?

The Prototype Carbon Fund (PCF) established by the World Bank in 1999 with contributions from interested governments and private companies was a first attempt to deal practically with this task. The underlying idea is to create a market for trading carbon dioxide emissions reductions between developed countries, on the one hand, and developing and transition countries, on the other. Developed countries contributing to the Fund sponsor the introduction of cleaner technologies in the less developed coun-

tries, the resulting emissions reductions are independently verified and certified, and the Fund's contributors are then allowed to count these reductions towards their Kyoto Protocol commitments. If this type of deal becomes widespread, many developing countries may additionally benefit from greater **foreign investment** and easier access to modern technologies, while the global problem of climate change prevention may be solved at a much lower cost.

The very first PCF deal happened to take place with Latvia, as part of the Liepaja Solid Waste Management Project. This project, financed jointly by the government of Latvia, the city of Liepaja, the World Bank, the Nordic Investment Bank, and the Swedish International Development Agency, is aimed at replacing several outdated landfills in the Liepaja region, many of which pose a risk to local groundwater resources, with a modern regional waste treatment facility. With the PCF contribution, a state-of-the-art energy cell system will be installed to collect landfill gases produced by decaying waste. These gases, containing 50 percent methane, will then be used to generate electricity and heat. It is expected that, over the project lifetime of 25 years, an equivalent of about 2 million tons of carbon dioxide will be prevented from entering the earth's atmosphere by (1) capturing the methane-containing landfill gases and (2) substituting this methane for natural gas in generating electricity for Latvia's power grid. In addition, the citizens of Liepaja will get a lower-cost, cleaner waste disposal facility using a minimum of land and sustainable for an indefinitely long time.

* * *

At the time of this writing, the Kyoto protocol has been ratified by many countries but still has not entered into legal force, because these countries represent less than 55 percent of all the 1990 greenhouse gases emissions of developed countries. Meanwhile, the need for action is truly urgent, given that any longer-term solution to reducing and stabilizing greenhouse gases emissions would require switching the world to alternative, zero-emission energy sources such as hydro, wind, and solar power. As of 1999, these sources accounted for only 5 percent of total energy production (mostly hydropower). Intensified research and development is still needed to make them economically competitive, and even then it might take 30-50 years more to completely replace the old energy-producing and energy-consuming stock of equipment and structures. If countries fail to commit to concerted emissions control without further delay, triggering catastrophic and irreversible climate change might become unavoidable.

15

Composite Indicators of Development

Can you suggest a better way to measure countries' development (than those described in this chapter)?

Comparing countries' **GNP (or GDP) per capita** is the most common approach to assessing their level of development. But higher per capita income in a country does not always mean that its people are better off than those in a country with lower income, because there are many aspects of human well-being that these indicators do not capture. (Can you give some examples? See Chapter 2.) Seeking a better measure of development success, experts use different methods of integrating data on average incomes with data on average health and education levels. These methods make it possible to assess a country's achievements in both **economic development** and human development (see Chapter 1).

"Development Diamonds"

Experts at the World Bank use so-called development diamonds to portray relationships among four socioeconomic indicators for a given country relative to the averages for that country's income group (low-income, lower-middle-income, upper-middle-income, or high-income). **Life expectancy at birth, gross primary** (or **secondary**) **enrollment, access to safe water,** and GNP

per capita are presented, one on each axis, then connected with bold lines to form a polygon. The shape of this "diamond" can easily be compared to the reference diamond (see colored diamonds), which represents the average indicators for the country's income group, each indexed to 100 percent. Any point outside the reference diamond shows a value better than the group average, while any point inside signals below-average achievement.

Botswana's development diamond has a triangular shape because data on the percentage of its population with access to safe water were unavailable in the World Bank (Figure 15.1). Think of another indicator, possibly even more important for Botswana's development, that you would use to compare it China. Use an indicator from the data tables at the back of this book to complete the development diamond for Botswana and one or two other countries of your choice.

Note that the development diamonds for India and Ethiopia, and Botswana and China were constructed using indexes based on average indicators for two different groups of countries: low-income and middle-income (see Figure 15.1). This approach makes it impossi-

Figure 15.1 **Development diamonds for selected countries: recent index values**

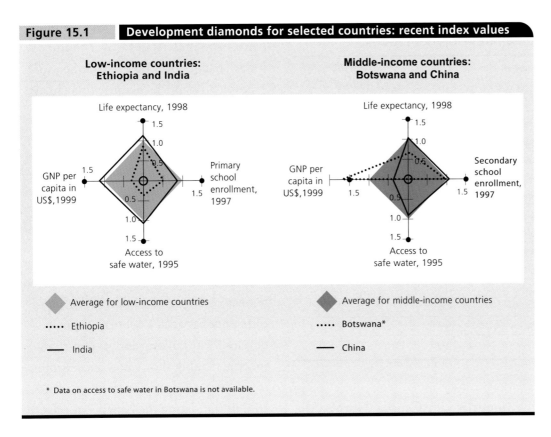

How can countries
use their wealth
more effectively
for the benefit
of their people?

ble to visually compare the development achievements of these two pairs of countries.

Human Development Index

United Nations experts prefer to use the human development index to measure a country's development. This composite index is a simple average of three indexes reflecting a country's achievements in health and longevity (as measured by life expectancy at birth), education (measured by **adult literacy** and combined primary, secondary, and tertiary enrollments), and **living standard** (measured by GDP per capita in **purchasing**

power parity terms). Achievement in each area is measured by how far a country has gone in attaining the following goal: life expectancy of 85 years, adult literacy and enrollments of 100 percent, and real GDP per capita of $40,000 in purchasing power parity terms. Although highly desirable, these goals have not yet been fully attained by any country, so the actual indicators are expressed as decimal shares of the ideal.

The advantage of the human development index relative to the development diamond method is that it allows countries to be ranked in order of their achievements in human development. In the ranking based on 1998 data, the top

Table 15.1   Differences between rankings by GNP per capita and by the human development index

Countries	Rank by real (PPP$) GNP per capita, 1999	Rank by index of human development, 1998	Real GNP per capita (PPP$) rank minus human development index rank
Botswana	84	122	–38
South Africa	69	103	–34
Namibia	92	115	–23
Switzerland	6	13	–7
United States	4	3	–1
Canada	16	1	15
Hungary	60	43	17
Sweden	28	6	22
China	128	99	29
Tajikistan	184	110	74

five countries were Canada, Norway, the United States, Australia, and Iceland. The bottom five countries were Sierra Leone, Niger, Burkina Faso, Ethiopia, and Guinea-Bissau. The top five developing economies were Singapore, Hong Kong (China), Brunei, Cyprus, and the Republic of Korea. (See Data Table 5)

The disadvantage of the human development index is that, as any aggregate index, it does not allow us to see the rel-

ative importance of its different components or to understand why a country's index changes over time—whether, for example, it happens because of a change in GNP per capita or because of a change in adult literacy.

The human development index ranking of some countries differs significantly from their ranking by real GNP (or GDP) per capita. For example, Sweden ranks only 28th in real GNP per capita but 6th in human development—a difference of 22 points (Table 15.1). The difference between a country's human development ranking and its per capita income ranking shows how successful it is (or isn't), compared with other countries in translating the benefits of **economic growth** into **quality of life** for its population (see Data Table 5). A positive difference means that a country is doing relatively better in terms of human development than in terms of per capita income. This outcome is often seen in former socialist countries and in the developed countries of Europe. A negative difference means the opposite. The most striking examples are Botswana and South Africa (see Table 15.1).

16

Indicators of Development Sustainability

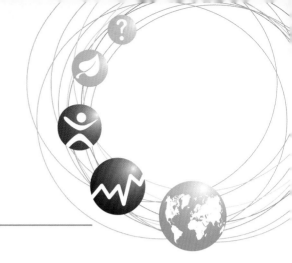

Classical economists consistently identified three sources and components of national wealth: land, labor, and capital. By contrast, Western economists of the 20th century preferred to focus on **capital,** understood to be human-made **physical capital** only—the stock of structures and equipment used for production. Thus expenses aimed at adding to this stock were the only expenses categorized as **investment.** Most other expenses, such as those for education or for environmental protection, were considered to constitute consumption and treated as deductions from potential capital accumulation.

A better understanding of the need for sustainable development first led to attempts to "green" national accounts—that is, to account for changes in **natural capital** in calculations of **gross domestic product** and **gross national product**—then to the development of statistical methods to account for changes in a country's **human capital.** Although valuation methods for natural and human capital are still imperfect, they allow experts to explore some critical development issues. These include the changing composition of a country's national wealth and operational indica-

tors of sustainable—or unsustainable—development.

Composition of National Wealth

According to a number of recent World Bank studies, physical capital (produced assets) is not the main—much less the only—component of a country's wealth. Most important for all countries are human resources, which consist of "raw labor," determined mainly by the number of people in a country's **labor force,** and human capital. Natural capital is another important component of every nation's wealth.

A country's level of development determines the roles played by the different components of its national wealth. The dominance of human capital is particularly marked in the most developed countries, where natural capital is calculated to account for just 2–5 percent of aggregate wealth. By contrast, in West Africa—one of the world's poorest regions—natural capital still prevails over physical capital, and the share of human resources is among the lowest in the world despite a large population (see Fig. 16.1). Comparing West Africa with Western

How does the structure of national wealth change as a country develops?

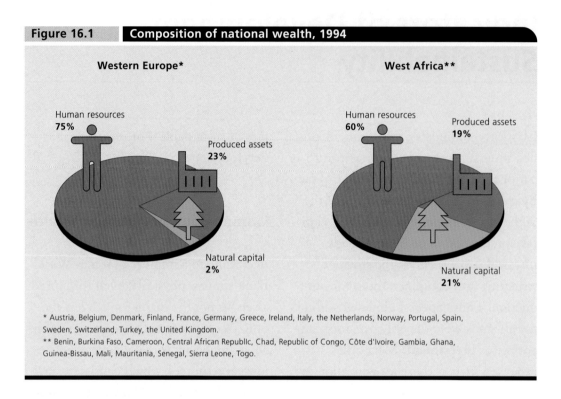

Figure 16.1 | **Composition of national wealth, 1994**

Western Europe*

Human resources
75%

Produced assets
23%

Natural capital
2%

West Africa**

Human resources
60%

Produced assets
19%

Natural capital
21%

* Austria, Belgium, Denmark, Finland, France, Germany, Greece, Ireland, Italy, the Netherlands, Norway, Portugal, Spain, Sweden, Switzerland, Turkey, the United Kingdom.
** Benin, Burkina Faso, Cameroon, Central African Republic, Chad, Republic of Congo, Côte d'Ivoire, Gambia, Ghana, Guinea-Bissau, Mali, Mauritania, Senegal, Sierra Leone, Togo.

Europe is particularly indicative because in absolute terms the two regions have roughly the same per capita value for natural capital. Thus the striking difference in the composition of their national wealth can be entirely attributed to the fact that the average West European has 13–14 times as much human and physical capital at his or her disposal.

Accumulation of National Wealth as an Indicator of Sustainable Development

Over the past 10 years the concept of sustainable development has become more comprehensive and measurable. A recent World Bank study defined sustainable development as "a process of

managing a portfolio of assets to preserve and enhance the opportunities people face." The assets that this definition refers to include not just traditionally accounted physical capital, but also natural and human capital. To be sustainable, development must provide for all these assets to grow over time—or at least not to decrease. The same logic applies to prudent management of a national economy as applies to prudent management of personal property.

With that definition in mind, one possible indicator of sustainable (or unsustainable) development might be the "genuine domestic saving rate" or "genuine domestic investment rate," a new statistical indicator being calculated by World Bank experts for most countries and for all the regions of the world. Standard measures of wealth accumulation ignore the depletion of, and damage to, **natural resources** such as forests and oil deposits, on the one hand, and investment in one of a nation's most valuable assets—its people—on the other. The genuine domestic **saving** (investment) rate is designed to correct for this shortcoming by adjusting the traditional domestic saving rate downward by an estimate of natural resource depletion and pollution damages (the loss of natural capital), and upward by growth in the value of human capital (which comes primarily from investing in education and basic health services). (See Fig. 16.2.)

Calculating genuine saving rates for different countries is extremely challenging, particularly because of difficulties in valuating changes in their human and natural capital. But the effort is considered worthwhile because of the potential importance of sustainable development indicators for informing and guiding practical policymaking. In Data Table 5, please see the genuine domestic saving rates estimated by World Bank economists taking into account net domestic saving (**gross domestic saving** less consumption of physical capital over the year), education expenditure, depletion of a nation's energy, mineral, and forest resources, and damage from CO_2 emissions.[1]

These preliminary estimates show that many of the most resource-dependent countries, including all the major oil exporters, have low or negative genuine domestic savings. That means that losses

How can countries make their development more sustainable?

[1]Note that these calculations do not account for such important negative factors as damage to water resources, degradation of soils, health losses from local pollution, depletion of fish stocks or such important positive factor as basic health expenditure.

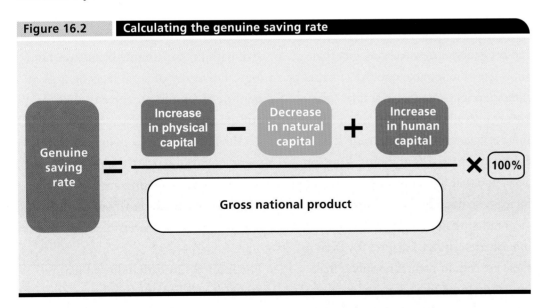

Figure 16.2   Calculating the genuine saving rate

of their national wealth caused by depletion of natural capital and damage done by CO_2 emissions outweigh the benefits from net domestic saving and education expenditure. Thus it is quite possible that in these countries the aggregate national wealth was actually decreasing, to the detriment of the people's quality of life and these countries' future development prospects. And such unsustainable development might be happening in spite of positive economic growth indicators, which are usually at the center of all governments' attention.

Note that this indicator of sustainable development assumes high substitutability among different components of national wealth. It is assumed, for example, that depletion of natural resources can be compensated for by investing incomes received from these resources in education (to build up national human capital) or in new enterprises (a country's physical capital). But this can only be true to the extent that these "compensatory" investments can bring about new technologies that allow use of renewable resources instead of nonrenewable ones (for example, solar energy instead of oil) or ensure much more efficient production, using less energy and materials as inputs. One can also hope that higher income levels would increase demand for "less material" services rather than for energy- and material-intensive goods (see Chapter 9). Even so, there are certain natural resources that humanity is not likely ever to be able to replace. Think, for example, of all the **ecospheric** resources that are vital for the

maintenance of the Earth's life support systems, such as the atmospheric **ozone** that protects all biological species from harmful solar radiation. Humans as a biological species would not survive without these kinds of services from nature. There are also many natural resources that have no known practical use to people as of now, but may prove indispensable at some time in the future. That is why, for example, there exists wide agreement on the importance of preserving all the existing biological species—the irreversible losses of biological diversity can seriously compromise the choices of both current and future generations.

Clearly there are certain critical limits or thresholds beyond which different kinds of natural capital cannot be replaced by anything else. Unfortunately, in most cases scientists cannot even tell us approximately where these critical limits are. Moreover, is "survivability" really a sufficient criterion for preserving natural resources? Even if humanity could survive without the unique beauty and biological diversity of coral reefs or tropical rainforests, would we agree to deprive our grandchildren of the opportunity to see them? That is why many development experts advocate the principle of precaution in depleting any natural resources, particularly where there is a risk of serious or irreversible damage.

The limited substitutability of natural capital (as well as of many forms of human capital) underlies the limitations of the genuine domestic saving rate as an

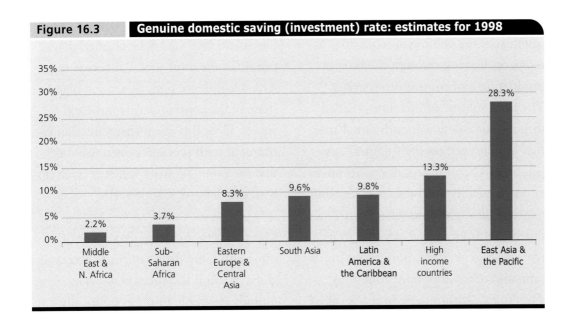

Figure 16.3 | **Genuine domestic saving (investment) rate: estimates for 1998**

indicator of sustainable development, even though these limitations are the flip side of the much-needed attempt to bring together all three aspects of sustainable development—economic, social, and environmental. On the one hand, this indicator can play an important role in attracting governments' attention to the issue of rational use of natural resources for the long-term benefit of their countries. It should be understood, however, that even those countries that appear to perform quite well in terms of this indicator might actually be very close to critical limits in using many of their natural resources. In Figure 16.3, based on Data Table 5, the groups of East Asian and high-income countries appear to be leading the world in the overall sustainability of their development. However, environmentalists point to the

dangerous deforestation, pollution, and loss of biodiversity that accompanied fast economic growth in East Asia. As for high-income countries, part of their relative environmental sustainability results from importing energy and mineral resources instead of depleting their own. That highlights another weakness of the indicator in question—its focus on country-level sustainability, while truly sustainable development can be only global.[2]

Material Throughput and Environmental Space

These indicators theoretically allow us to measure and monitor sustainability on the global scale but, unlike the genuine domestic saving rate, they focus solely on environmental sustainability.

[2]Note that, in spite of economic globalization, governments still bear the main responsibility for the rational use of natural resources within their national territories. Thus, country-level indicators of sustainability are important for practical policymaking, but arguably need to be supplemented by global-level indicators.

Is development possible without growth of material throughput?

Theoretically it should be possible to measure the volume of material resources flowing through the human production and consumption cycle. The total volume of this flow—called throughput—determines the total stress that humans put on their natural environment. Then the task of environmental sustainability can be seen as limiting material throughput to what nature can tolerate without serious damage to its resource-regeneration, pollution-absorption, and other important functions. The "space" within these limits is called "environmental space," shared by all humanity. Then to determine whether a certain country is developing in an environmentally sustainable way, its use of natural resources and its pollution can be compared with the environmental space that belongs to that country.[3]

In fact, different countries use the limited global environmental space very unequally. High-income countries with less than one-fifth of the world population consume about three-quarters of the raw materials and energy traded in the world and are responsible for a disproportionately large share of all pollution in the world (see, for example, Fig. 14.3). Some environmentalists have calculated that if all the people on Earth were to consume natural resources in the same quantities as people in high-income countries do

today, they would need 10 planets like Earth, not one. Can it be claimed that people in the most successful economies have a legitimate right to a much bigger share of the common environmental space? Does this mean that natural environment itself precludes the possibility that the poor countries will ever catch up with the rich (see Chapter 4)?

Many development experts agree that more equitable distribution of access to global natural resources is not only morally desirable but also politically necessary to create the conditions for successful cooperation between developed and developing countries in dealing with multiple global challenges of sustainable development. But the practical—political, economic, and technological—possibility of radically reducing the use of environmental space by high-income countries is much more disputable. Such a radical change would require a strong political commitment to creating economic incentives for shifting the focus of technological development from saving labor to saving natural resources. Then economic growth in both developed and developing countries would continue with stable or even decreasing material throughput. Interestingly, some environmentalists point out that many of the technologies needed for uncoupling

[3]A rather similar concept of *ecological footprint* looks at the area of land that a particular group of consumers uses. This concept works reasonably well with some issues, for example, when different ways of producing food or paper are examined, but is less helpful in dealing with other issues, such as global warming (see Chapter 14) or water pollution.

economic growth from throughput growth already exist, but suboptimal economic conditions prevent their use.

Material throughput and environmental space as indicators of global environmental sustainability show that developed countries need to change their modes of production and consumption beyond those changes already under way in the course of their postindustrialization (see Chapter 9).

Social Capital and Public Officials' Corruption

Measuring and monitoring social sustainability is probably even more challenging than measuring environmental sustainability because of the lack of a widely accepted unifying concept similar to that of environmental space. Experts know how to measure many of the negative factors undermining social sustainability, such as unemployment, income inequality (see Chapter 5), or poverty (see Chapter 6). The population's education (see Chapter 7) and health status (see Chapter 8) are also understood to affect social sustainability. But any of these factors taken separately fails to explain why some countries and communities consistently tend to use all their **production resources (human, physical, and natural capital)** much more **efficiently** than do others and so are developing more successfully. The recently introduced concept of "social

capital" might be able to answer this question and "capture" most aspects of a country's social development.

Refer to Figure 16.1 once again. What this picture fails to acknowledge is perhaps the most critical factor in any society's development: the way people interact, cooperate, and resolve their conflicts. This is what conventional statistical indicators have trouble measuring. And this is what researchers have recently come to call the *social capital* of society.

Social capital refers to organizations and associations (including public, private, and nonprofit) as well as to norms and relationships (such as laws, traditions, and personal networks). It is the glue that holds societies together—what social cohesion depends on. Abundant social capital considerably lowers the costs of doing business and increases productivity by promoting trust, coordination, and cooperation at all levels. By contrast, a lack of social capital leads to conflicts and inefficiencies.

Because social capital is so multidimensional, there can hardly be a single "best" way of measuring it. But that does not mean that measurement is impossible. Researchers measure social capital in a number of creative ways, usually by calculating composite indexes based on a range of data collected through surveys. The data used for these calculations generally reflect the number of formal and

How can countries build their social capital?

Table 16.1   The 2000 Corruption Perception Index (selected countries)

Country rank	1	2	3	5	6	10	14	17
Country	Finland	Denmark	New Zealand, Sweden	Canada	Singapore	United Kingdom	USA	Germany
CPI score	10.0	9.8	9.4	9.2	9.1	8.7	7.8	7.6
Country rank	21	23	27	28	32	34	42	43
Country	France	Japan	Estonia	Taiwan (China)	Hungary, Tunisia	South Africa	Czech Republic	Poland, El Salvador
CPI score	6.7	6.4	5.7	5.5	5.2	5.0	4.3	4.2
Country rank	49	52	57	63	65	68	76	79
Country	Brazil	Argentina, Ghana	Latvia, Zambia	China, Egypt	Kazakhstan, Zimbabwe	Romania	Tanzania, Vietnam	Uzbekistan
CPI score	3.9	3.5	3.4	3.1	3.0	2.9	2.5	2.4
Country rank	82	85	87	89	90			
Country	Kenya, Russia	Angola, Indonesia	Azerbaijan, Ukraine	Yugoslavia	Nigeria			
CPI score	2.1	1.7	1.5	1.3	1.2			

Source: Transparency International Press Release, Berlin, September 13, 2000

informal groups and networks that people call upon, prevailing norms of cooperation and reciprocity, and people's subjective trust in others, in public and private institutions, and in governments.

Mounting evidence suggests that social capital is critical for economies to grow and for people to prosper. However, radical reforms or even rapid but unbalanced development often undermine existing forms of social capital without replacing them with new ones. Such degradation of social capital threatens social cohesion and renders development unsustainable. Some development experts believe that this is what has happened recently in many transition countries.

One red flag of social capital degradation is corruption among public servants, including bribery, misappropriation of public funds, and misuse of authority. Corruption not only wastes resources by distorting government policies away from the interests of the majority, it also generates apathy and cynicism among citizens, makes laws dysfunctional, and contributes to a rise in crime. Eventually, corruption discredits political democracy, which is essential for development, and undermines broad public support for economic reforms. It is no wonder that, according to some studies, countries suffering from high levels of corruption typically exhibit lower rates of economic growth. Such elements of social capital as good governance and the rule of law are no less important for sustainable **economic development** than such basic economic conditions as sufficient **saving** and **investment** (see Chapter 6) or strong incentives for efficiency (see Chapter 11).

Corruption among government officials is widely seen to be particularly widespread in some African countries and in **transition countries,** where it became hard to control owing to simultaneous political and economic reforms carried out amid a massive redistribution of state assets. Table 16.1 shows selected Corruption Perception Indexes (CPI), calculated by an influential nongovernmental organization (NGO), Transparency International, based on the results of multiple surveys among businesspeople, international analysts, and the general public. These indexes range between 10 (highly clean from corruption) and 0 (highly corrupt). The 2000 CPI table ranked 90 countries for which data were available, from Finland (most clean) to Nigeria (most corrupt).

Note that the nature of corruption can differ significantly among countries. One of the ways of classifying various corrupt behaviors is based on how deep the corrupt transaction reaches into the operations of the state. So-called *administrative corruption* refers to intentional misimplementation of existing laws, rules, and regulations by public officials to provide advantages to selected individuals, groups, or firms in exchange for illicit

and nontransparent private gains (bribes). Some of the most common examples of administrative corruption, reported in enterprise surveys, are bribe payments to obtain state licenses and permits, to deal with taxes, and to gain government contracts. Household surveys show bribery in the police force, particularly the traffic police, as well as in the health and education systems as most common. On the other hand, so-called *state capture* refers to the actions of individuals, groups, or firms to *influence the formation* of laws, rules, and regulations to their own advantage by means of illicit and nontransparent provision of private benefits to public officials. The "sales" to private interests of parliamentary votes, presidential decrees, or civil and criminal court decisions are some of the most common examples of state capture.

Researchers explain the different typology of corruption in the group of transition countries (see Fig. 16.4) by the differences in their historical legacies and economic realities. Administrative corruption is typically lower in countries with longer experience of sovereignty (within recent history) and closer links to European standards of civil service. These countries tend to benefit from relatively developed systems of public administration and better-trained public officials. As for state capture, it is explained mostly as a result of high concentration of economic power. Thus countries richly endowed with natural resources (like Azerbaijan and Russia) or

How can countries fight the curse of government corruption?

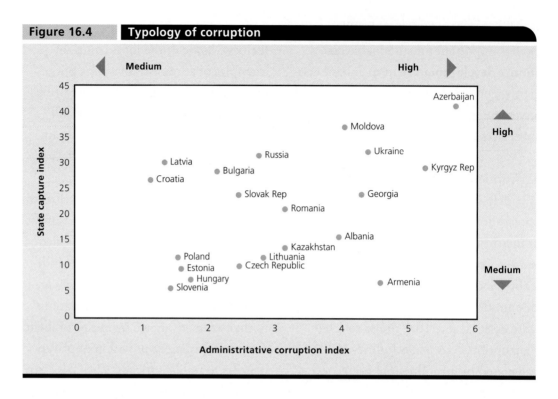

Figure 16.4 | **Typology of corruption**

well placed to serve as transit routes for the distribution of these resources (like Latvia) are the most fertile ground for state capture. In these countries there is always a risk that dominant private or public firms will develop close ties to political leaders and succeed in furthering their own interests at the expense of the broader public interest.

To control corruption and minimize its harmful effect on a country's development, governments can use different strategies. Reforming public administration to reduce opportunities and incentives for corruption and to increase transparency and accountability in government decisionmaking is usually necessary but insufficient. Other necessary measures include strengthening the independence and efficiency of the judicial system; giving more voice to NGOs

representing various groups of the population; fostering truly independent mass media; and creating a competitive private sector, free from excessive government regulation as well as from monopolization. **Market liberalization** and de-monopolization are often seen as particularly effective means of reducing the opportunities for different forms of corruption.

* * *

Think of the other possible ways to measure and monitor the sustainability of development at local, national, and global levels. In your opinion, which issues in sustainable development appear to be the most urgent? Awareness of which indicators could help people, governments, and the international community to deal with these issues?

17

Development Goals and Strategies

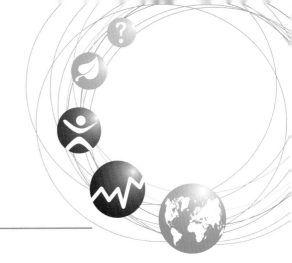

Over the past several decades some **developing countries** have achieved high **economic growth** rates, significantly narrowing the gap between themselves and the most **developed countries.** But many more developing countries have actually seen the economic gap widen (see Fig. 4.4). Thus, while accelerated growth and development leading to convergence with developed countries are possible, these are in no way guaranteed. In fact there is a high risk that today's gap between the rich and the poor countries—with 80 percent of the world's population commanding less than 20 percent of global GDP—will become even wider. There is also a high risk that the number of people living in extreme poverty—on less than US$1 a day—will not substantially decrease (see Chapter 6). All these risks are aggravated by the growth of the world's population, which in the next 30 years is projected to expand by two billion people, almost all of them expected to be born in developing countries (see Chapter 3).

Whose responsibility is it to stop the global spread of poverty?

And what can governments do to catalyze their countries' development?

To begin to answer those questions, it is important to remember that development is far more complex than simply economic growth or the quantitative accumulation of national **capital,** even in the broader meaning of the term (as described in Chapter 16, for instance). Development is also the qualitative transformation of a whole society, a shift to new ways of thinking, and, correspondingly, to new relations and new methods of production. Moreover, as you will probably agree, transformation qualifies as development only if it benefits most people—improves their **quality of life** and gives them more control over their destinies (see Chapter 1). This comprehensive process of change has to involve most of the population and cannot be imposed from outside the country or from above—for example, by means of unpopular government policy or by means of foreign aid.

Millennium Development Goals

The 1992 Earth Summit in Rio de Janeiro issued the famous Agenda 21 (for the 21st century), which—in its 40 chapters—provided the main framework for international understanding of and

Which other goals and targets would you add to the list of Millennium Development Goals?

cooperation on the issues of sustainable development. Notably, Agenda 21 recognized combating poverty as a basic condition for ensuring sustainability—social, economic, and even environmental. Since 1992 international agreement on the key issues of sustainable development has deepened and a wide consensus on the urgent need to combat poverty in its many forms has arisen. A number of world conferences organized by the United Nations following the Rio Earth Summit discussed the so-called International Development Goals, which were meant to help focus and coordinate the efforts of donor countries, international development agencies, and the governments of developing countries themselves. In September 2000 many of those goals were incorporated into the resolutions of the UN Millennium General Assembly in New York (also called the Millennium Summit) and endorsed by 189 countries as Millennium Development Goals.

There are eight major Millennium Development Goals, seven of which formulate far-reaching improvements in some of the most important indicators of development, followed by concrete targets to be achieved by 2015, in comparison with the figures for 1990. The eighth goal specifies some of the main means of achieving the first seven goals in the portion of the work that requires joint effort by international development partners—the governments of

developed and developing countries, as well as the private sector.

In summary form, the Millennium Development Goals and their related targets call for achieving the following outcomes by 2015:

1. Decreasing by half the proportion of people living in extreme poverty (on less than US$1 a day) and suffering from hunger.
2. Achieving universal primary education.
3. Eliminating gender disparity at all levels of education.
4. Reducing the under-five mortality rate by two-thirds.
5. Reducing the maternal mortality ratios by three-quarters.
6. Halting and beginning to reverse the spread of HIV/AIDS, malaria, and other diseases.
7. Ensuring improved environmental sustainability (by integrating sustainable development into country policies, reversing the loss of environmental resources, and halving the proportion of people without access to potable water and basic sanitation).
8. Building a Global Partnership for Development.

(In Annex 3, see the exact list of eight long-term goals along with concrete targets and indicators for tracking progress towards these targets.)

The eighth goal was added in 2001, and its specific targets and indicators continue to be actively discussed and formulated under the leadership of the main international development agencies. As of early 2002, wide agreement seemed to be achieved on the following targets:

- Further develop open and nondiscriminatory trading and financial systems, which would include an increased level of official development assistance (up to 0.7 percent of the donor countries' GDP),
- Address the special needs of the **least developed countries** and those of the landlocked and small island developing countries (which have greater difficulty competing in the global economy),
- Deal comprehensively with the problem of the unsustainable foreign debt of developing countries,
- Develop and implement strategies for reducing youth unemployment,
- Provide access to affordable essential drugs in developing countries,
- Spread more widely the benefits of new technologies, especially information and communication technologies (ICT).

Note that success in the first three components of Goal 8 will depend mostly on the partnership between the governments of developed and developing countries, while attainment of the last three will also require good will and active participation on the part of the private sector, including the leading pharmaceutical and ICT companies.

It is important to understand that all of the Millennium Development Goals are closely interconnected, so that achieving one of them can be expected to contribute to achieving the others. For example, reducing the share of people living in extreme poverty from about 30 percent of the developing world's population to about 15 percent would certainly help to deal with the health and education challenges, but achieving health and education goals would also contribute to the fight against poverty. It can also be shown that providing for environmental sustainability, although it may initially require some additional spending, will ultimately more than pay for itself in terms of better health, longer lives, and more natural resources available for poverty reduction. Unfortunately, failure to achieve some of these goals can also preclude the achievement of many or all of the others. Particularly devastating can be the effects of an unchecked HIV/AIDS epidemic, which, by killing adults in their most productive years, exposes millions to extreme deprivation. And a failure to build an effective Global Partnership for Development can make the challenge of attaining the Millennium Development Goals disproportionately hard for many developing countries, particularly the poorest of them.

What will be the main difficulties in building an effective Global Partnership for Development?

The last decade of the 20th century has brought some progress toward all the Millennium Goals, but if improvements are not accelerated, these goals will not be achieved by the 2015 deadline in many or even in most developing countries. For example, if the average rate of economic growth of the 1990s (1.7 percent a year) is not increased, the average proportion of people living on less than US$1 a day will probably not decline below 19 percent. Moreover, most improvements are likely to occur in China and India, while in countries of Sub-Saharan Africa the number of poor may actually continue to rise. Overall, according to the World Bank estimate made in 2002, only 22 developing countries seemed to be on target to meet this goal, while 65 other countries were unlikely to meet it without additional external assistance or their governments' policy changes or both. Progress in reducing under-five mortality has also been uneven across countries: although 26 developing countries were well on track to reach or exceed the goal by 2015, 11 other countries experienced increased morality rates. Most of the latter countries are in Sub-Saharan Africa, where HIV/AIDS has significantly aggravated the problem. Sub-Saharan Africa also has the largest proportion of children out of school (see Data Table 2) and is lagging behind other developing world regions in narrowing the gap between girls' and boys' school enrollments, even though it has traditionally had lower barriers to girls' schooling than some other places.

The main precondition for achieving the Millennium Goals is sufficiently fast and equitable economic growth in developing countries to provide the material resources for reducing all kinds of poverty, including human poverty (poverty in health and education). The main responsibility for meeting this challenge lies with the governments of developing countries, but donor countries and international development agencies can have important roles to play by building a Global Partnership for Development to complement these efforts. In addition to increasing the amount of official development assistance and improving its effectiveness in poverty reduction, developed countries can make a big contribution by removing the remaining barriers to imports from developing countries, thus helping to accelerate their economic growth.

According to the World Bank's preliminary estimates, reducing **protectionism** by half worldwide would yield developing countries a gain in welfare approximately equivalent to US$200 billion in 2015, much more than any expected official assistance. However, this gain would not substitute for development assistance because of its unequal distribution among developing countries— most of the new trade opportunities would be taken by middle-income, already high-trading economies. The need for additional development assistance is estimated by various international agencies to be in the range of US$40-60 billion a year, which would mean practically doubling the existing levels of assistance. Is it realistic to expect such an increase?

The International Conference on Financing for Development (Monterrey, Mexico, March 2002) appears to have marked a turning point in the way the main donor countries view the role of development assistance. As expressed by World Bank President James Wolfensohn, in 2002 an "imaginary wall" that has long separated the rich world from the poor came crashing down, and it became clear that there are not two worlds, but one. "We are linked by trade, investment, finance, by travel and communication, by disease, by crime, by migration, by environmental degradation, by drugs, by financial crisis, and by terror." Thus development assistance should be provided not because it is ethically right, not as charity, but in order to build a better and safer world for all of us, our children, and our grandchildren.

Notably, in preparation for the Monterrey Conference, the **European Union** countries committed themselves to raising their official development assistance to the average level of 0.39 percent of GDP by 2006, which will represent at least an extra US$7 billion in that year. For its part, the United States pledged to begin increasing its allocations for development assistance so as to bring the increase up to US$5 billion a year by 2006. Australia, Canada, Norway, and Switzerland also made new commitments on aid. Overall, these initiatives are expected to raise official development assistance by about US$15 billion by 2006 and from 0.22 percent of donor countries' GDP to 0.26 percent (see Chapter 13). These new commitments were welcomed by all the development stakeholders, even though it is widely understood that much more needs to be done to ensure the achievement of the Millennium Development Goals. More efforts will be needed from both donor countries and developing countries themselves.

The Role of National Development Policies

The governments of developing countries are the most important actors in the development process, and no amount of foreign aid can be effective in a country where the government is corrupt (see Chapter 16) or fails to implement good policies enabling national economies to grow. However, even governments truly seeking to accelerate their countries' development face a lot of difficult choices, if only because they have to operate with limited resources. While

Which roles in national development should the government play? How can the government catalyze national development?

Does your country have a national sustainable development strategy? If so, what are its main goals?

development is by its nature a comprehensive process of change, governments must, nevertheless, identify and focus on a few areas where their limited action can make the biggest difference. In addition to making up for multiple **market failures** (see Chapter 11), including those in the area of environmental protection, government can also play an important role in coordinating the involvement of all development agents—private firms, public agencies, and civic associations—within the framework of a national sustainable development strategy. Government can help different segments of society arrive at a common vision of the country's medium-term and long-term future, build broad national consensus on ways of making this vision a reality, and enable all the development agents to act in accordance with their social responsibilities. Formulating comprehensive national development priorities and coordinating their achievement is a crucial task that can never be entrusted to the private sector or to any foreign aid providers.

Note that in early 2002 around 50 countries reported to the World Summit on Sustainable Development (Johannesburg, South Africa) that they had already adopted or were developing national sustainable development strategies, integrating economic, social, and environmental goals. In some cases, national poverty reduction strategies were comprehensive enough to stand for sustainable development strategies. But in some others, social policies aimed at poverty reduction were formulated without adequate consideration of economic and environmental policies, even though the poor were known to be badly hurt by environmental losses. At the same time, policies for agricultural and industrial development in many cases have failed to take into account poverty reduction and environmental protection priorities. Agenda 21 and the Millennium Development Goals are meant to help developing countries' governments to formulate their specific national development strategies in a comprehensive manner, with due regard for complex interactions among all the aspects of sustainable development.

Note that the roles of the government and the private sector in implementing the national development strategy cannot be the same in all countries. They depend on the maturity and capabilities of the country's private sector, on the one hand, and on the organizational and financial capabilities of the government, on the other. But there are certain areas where government involvement is indispensable: providing for universal basic health care and primary education, protecting the economically vulnerable, creating and maintaining an effective legal system with strong law enforcement and independent, well-functioning courts. Supporting the preservation and development of national culture is another important role for government, particularly where the private sector and civic associations are weak. Cultural values can serve as a strong cohesive force when other forces are being weakened by war or by rapid social change. Cultural development is not a luxury, but a way to strengthen social capital and thus one of the keys to successful development.

In the economic sphere, the government is indispensable in promoting and safeguarding market competition in the private sector. The government can also play an important role in improving public access to the information and knowledge needed for development— for example, by supporting modern means of communication (telephones, faxes, Internet), investing in basic research, and creating a favorable environment for independent media and civic associations.

Some government roles are still highly debatable, however. For example, it is not clear to what extent governments should support and protect from foreign competition those industries identified as areas of a country's **comparative advantage** (see Chapter 12). Nor is it clear if there is any universal optimal level of redistribution of incomes through the government budget—via taxation and various social programs— in the interests of social equity (see Chapter 5).

Difficult Choices

Every country faces many choices in dealing with its development issues. These choices are made daily in more or less coordinated and more or less democratic ways, with a longer- or shorter-term perspective in mind. They entail big risks or big benefits for entire nations, but there is a lot of uncertainty in every choice. Learning from historical experience, national as well as global, may be the best way to minimize this uncertainty. The author of this book hopes that it will help you start thinking about your country's development in a global context—comparing countries and searching for useful lessons of development experience from around the world—and looking forward to what can realistically be achieved in 10, 20, or 50 years.

The author also hopes that this book will encourage you to play an active role in your country's development efforts, including discussions on the vision for its future and on its unique path of development. Your attitude—active or passive, optimistic or pessimistic—is part of your country's social capital, too. The Rio Declaration adopted by the Earth Summit specifically pointed out that the "creativity, ideals, and courage of the youth of the world should be mobilized to forge a global partnership in order to achieve sustainable development and ensure a better future for all." You can in fact make a real difference by developing informed opinions and making them known to other people, by influencing the course of public debates and eventually the choice of government policies. The experience of many countries shows that policies can be sustained over the long term only if they are understood and supported by most of the population. Only if the changes that these policies bring about do not contradict most people's values and sense of fairness can the ongoing process of change be broadly acknowledged as development. That is why your participation, and that of your peers, in shaping and implementing a national development strategy is so important for your country's future success.

Glossary

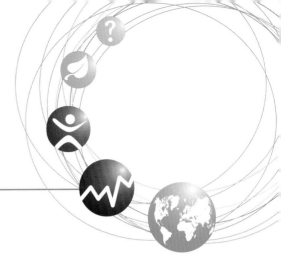

Absolute advantage. An advantage that a country has in producing certain goods or *services* relative to all or many other countries due to specific factors of production at its disposal—such as rich farmland and a favorable climate for agricultural production or a highly educated labor force for high-tech *manufacturing*. A country's absolute advantage means that it can produce certain goods or services at a lower cost than would be possible for other countries. Thus it is clearly beneficial for this country to specialize in producing and exporting these goods and services. But even countries that do not have any absolute advantages can benefit from international trade; see *comparative advantage*.

Access to safe water. The percentage of the population with reasonable means of getting safe water—either treated surface water or clean untreated water from springs, wells, or protected boreholes.

Accumulation of capital. Using *investment* to build *capital* assets.

Adult illiteracy. The percentage of the population 15 and older who cannot, with understanding, read and write a simple statement about their everyday life.

Age dependency ratio. The ratio of the nonworking population—people under 15 or over 65-to the working population—people 15-64. In 1996 the average ratio for *low-income countries* was 0.7, for middle-income countries 0.6, and for *high-income countries* 0.5.

Agriculture. The sector of an economy that includes crop production, animal husbandry, hunting, fishing, and forestry.

Birth rate. The number of live births in a year expressed as a percentage of the population or per 1,000 people.

Capital (capital assets). A stock of wealth used to produce goods and *services*. Modern economists divide capital into *physical capital* (also called *produced assets*), *natural capital*, and *human capital*.

Carbon dioxide emissions per capita. The amount of carbon dioxide a country releases into the atmosphere during a certain period—usually one year—divided by the total population of that country. Large amounts of carbon dioxide are released when people burn *fossil fuels* and biomass—fuelwood, charcoal, dung—to produce energy.

Child mortality rate (under-five mortality rate). The probability that a newborn baby will die before reaching age five. Expressed as a number per 1,000 live births.

Chlorofluorocarbons (CFCs).
Inexpensive synthetic gases often used as coolants in refrigerators and air conditioners and as propellants in aerosol spray cans. Although originally considered harmless, CFCs are now known to accumulate in the earth's atmosphere, where they destroy the protective *ozone* layer and trap the sun's heat—contributing to the greenhouse effect (see *greenhouse gases*). The use of CFCs is now controlled by the Montreal Protocol, an agreement signed by many countries.

Comparative advantage. The concept, formulated by British economist David Ricardo, according to which economic agents—people, firms, countries—are most efficient when they do the things that they are best at doing. Comparative advantage is particularly important in global markets, where countries benefit most by producing and exporting goods and *services* that they can produce more efficiently (at a lower cost, by using less *physical, human,* and *natural capital*) than other goods and services. In particular, Ricardo showed that a country can benefit from international trade even if it has higher costs of production for all traded goods and services relative to the countries it trades with—that is, even if it has

no *absolute advantages* whatsoever. This can be done by correctly choosing the country's international specialization in accordance with its comparative advantages. In this case, by using export earnings to import other goods and service at prices that are lower than the costs of their domestic production, the country will maximize the overall value of national production and consumption.

Countries with transition economies (transition countries, transition economies). Countries moving from centrally planned to market-oriented economies. These countries—which include China, Mongolia, Vietnam, former republics of the Soviet Union, and the countries of Central and Eastern Europe—contain about one-third of the world's population.

Death rate. The number of deaths in a year expressed as a percentage of the population or per 1,000 people.

Demography. The scientific study of human populations, including their size, composition, distribution, density, and growth as well as the causes and socioeconomic consequences of changes in these factors.

Developed countries (industrial countries, industrially advanced countries). *High-income countries,* in which most people have a high *standard of living.* Sometimes also defined as countries with a

measure called **net domestic product (NDP)**, also known as **national income**. The words "product" and "income" are often used interchangeably, so *GNP per capita* is also called *income per capita.*

Gross primary school enrollment ratio. The ratio of primary school enrollment to the number of primary school-aged children (usually children 6-11). The **gross secondary school enrollment ratio** is calculated in the same way, except that the corresponding age group is 12-17. For the **gross tertiary education enrollment ratio,** calculations are based on the number of young people in the five-year age group following the secondary school leaving age. Gross enrollment ratios can be higher than 100 percent because some students are younger or older than the corresponding age group.

High-income countries. Classified by the *World Bank* as countries whose *GNP per capita* was $9,266 or more in 1999. The group includes both *developed countries* and *high-income developing economies.*

High-income developing economies. Economies that the United Nations classifies as developing even though their per capita incomes would place them with *developed countries.* This classification may be based on their economic structure or the official opinion of their gov-ernments. In 1995 this group included Hong Kong (China), Israel, Kuwait, Singapore, and the United Arab Emirates.

Human capital. People's innate abilities and talents plus their knowledge, skills, and experience that make them economically *productive.* Human capital can be increased by *investing* in health care, education, and job training.

Human development index (HDI). A composite of several social indicators that is useful for broad cross-country comparisons even though it yields little specific information about each country. First used in the United Nations Development Programme's Human Development Report 1990.

Human resources. The total quantity and quality of human effort available to produce goods and services. The muscle power and brain power of human beings. Human resources can be viewed as consisting of "raw labor"—determined mostly by the number of people in a country's *labor force*—combined with *human capital.*

Import quotas. Government-imposed limits on the quantities of certain goods and *services* allowed to be imported. Like *import tariffs,* import quotas are used by governments to protect domestic industries from foreign competition. See *protection.*

Import tariffs. Taxes imposed on certain imported goods or *services*. May be levied as a percentage of the value of imports or as a fixed amount per unit. Used to increase government revenue and protect domestic industries from foreign competition. See *protection*.

Income per capita. Another term for *GNP per capita*.

Industrial countries. See *developed countries*.

Industrialization. The phase of a country's *economic development* in which *industry* grows faster than *agriculture* and gradually comes to play the leading role in the economy.

Industry. The sector of an economy that includes mining, construction, manufacturing, electricity, gas, and water.

Infant mortality rate. Of every 1,000 infants born, the number that die before reaching their first birthday.

International Monetary Fund (IMF). An international institution founded in 1944—together with the *World Bank*—to promote international monetary cooperation and facilitate balanced growth of trade by encouraging the removal of foreign exchange restrictions, promoting exchange rate stability, and expediting payments among member countries.

International poverty line. An income level established by the *World Bank* to determine which people in the world are poor—set at $1 a day per person in 1985 international *purchasing power parity (PPP)* prices (equivalent to $1.08 in 1993 PPP prices). A person is considered poor if he or she lives in a household whose daily income or consumption is less than $1 per person. Although this *poverty line* is useful for international comparisons, it is impossible to create an indicator of poverty that is strictly comparable across countries. The level of $1 a day per person is close to national *poverty lines* in *low-income countries* but considerably lower than those in *high-income countries*. For comparing poverty levels across *middle-income countries,* international poverty lines of $2, $4, and $11 a day per person are considered to be more appropriate.

Investment. Outlays made by individuals, firms, or governments to add to their capital. From the viewpoint of individual economic agents, buying property rights for existing capital is also an investment. But from the viewpoint of an economy as a whole, only creating new capital is counted as an investment. Investment is a necessary condition for *economic growth.* See *savings, gross domestic saving rate,* and *gross domestic investment rate.*

Labor force. All the economically active people in a country between 15 and 65. Includes all employed persons, the unemployed, and members of the armed services, but excludes students and unpaid caregivers such as homemakers.

Least developed countries. *Low-income countries* where, according to the United Nations, *economic growth* faces long-term impediments—such as low *human resources* development. A category used to guide donors and countries in allocating foreign assistance.

Life expectancy at birth. The number of years a newborn baby would live if, at each age he/she passes through, the chances of survival were the same as they were for that age group in the year of his/her birth. The change in this indicator reflects changes in the overall health of a country's population, in people's living conditions (environmental, economic, social) and in the quality of health care.

Living standard. See *standard of living.*

Low-income countries. Classified by the *World Bank* as countries whose *GNP per capita* was $755 or less in 1999.

Manufactured goods. Goods produced using *primary goods.* Include petroleum, steel, textiles, baked goods, and others.

Market failures. Cases when a market economy fails to provide people with a desirable supply of certain kinds of goods and *services.* Market failures can occur in a market economy when it does

not produce enough *public goods* and goods with positive *externalities,* when it produces too many goods with negative externalities, when goods are overpriced by *natural monopolies,* and when market agents do not have access to sufficient information, such as information about the quality of some consumer goods. These market failures usually justify economic intervention by the government. But there is always the risk of government failure—in which faulty political processes or institutional structures prevent government measures from improving social welfare (see Chapter 11).

Maternal mortality rate. The annual number of women who die from pregnancy-related causes during pregnancy and childbirth, per 100,000 live births. The data are particularly difficult to collect, so expert estimates based on available data are often used instead.

Market liberalization. Removing and abstaining from using state controls that impede the normal functioning of a market economy—for example, lifting price and wage controls and *import quotas* or lowering taxes and *import tariffs.* Market liberalization usually does not mean that a government completely abstains from interfering with market processes.

Middle-income countries. Classified by the *World Bank* as countries whose *GNP per capita* was between $756 and $9,265 in 1999. These countries are further divided into lower-middle-income countries ($756–$2,995) and upper-middle-income countries ($2,996–$$9,265).

Natural capital. A stock of *natural resources*—such as land, water, and minerals—used for production. Can be either *renewable* or *nonrenewable.*

Natural monopoly. A situation that occurs when one firm in an industry can serve the entire market at a lower cost than would be possible if the industry were composed of many smaller firms. Gas and water utilities are two classic examples of natural monopolies. These monopolies must not be left to operate freely; if they are, they can increase prices and profits by restricting their output. Governments prevent such a scenario by regulating utility monopolies or providing utility *services* themselves.

Natural population increase. The difference between the *birth rate* and the *death rate* over a period of time. See also *population growth rate.*

Natural resources. All "gifts of nature"—air, land, water, forests, wildlife, topsoil, minerals—used by people for production or for direct consumption. Can be either *renewable* or *nonrenewable.* Natural resources include *natural capital* plus those gifts of nature that cannot be stocked (such as sunlight) or cannot be used in production (such as

picturesque landscapes). See also *ecosphere.*

Net official assistance. The sum of grants and concessional loans from donor country governments to recipient countries, minus any repayment of loan principal during the period of the loans.

Net private flows. Privately financed capital flows that enter a country on market terms, minus such flows that leave the country. An example of a net private flow is net portfolio investment—the value of stocks and bonds bought by foreign investors minus the value of stocks and bonds sold by them. See also *portfolio investment.*

Nominal indicator. An indicator measured using the prices prevailing at the time of measurement. A change in a nominal indicator sometimes reflects changing market prices more than any other changes (changes in the *real indicator*). For example, during periods of inflation, nominal wages can increase while their real value decreases. In making cross-country comparisons, this term also applies to the conversion of indicators calculated in local currency units into some common currency, most often US dollars. Nominal indicators are those converted into US dollars using current exchange rates, while real indicators are calculated based on *purchasing power parity (PPP)* conversion factors.

Nonrenewable natural resources. *Natural resources* that cannot be replaced or replenished. See *renewable natural resources.*

Organisation for Economic Cooperation and Development (OECD). An organization that coordinates policy mostly among *developed countries.* OECD member countries exchange economic data and create unified policies to maximize their countries' *economic growth* and help nonmember countries develop more rapidly. The OECD arose from the Organisation for European Economic Cooperation (OEEC), which was created in 1948 to administer the Marshall Plan in Europe. In 1960, when the Marshall Plan was completed, Canada, Spain, and the United States joined OEEC members to form the OECD.

Ozone. A gas that pollutes the air at low altitudes, but that high in the atmosphere forms a thin shield protecting life on earth from harmful solar radiation. *Chlorofluorocarbons (CFCs)* destroy this high-level ozone layer.

Physical capital (produced assets). Buildings, machines, and technical equipment used in production plus inventories of raw materials, half-finished goods, and finished goods.

Population growth rate. The increase in a country's population during a certain period—usually one year—expressed as a percentage of the population when the period began. The population growth rate is the sum of the difference between the *birth rate* and the *death rate*—the *natural population increase*—and the difference between the population entering and leaving the country—the net migration rate.

Portfolio investment. Stock and bond purchases that, unlike direct investment, do not create a lasting interest in or effective management control over an enterprise. See *foreign direct investment.*

Postindustrialization. The phase in a country's *economic development* that follows *industrialization* and is characterized by the leading role of *service sector* in the national economy.

Poverty line (national). The income level below which people are defined as poor. The definition is based on the income level people require to buy life's basic necessities—food, clothing, housing—and satisfy their most important sociocultural needs. The poverty line changes over time and varies by country. Also called *subsistence minimum.* Official national poverty line is determined by a country's government. See also *international poverty line.*

Primary goods. Goods that are sold (for consumption or production) just as they were found in nature. Include oil, coal, iron, and agricultural products like wheat or cotton. Also called commodities.

Produced assets. See *physical capital*.

Production resources. The main inputs for any production. Traditionally, economists identified three factors of production: labor, land, and capital. More recently, economists came to use the concept of three types of capital: *physical (or produced) capital, human capital,* and *natural capital.*

Productivity (economic productivity, efficiency). Output of goods and *services* per unit of input—for example, per unit of labor (labor productivity), per unit of energy (such as GNP per unit of energy use), or per unit of all *production resources* combined (see Chapter 2).

Protection, protectionism. The imposition of *import tariffs, import quotas,* or other barriers that restrict the flow of imports. The opposite of *free trade.* Used to:

- Protect "strategically important" industries, without which a country would be vulnerable in times of war.
- Protect new industries until they are strong enough to compete in international markets.
- Retaliate against protectionist policies of trade partners. Since World War II protectionist policies have been significantly reduced in most

countries through negotiations under the *General Agreement on Tariffs and Trade (GATT).*

Public goods. Goods that are nonrival—consumption by one person does not reduce the supply available for others—and nonexcludable—people cannot be prevented from consuming them. These characteristics make it impossible to charge consumers for public goods, so the private sector is not interested in supplying them. Instead, they are often supplied by government. Public goods are usually national or local. Defense is a national public good—benefiting the entire population of a country. Rural roads are local public goods, benefiting a smaller group of people. There can also be global public goods, benefiting most of the world's population, for example global peace and security, or information needed to prevent global climate change. Providing such goods (and *services*) is a function of international organizations.

Purchasing power parity (PPP) conversion factor. The PPP conversion factor shows how much of a country's currency is needed in that country to buy what $1 would buy in the United States. By using the PPP conversion factor instead of the currency exchange rate, we can convert a country's GNP per capita calculated in national currency units into *GNP per capita* in U.S. dollars while taking into account the difference in domestic prices for the same goods. Thus PPP helps us compare GNPs of different countries more accurately. Because prices are usually lower in developing countries, their GNP per capita expressed in PPP dollars is higher than their *GNP per capita* expressed in U.S. dollars. In *developed countries* the opposite is true (see Chapter 2).

Quality of life. People's overall well-being. Quality of life is difficult to measure (whether for an individual, group, or nation) because in addition to material well-being (see *standard of living*) it includes such intangible components as the quality of the environment, national security, personal safety, and political and economic freedoms.

Real indicator (price, income, other). An economic indicator that uses the prices from some base year. This approach controls for fluctuating market prices so that other economic changes can be seen more clearly. In cross-country comparisons, this term also applies to the conversion of indicators calculated in local currency units into some common currency, most often US dollars. Real indicators are calculated with the help of *purchasing power parity (PPP) conversion factors*, while *nominal indicators* are those converted into US dollars using current exchange rates.

Renewable natural resources. *Natural resources* that can be replaced or replenished by natural processes or human action. Fish and forests are renewable natural resources. Minerals and fossil fuels are *nonrenewable natural resources* because they are regenerated on a geological, rather than human, time scale. Some aspects of the environment—soil quality, assimilative capacity, ecological support systems—are called semirenewable because they are regenerated very slowly on a human time scale.

Savings. Income not used for current consumption. See also *gross domestic saving rate* and *gross domestic investment rate.*

Services. Intangible goods that are often produced and consumed at the same time. An example is education: students consume a lesson—an educational service—at the same time a teacher produces it. The service sector of the economy includes hotels, restaurants, and wholesale and retail trade; transport, storage, and communications; financing, insurance, real estate, and business *services;* community and social *services* (such as education and health care); and personal services.

Shadow economy. See *gray economy.*

Standard of living. The level of well-being (of an individual, group or the population of a country) as measured by the level of income (for example, *GNP per capita*) or by the quantity of various goods and *services* consumed (for example, the number of cars per 1,000 people or the number of television sets per capita). See also *quality of life.*

Subsistence minimum. Another term for *poverty line.*

Sustainable development. According to the United Nations World Commission on Environment and Development (1987), sustainable development is "development that meets the needs of the present without compromising the ability of future generations to meet their own needs." According to the more operational (practice-oriented) definition used by the *World Bank,* sustainable development is "a process of managing a portfolio of assets to preserve and enhance the opportunities people face." Sustainable development includes economic, environmental, and social sustainability, which can be achieved by rationally managing *physical, natural,* and *human capital* (see Chapters 1 and 16).

Terms of trade. The ratio of export prices to import prices. A high ratio benefits an economy, because then the country can pay for many imports by selling a small amount of exports. If terms of trade worsen, the country needs to sell more exports to buy the same amount of imports.

Transfer payments. Payments from the government to individuals used to redistribute a country's wealth. Examples are

pensions, welfare, and unemployment benefits.

Transition countries. See *countries with transition economies.*

Under-five mortality rate. See *child mortality rate.*

Undernourished people. People whose food intake is chronically insufficient to meet their minimum energy requirements.

World Bank. An international lending institution that aims to reduce poverty and improve people's lives by strengthening economies and promoting *sustainable development.* Owned by the governments of its 181 member countries, the Bank lends about $20 billion a year to development projects, provides technical assistance and policy advice, and acts as a catalyst for investment and lending from other sources. The *World Bank's* poorest members receive loans for up to 50 years without interest. Other needy members receive loans for 15-20 years at lower interest rates than are charged by commercial banks.

World Trade Organization (WTO). An international organization established on January 1, 1995, to succeed the *General Agreement on Tariffs and Trade (GATT).* Serves as a forum for multilateral trade negotiations and helps resolve its members' trade disputes.

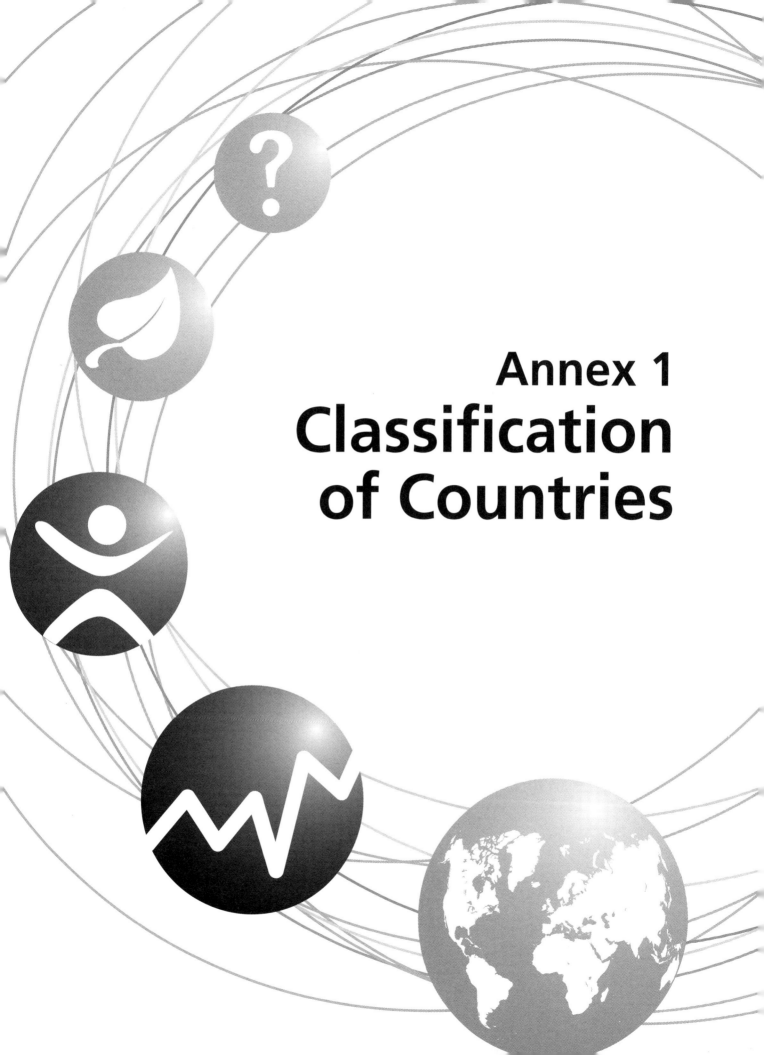

Annex 1
Classification of Countries

Classification of Economies by Income and Region, 2000

Income group	Subgroup	Sub-Saharan Africa		Asia		Europe and Central Asia		Middle East and North Africa		Americas
		East and Southern Africa	West Africa	East Asia and Pacific	South Asia	Eastern Europe and Central Asia	Rest of Europe	Middle East	North Africa	
1	2	3	4	5	6	7	8	9	10	11
Low-income		Angola Burundi Comoros Congo, Dem. Rep. Eritrea Ethiopia Kenya Lesotho Madagascar Malawi Mozambique Rwanda Somalia Sudan Tanzania Uganda Zambia Zimbabwe	Benin Burkina Faso Cameroon Central African Rep. Chad Congo, Rep. Côte d'Ivoire Gambia, The Ghana Guinea Guinea-Bissau Liberia Mali Mauritania Niger Nigeria São Tomé and Principe Senegal Sierra Leone Togo	Cambodia Indonesia Korea, Dem. Rep. Lao PDR Mongolia Myanmar Solomon Islands Vietnam	Afghanistan Bangladesh Bhutan India Nepal Pakistan	Armenia Azerbaijan Georgia Kyrgyz Rep. Moldova Tajikistan Turkmenistan Ukraine Uzbekistan		Yemen, Rep.		Haiti Nicaragua
Middle-income	Lower	Namibia Swaziland	Cape Verde Equatorial Guinea	China Fiji Kiribati Marshall Islands Micronesia, Fed. Sts. Papua New Guinea Philippines Samoa Thailand Tonga Vanuatu	Maldives Sri Lanka	Albania Belarus Bosnia and Herzegovina Bulgaria Kazakhstan Latvia Lithuania Macedonia, FYR[a] Romania Russian Federation Yugoslavia, Fed. Rep.[b]	Turkey	Iran, Islamic Rep. Iraq Jordan Syrian Arab Rep. West Bank and Gaza	Algeria Djibouti Egypt, Arab Rep. Morocco Tunisia	Belize Bolivia Colombia Costa Rica Cuba Dominican Republic Ecuador El Salvador Guatemala Guyana Honduras Jamaica Paraguay Peru St. Vincent and the Grenadines Suriname

1	2	3	4	5	6	7	8	9	10	11
Middle-income	Upper	Botswana Mauritius Mayotte Seychelles South Africa	Gabon	American Samoa Korea, Rep. Malaysia Palau		Croatia Czech Rep. Estonia Hungary Poland Slovak Rep.	Isle of Man	Bahrain Lebanon Oman Saudi Arabia	Libya Malta	Antigua and Barbuda Argentina Barbados Brazil Chile Dominica Grenada Mexico Panama Puerto Rico St. Kitts and Nevis St. Lucia Trinidad and Tobago Uruguay Venezuela, RB
	OECD countries			Australia Japan New Zealand			Austria Belgium Denmark Finland France[c] Germany Greece Iceland Ireland Italy Luxembourg Netherlands Norway Portugal Spain Sweden Switzerland United Kingdom			Canada United States
High-income	Non-OECD countries			Brunei French Polynesia Guam Hong Kong, China[d] Macao, China[e] New Caledonia N. Mariana Islands Singapore Taiwan, China		Slovenia	Andorra Channel Islands Cyprus Faeroe Islands Greenland Liechtenstein Monaco	Israel Kuwait Qatar United Arab Emirates		Aruba Bahamas, The Bermuda Cayman Islands Netherlands Antilles Virgin Islands (U.S.)
Total	207	25	23	35	8	27	27	14	7	41

a. Former Yugoslav Republic of Macedonia. b. Federal Republic of Yugoslavia (Serbia/Montenegro). c. The French overseas departments French Guiana, Guadeloupe, Martinique, and Réunion are included in France. d. On 1 July 1997 China resumed its exercise of sovereignty over Hong Kong. e. On 20 December 1999 China resumed it exercise of sovereignty over Macao.

Annex 2
Data Tables

Table 1. Indicators to chapters 1–5

COUNTRY or REGION	Gross domestic product $ millions		Average annual GDP growth %		Population millions		Fertility rate births per woman		Birth rate per 1,000 people	
	1990	1999	1980-90	1990-99	1980	1999	1980	1999	1980	1999
Afghanistan	..	..	..	..	15.95	23.48	7.0	6.7	50	47
Albania	2,102	3,058	1.5	2.3	2.67	3.40	3.6	2.4	29	16
Algeria	61,902	47,015	2.7	1.6	18.67	30.50	6.7	3.4	42	25
American Samoa	..	..	..	..	0.03	0.06	..	..	..	..
Andorra	..	..	..	..	..	0.07	..	..	..	..
Angola	10,260	5,861	3.4	0.8	7.02	12.40	6.9	6.7	34	48
Antigua and Barbuda	..	..			0.06	0.07	2.1	1.7	17	20
Argentina	141,352	281,942	-0.7	4.9	28.11	36.60	3.3	2.5	24	19
Armenia	4,124	1,911	..	-3.1	3.10	3.80	2.3	1.3	23	11
Aruba	..	..	..	..	..	0.09	..	..	..	..
Australia	297,204	389,691	3.4	3.8	14.69	18.05	1.9	1.8	15	13
Austria	159,499	208,949	2.2	2.0	7.55	8.10	1.6	1.3	12	10
Azerbaijan	9,837	4,457	..	-9.0	6.17	8.00	3.2	2.0	25	15
Bahamas, The	..	..	..	.	0.21	0.30	3.3	2.2	24	19
Bahrain	..	..	..	..	0.33	0.58	5.2	..	34	20
Bangladesh	29,855	45,779	4.3	4.8	86.70	127.70	6.1	3.2	44	28
Barbados	..	..	..	..	0.25	0.27	2.0	1.8	17	1
Belarus	34,911	25,693	..	-4.3	9.64	10.02	2.0	1.3	16	9
Belgium	196,134	245,706	1.9	1.7	9.85	10.02	1.7	1.6	13	11
Belize	..	..	..	..	0.15	0.25	..	..	..	30
Benin	1,845	2,402	2.5	4.7	3.46	6.10	7.0	5.6	49	40
Bermuda	..	..	..	..	0.05	0.06	..	..	..	..
Bhutan	..	..	..	..	0.49	0.78	..	5.7	..	38
Bolivia	4,868	8,516	-0.2	4.2	5.36	8.10	5.5	4.0	39	32
Bosnia and Herzegovina	..	..	..	..	4.09	3.88	2.1	1.6	19	13
Botswana	3,766	5,996	10.3	4.3	0.90	1.60	6.1	4.1	45	33
Brazil	464,989	760,345	2.7	2.9	121.70	168.10	3.9	2.2	31	20
Brunei	..	..	..	..	0.19	0.32	4.0	2.7	31	21
Bulgaria	20,726	12,103	3.4	-2.7	8.86	8.20	2.0	1.1	15	8
Burkina Faso	2,765	2,643	3.6	3.8	6.96	11.00	7.5	6.6	47	44
Burundi	1,132	701	4.4	-2.9	4.13	6.70	6.8	6.1	46	41
Cambodia	1,115	3,117	..	4.8	6.80	11.80	4.7	4.4	40	32
Cameroon	11,152	8,781	3.4	1.3	8.70	14.70	6.4	4.9	45	38
Canada	572,673	612,049	3.3	2.3	24.59	30.60	1.7	1.5	15	11
Cape Verde	..	..	..	..	0.29	0.43	6.5	3.8	37	36
Cayman Islands	..	..	..	..	..	0.04	..	..	..	.
Central African Republic	1,488	1,053	1.4	1.8	2.31	3.50	5.8	4.7	43	36
Chad	1,739	1,574	6.1	2.3	4.48	7.50	6.9	6.3	44	45
Channel Islands	..	..	..	..	0.13	0.15	1.4	1.8	12	11
Chile	30,307	71,092	4.2	7.2	11.14	15.00	2.8	2.2	23	18
China	354,644	991,203	10.1	10.7	981.24	1,249.70	2.5	1.9	18	16
Hong Kong, China	74,784	158,611	6.9	3.9	5.04	6.90	2.0	1.0	17	8
Macao, China	..	..	..	..	0.29	0.47	2.3	1.4	20	10
Colombia	46,907	88,596	3.6	3.3	27.89	41.50	3.9	2.7	31	23
Comoros	..	..	..	..	0.34	0.54	7.2	4.4	..	34
Congo, Dom. Rep.	9,348	6,964	1.6	-5.1	27.01	49.80	6.6	6.2	48	45
Congo, Rep.	2,799	2,273	3.3	0.9	1.67	2.90	6.3	5.9	45	43
Costa Rica	5,713	11,076	3.0	4.1	2.28	3.60	3.6	2.5	31	21
Côte d'Ivoire	10,796	11,223	0.7	3.7	8.19	14.70	7.4	4.9	51	37
Croatia	13,370	21,752	..	-0.4	4.59	4.50	..	1.5	..	10

Death rate per 1,000 people		Average annual population growth %		GNP per capita		GDP per capita growth average annual real growth %	Gini index	
				$	PPP $			
1980	1999	1980-99	1999-2015	1999	1999	1990-1999	Survey year	
23	19	..	..	..	..	..	..	..
6	5	1.2	1.0	870	2,892	2.8		
12	6	2.5	1.7	1,550	4,753	-0.5	1995	35.3
..	..	..	..	..	..	..	..	..
..	..	..	..	..	..	..	..	..
23	19	3.0	2.7	220	632	-2.8	..	..
6	5	..	1.0	..	..	2.7	..	..
9	8	1.4	1.0	7,600	11,324	3.6	..	..
6	6	1.1	0.4	490	2,210	-3.9	..	..
..	..	..	..	..	..	..	..	..
7	7	1.3	0.8	20,050	22,448	2.9	1994	35.2
12	10	0.4	-0.1	25,970	23,808	1.4	1987	23.1
7	6	1.4	0.9	550	2,322	-10.7	..	..
7	5	..	..	..	..	-0.1	..	..
6	3	..	..	..	..	0.8	..	..
18	9	2.0	1.6	370	1,475	3.1	1995-96	33.6
8	9	..	..	..	..	1.5	..	..
10	14	0.2	-0.4	2,630	6,518	-2.9	1998	21.7
12	10	0.2	0.0	24,510	24,200	1.4	1992	25.0
..	5	..	..	2,730	4,492	0.7	..	..
19	13	3.0	2.4	380	886	1.8	..	..
..	..	..	..	..	..	..	..	..
..	9	..	..	510	1,496	3.4	..	..
15	9	2.2	1.8	1,010	2,193	1.8	1990	42.0
7	7	-0.3	0.6	..	..	32.7	..	..
10	18	3.0	0.6	3,240	6,032	1.8	..	..
9	7	1.7	1.1	4,420	6,317	1.5	1996	60.0
5	3	..	..	..	..	-0.5	..	..
11	14	-0.4	-0.7	1,380	4,914	-2.1	1995	28.3
20	19	2.4	2.1	240	898	1.4	1994	48.2
18	20	2.5	1.7	120	553	-5.0	1992	33.3
27	12	2.9	1.4	260	1,286	1.9	1997	40.4
16	13	2.8	1.8	580	1,444	-1.5	..	..
7	7	1.1	0.6	19,320	23,725	1.7	1994	31.5
11	6	..	..	1,330	3,497	3.2	..	..
..	..	..	..	..	..	..	..	..
19	19	2.2	1.4	290	1,131	-0.3	1993	61.3
22	16	2.7	2.8	200	816	-0.9	..	..
12	10	..	..	..	..	..	..	..
7	5	1.6	1.0	4,740	8,370	5.6	1994	56.5
6	7	1.3	0.7	780	3,291	9.5	1998	40.3
5	5	1.5	0.7	23,520	20,939	1.9	..	..
7	3	..	..	..	..	0.7	..	..
7	6	2.0	1.3	2,250	5,709	1.4	1996	57.1
..	9	..	..	350	1,360	-3.1	..	..
16	15	3.2	2.6	..	..	-8.1	..	..
16	16	2.8	2.6	670	897	-3.3	..	..
4	4	2.4	1.3	2,740	5,770	3.0	1996	47.0
17	17	3.4	1.7	710	1,546	0.6	1995	36.7
..	12	-0.1	-0.2	4,580	6,915	1.0	1998	26.8

Table 1. Indicators to chapters 1–5 (continued)

COUNTRY or REGION	Gross domestic product $ millions		Average annual GDP growth %		Population millions		Fertility rate births per woman		Birth rate per 1,000 people	
	1990	1999	1980-90	1990-99	1980	1999	1980	1999	1980	1999
Cuba	..	..	..	..	9.72	11.15	2.0	1.6	14	13
Cyprus	..	..	..	..	0.61	0.76	2.5	1.9	20	13
Czech Republic	34,880	56,379	1.7	0.9	10.23	10.30	2.1	1.2	15	9
Denmark	133,361	174,363	2.3	2.8	5.12	5.30	1.5	1.8	11	12
Djibouti	..	..	..	..	0.28	0.65	6.6	5.2	48	37
Dominica	..	..	..	..	0.07	0.07	..	1.9	25	20
Dominican Republic	7,074	17,125	3.1	5.7	5.70	8.40	4.2	2.8	33	24
Ecuador	10,686	18,712	2.0	2.2	7.96	12.50	5.0	3.1	36	24
Egypt, Arab Rep.	43,130	92,413	5.4	4.4	40.88	62.40	5.1	3.3	39	26
El Salvador	4,807	12,229	0.2	4.9	4.55	6.20	4.9	3.2	36	27
Equatorial Guinea	..	..	..	..	0.22	0.44	5.7	5.3	43	40
Eritrea	437	670	..	5.2	..	4.00	..	5.6	..	39
Estonia	6,760	5,101	2.2	-1.3	1.48	1.40	2.0	1.2	15	9
Ethiopia	,842	6,534	1.1	4.8	37.72	62.80	6.6	6.3	48	44
Faeroe Islands	..	..	..	..	..	0.04	..	..	..	..
Fiji	..	..	..	..	0.63	0.80	3.5	2.8	30	22
Finland	134,806	126,130	3.3	2.5	4.78	5.20	1.6	1.8	13	11
France	1,195,438	1,410,262	2.3	1.7	53.88	59.10	1.9	1.8	15	13
French Polynesia	..	..	..	..	0.16	0.23	..	2.7	31	22
Gabon	..	..	..	..	0.69	1.25	4.5	5.1	33	36
Gambia, The	..	..	..	..	0.64	1.11	6.5	5.5	48	41
Georgia	12	4,192	0.4	-10.3	5.07	5.50	2.3	1.3	18	9
Germany	1,719,510	2,081,202	2.2	1.5	78.30	82.00	1.4	1.4	11	9
Ghana	5,886	7,606	3.0	4.3	10.74	18.90	6.5	4.3	45	30
Greece	82,914	123,934	1.8	1.9	9.64	10.50	2.2	1.3	15	9
Greenland	..	..	..	..	..	0.06	..	..	..	..
Grenada	..	..	..	..	0.09	0.10	..	3.4	..	25
Guam	..	..	..	..	0.11	0.15	..	3.9	28	28
Guatemala	7,650	18,016	0.8	4.2	6.92	11.10	6.3	4.7	43	34
Guinea	2,818	3,693	..	4.2	4.46	7.20	6.1	5.3	46	40
Guinea-Bissau	..	..	..	..	0.81	1.19	5.8	5.5	43	41
Guyana	..	..	..	..	0.76	0.86	3.5	2.3	30	21
Haiti	2,981	3,871	-0.2	-1.7	5.35	7.80	5.9	4.1	37	31
Honduras	3,049	5,342	2.7	3.2	3.66	6.30	6.5	4.0	43	32
Hungary	33,056	48,355	1.3	1.0	10.71	10.10	1.9	1.3	14	9
Iceland	..	..	..	..	0.23	0.28	2.5	2.0	20	15
India	322,737	459,765	5.8	6.1	687.33	997.50	5.0	3.1	34	26
Indonesia	114,426	140,964	6.1	4.7	148.30	207.00	4.3	2.6	34	22
Iran, Islamic Rep.	120,404	101,073	1.7	3.4	39.12	63.00	6.7	2.7	44	21
Iraq	..	..	..	..	13.01	22.80	6.4	4.4	41	32
Ireland	45,527	84,861	3.2	7.9	3.40	3.70	3.2	1.9	22	14
Isle of Man	..	..	..	..	..	0.08	..	..	..	..
Israel	52,490	99,068	3.5	5.1	3.88	6.10	3.2	2.9	24	21
Italy	1,093,947	1,149,958	2.4	1.2	56.43	57.60	1.6	1.2	11	9
Jamaica	4,239	6,134	2.0	0.1	2.13	2.60	3.7	2.5	28	22
Japan	2,970,043	4,395,083	4.0	1.4	116.78	126.60	1.8	1.4	14	10
Jordan	4,020	7,616	2.5	4.8	2.18	4.70	6.8	3.7	..	30
Kazakstan	40,304	15,594	..	-5.9	14.91	15.40	2.9	2.0	24	14
Kenya	8,533	10,603	4.2	2.2	16.56	30.00	7.8	4.5	51	35
Kiribati	..	..	..	..	0.06	0.09	4.6	4.0	..	30

Death rate per 1,000 people		Average annual population growth %		GNP per capita		GDP per capita growth average annual real growth %	Gini index	
1980	1999	1980-99	1999-2015	$ 1999	PPP $ 1999	1990-1999	Survey year	
6	7	0.7	0.3	..	..	..	..	..
8	8	..	..	11,960	18,395	2.8	..	..
13	11	0.0	-0.2	5,060	12,289	0.9	1996	25.4
11	11	0.2	0.0	32,030	24,280	2.0	1992	24.7
20	17	..	..	790	..	-5.1	..	..
5	6	..	..	3,170	4,825	1.8	..	..
7	5	2.0	1.3	1,910	4,653	3.9	1996	48.7
9	6	2.3	1.5	1,310	2,605	0.0	1995	43.7
13	7	2.2	1.5	1,400	3,303	2.4	1995	28.9
11	6	1.5	1.6	1,900	4,048	2.8	1996	52.3
22	16	..	..	1,170	..	16.3	..	..
..	13	2.7	2.2	200	1,012	2.2	..	..
12	13	-0.1	-0.5	3,480	7,826	-0.3	1995	35.4
22	20	2.7	2.1	100	599	2.4	1995	40.0
..	..	..	..	..	..	..	..	..
6	6	..	..	2,210	4,536	1.2	..	..
9	10	0.4	0.1	23,780	21,209	2.0	1991	25.6
10	9	0.4	0.3	23,480	21,897	1.1	1995	32.7
6	5	..	..	..	..	-0.1	..	..
18	16	2.9	2.1	3,350	5,325	0.6	..	..
24	13	3.5	2.2	340	1,492	-0.6	..	..
9	8	0.4	-0.1	620	3,606	..	..	..
12	10	0.2	-0.2	25,350	22,404	1.0	1994	30.0
15	10	2.9	1.7	390	1,793	1.6	1997	32.7
9	10	0.5	-0.1	11,770	14,595	1.8	1993	32.7
..	..	..	..	..	..	..	..	..
..	7	..	..	3,450	5,847	2.2	..	..
4	4	..	..	..	..	..	..	..
11	7	2.6	2.4	1,660	3,517	1.5	1989	59.6
24	17	2.6	1.9	510	1,761	1.5	1994	40.3
25	21	2.1	1.8	160	595	-1.9	..	..
7	8	..	..	760	3,242	5.2	..	..
15	13	2.0	1.6	460	1,407	-3.4	..	..
10	5	3.0	2.1	760	2,254	0.3	1996	53.7
14	14	-0.3	-0.4	4,650	10,479	1.4	1996	30.8
7	7	..	..	29,280	26,283	1.8	..	..
13	9	2.0	1.3	450	2,149	4.1	1997	37.8
12	7	1.8	1.2	580	2,439	3.0	1996	36.5
11	6	2.5	1.7	1,760	5,163	1.9	..	..
9	10	3.0	2.0	..	..	..	..	..
10	9	0.5	0.8	19,160	19,180	6.1	1987	35.9
..	..	..	..	..	..	..	..	..
7	6	2.4	1.6	..	..	2.3	1992	35.5
10	10	0.1	-0.3	19,710	20,751	1.2	1995	27.3
7	6	1.0	0.9	2,330	3,276	-0.6	1996	36.4
6	8	0.4	-0.1	32,230	24,041	1.1	1993	24.9
..	4	4.1	2.3	1,500	3,542	1.1	1997	36.4
8	10	0.0	0.1	1,230	4,408	-4.9	1996	35.4
13	13	3.0	1.5	360	975	-0.3	1994	44.5
..	8	..	..	910	3,186	1.0	..	..

Table 1. Indicators to chapters 1–5 (continued)

COUNTRY or REGION	Gross domestic product $ millions		Average annual GDP growth %		Population millions		Fertility rate births per woman		Birth rate per 1,000 people	
	1990	1999	1980-90	1990-99	1980	1999	1980	1999	1980	1999
Korea, Dem. Rep.	..	..	..	..	18.26	23.41	2.8	2.0	22	20
Korea, Rep.	252,622	406,940	9.4	5.7	38.12	46.80	2.6	1.6	22	14
Kuwait	18,428	29,572	1.3	..	1.38	1.90	5.3	2.7	37	22
Kyrgyz Republic	..	1,629	..	-7.4	3.63	4.70	4.1	2.7	30	21
Lao PDR	865	1,373	3.7	6.4	3.21	5.10	6.7	5.4	45	37
Latvia	12,490	6,664	3.7	-4.8	2.54	2.40	2.0	1.1	15	8
Lebanon	2,838	17,229	..	7.7	2.83	4.30	4.0	2.4	30	21
Lesotho	622	874	4.6	4.4	1.37	2.10	5.5	4.5	41	34
Liberia	..	..	..	..	1.88	3.04	6.8	6.1	47	45
Libya	..	..	..	..	3.04	5.42	7.3	3.6	46	28
Liechtenstein	..	..	..	..	..	0.03	..	..	..	..
Lithuania	13,264	10,454	..	-3.9	3.41	3.70	2.0	1.4	16	10
Luxembourg	..	..	..	..	0.36	0.43	1.5	1.7	11	13
Macedonia, FYR	2,635	3,445	..	1.9	1.89	2.00	2.5	1.8	21	14
Madagascar	3,081	3,733	1.1	1.7	8.71	15.10	6.6	5.6	47	41
Malawi	1,803	1,820	2.5	4.0	6.14	10.80	7.6	6.3	57	46
Malaysia	42,775	74,634	5.3	6.3	13.76	22.70	4.2	3.0	31	24
Maldives	..	..	..	..	0.16	0.28	6.9	4.3	42	29
Mali	2,421	2,714	0.8	3.6	6.59	10.90	7.1	6.4	49	46
Malta	..	..	..	..	0.36	0.38	2.0	1.8	15	12
Marshall Islands	..	..	..	..	..	0.06	..	..	..	..
Martinique	..	..	..	..	0.33	0.38	..	..	..	..
Mauritania	1,020	959	1.8	4.1	1.55	2.60	6.3	5.3	43	39
Mauritius	..	..	.	..	0.97	1.17	2.7	2.0	24	17
Mayotte	..	..	..	..	..	0.13	..	..	..	..
Mexico	262,710	474,951	1.1	2.7	66.56	97.40	4.7	2.8	33	27
Micronesia, Fed. Sts.	..	..	..	..	0.07	0.12	..	3.8	..	27
Moldova	10,583	1,092	3.0	-11.5	4.00	4.30	2.4	1.7	20	12
Monaco	..	..	..	..	..	0.03	..	..	..	..
Mongolia	..	905	5.4	0.7	1.66	2.60	5.3	2.7	38	21
Morocco	25,821	35,238	4.2	2.3	19.38	28.20	5.4	2.9	38	25
Mozambique	2,512	4,169	-0.1	6.3	12.10	17.30	6.5	5.2	46	40
Myanmar	..	..	0.6	6.3	33.82	45.00	4.9	3.1	36	26
Namibia	2,340	3,075	1.3	3.4	1.03	1.70	5.9	4.7	41	35
Nepal	3,628	4,904	4.6	4.8	14.64	23.40	6.1	4.3	44	34
Netherlands	283,672	384,766	2.3	2.7	14.15	15.80	1.6	1.6	13	13
Netherlands Antilles	..	..	..	..	0.17	0.22	2.4	2.2	..	16
New Caledonia	..	..	..	..	0.14	0.21	3.3	2.6	26	21
New Zealand	43,103	53,622	1.7	2.9	3.11	3.60	2.0	2.0	16	15
Nicaragua	1,009	2,302	-1.9	3.2	2.80	4.90	6.3	3.6	45	30
Niger	2,481	2,067	-0.1	2.5	5.52	10.50	7.4	7.3	51	51
Nigeria	28,472	43,286	1.6	2.4	71.15	123.90	6.9	5.2	50	40
Northern Mariana Islands	..	..	..	..	..	0.07	..	..	..	..
Norway	115,453	145,449	2.8	3.7	4.09	4.50	1.7	1.8	12	13
Oman	..	..	..	..	1.10	2.35	9.9	4.5	45	28
Pakistan	40,010	59,880	6.3	4.0	82.70	134.80	7.0	4.8	47	34
Palau	..	..	..	..	..	19.00	..	..	..	..
Panama	5,313	9,606	0.5	4.2	1.96	2.80	3.7	2.5	29	21
Papua New Guinea	3,221	3,571	1.9	4.0	3.09	4.70	5.8	4.2	36	31
Paraguay	5,265	8,065	2.5	2.4	3.14	5.40	5.2	4.0	36	30

Death rate per 1,000 people		Average annual population growth %		GNP per capita		GDP per capita growth average annual real growth %	Gini index	
1980	1999	1980-99	1999-2015	$ 1999	PPP $ 1999	1990-1999	Survey year	
6	10	1.5	0.6	..	..	..	..	..
6	6	1.1	0.5	8,490	14,637	4.7	1993	31.6
4	2	1.8	2.5	..	..	..	..	..
9	7	1.5	1.1	300	2,223	-6.4	1997	40.5
20	13	2.4	2.2	280	1,726	3.8	1992	30.4
13	14	-0.2	-0.7	2,470	5,938	-3.7	1998	32.4
9	6	1.9	1.2	3,700	4,129	5.7	..	..
15	13	2.4	0.9	550	2,058	2.1	1986-87	56.0
17	17	..	..	..	..	..	..	..
12	4	3.0	2.0	..	..	..	..	..
..	..	..	..	..	..	..	..	..
10	11	0.4	-0.1	2,620	6,093	-3.9	1996	32.4
11	9	..	..	44,640	38,247	3.8	..	..
7	8	0.4	0.4	1,690	4,339	-1.5	..	..
16	12	2.8	2.5	250	766	-1.2	1993	46.0
23	24	2.9	1.8	190	581	0.9	..	..
6	4	2.6	1.6	3,400	7,963	4.7	1995	48.5
13	5	..	..	1,160	3,545	3.9	..	..
22	19	2.5	2.2	240	693	1.1	1994	50.5
9	8	..	..	15,066	3	4.2	..	..
..	..	..	..	..	-3	..	..	..
7	..	..	..	..		..	..	..
19	13	2.7	2.2	380	1,522	1.3	1995	38.9
6	7	1.0	0.9	3,590	8,652	3.9	..	..
..	..	..	..	..	..	..	..	..
7	5	1.9	1.3	4,400	7,719	1.0	1995	53.7
..	6	..	..	1,810	..	-1.8	..	..
10	11	0.4	-0.2	370	2,358	-10.8	1992	34.4
..	..	..	..	..	..	..	..	..
11	6	1.9	1.5	350	1,496	-0.6	1995	33.2
12	7	2.0	1.4	1,200	3,190	0.4	1998-99	39.5
20	20	1.9	1.7	230	797	3.8	1996-97	39.6
14	10	1.5	1 1	..	..	5.1	..	..
14	15	2.6	1.1	1,890	5,369	0.8	..	..
18	10	2.5	2.1	220	1,219	2.3	1995-96	36.7
8	9	0.6	0.4	24,320	23,052	2.1	1994	32.6
..	6	..	..	..	..	..	..	..
7	5	..	..	..	..	-0.8	..	..
9	7	1.1	0.6	13,780	16,566	1.8	1991	43.9
11	5	2.7	2.1	430	2,154	0.4	1993	50.3
23	18	3.3	3.0	190	727	-1.0	1995	50.5
18	16	2.9	2.0	310	744	-0.5	1996-97	50.6
..	..	..	..	..	..	..	..	..
10	10	0.5	0.4	32,880	26,522	3.2	1995	25.8
10	3	4.0	2.2	..	..	0.3	..	..
15	8	2.6	2.2	470	1,757	1.3	1996-97	31.2
..	..	..	..	..	..	..	..	..
6	5	1.9	1.2	3,070	5,016	2.4	1997	48.5
14	10	2.2	1.7	800	2,263	2.3	1996	50.9
8	5	2.9	2.1	1,580	4,193	-0.2	1995	59.1

Table 1. Indicators to chapters 1–5 (continued)

COUNTRY or REGION	Gross domestic product $ millions		Average annual GDP growth %		Population millions		Fertility rate births per woman		Birth rate per 1,000 people	
	1990	1999	1980-90	1990-99	1980	1999	1980	1999	1980	1999
Peru	32,802	57,318	-0.3	5.4	17.30	25.20	4.5	3.1	35	24
Philippines	44,331	75,350	1.0	3.2	48.32	76.80	4.8	3.5	35	27
Poland	61,197	154,146	2.2	4.7	35.58	38.70	2.3	1.4	20	10
Portugal	69,132	107,716	3.1	2.5	9.77	10.00	2.2	1.5	16	12
Puerto Rico	..	..	..	..	3.21	3.89	2.6	1.9	23	16
Qatar	..	..	..	..	0.23	0.76	5.6	2.7	29	14
Romania	38,299	33,750	0.5	-1.2	22.20	22.50	2.4	1.3	18	10
Russian Federation	579,068	375,345	..	-6.1	139.01	146.50	1.9	1.3	16	9
Rwanda	2,584	1,956	2.2	-1.5	5.16	8.30	8.3	6.0	51	45
Samoa	..	..	..	..	0.16	0.17	..	4.4	..	30
Sao Tome and Principe	..	..	..	..	0.09	0.15	..	4.5	39	32
Saudi Arabia	104,670	128,892	0.0	1.6	9.37	21.40	7.3	5.5	43	34
Senegal	5,698	4,791	3.1	3.2	5.54	9.30	6.8	5.4	46	38
Seychelles	..	..	..	..	0.06	0.08	..	2.1	29	18
Sierra Leone	897	669	1.2	-4.8	3.24	4.90	6.5	5.9	49	45
Singapore	36,638	84,945	6.7	8.0	2.28	3.20	1.7	1.5	17	13
Slovak Republic	15,485	19,307	2.0	1.9	4.98	5.40	2.3	1.4	19	10
Slovenia	12,673	20,653	..	2.4	1.90	2.00	2.1	1.2	15	9
Solomon Islands	..	..	..	..	0.23	0.43	6.7	4.6	44	34
Somalia	..	..	..	..	6.71	9.39	7.3	7.1	52	51
South Africa	111,997	131,127	1.0	1.9	29.17	42.10	4.6	2.9	36	26
Spain	491,938	562,245	3.0	2.2	37.39	39.40	2.2	1.2	15	9
Sri Lanka	8,032	15,707	4.0	5.3	14.74	19.00	3.5	2.1	28	17
St. Kitts and Nevis	..	..	..	..	0.04	0.04	..	2.3	27	19
St. Lucia	..	..	..	..	0.12	0.15	4.4	2.4	31	19
St. Vincent and the Grenadines	..	..	..	..	0.10	0.11	..	2.2	28	18
Sudan	..	..	..	..	18.68	28.99	6.5	4.5	45	33
Suriname	..	..	..	..	0.36	0.41	3.9	2.4	28	24
Swaziland	..	..	..	..	0.57	1.02	6.2	4.5	44	36
Sweden	229,756	226,388	2.3	1.5	8.31	8.90	1.7	1.5	12	10
Switzerland	228,415	260,299	2.0	0.5	6.32	7.10	1.5	1.5	12	11
Syrian Arab Republic	12,309	19,380	1.5	5.7	8.70	15.70	7.4	3.7	46	29
Tajikistan	4,857	1,778	..	-9.8	3.97	6.20	5.6	3.3	37	22
Tanzania	4,220	8,777	..	3.1	18.58	32.90	6.7	5.4	47	40
Thailand	85,345	123,887	7.6	4.7	46.72	61.70	3.5	1.9	28	17
Togo	1,628	1,506	1.7	2.5	2.62	4.60	6.8	5.1	45	38
Tonga	..	..	..	..	0.09	0.10	4.9	3.8	29	26
Trinidad and Tobago	..	..	..	..	1.08	1.29	3.3	1.8	29	15
Tunisia	12,291	21,188	3.3	4.6	6.38	9.50	5.2	2.2	35	17
Turkey	150,721	188,374	5.4	4.1	44.44	64.40	4.3	2.4	32	21
Turkmenistan	6,333	2,708	..	-3.5	2.86	4.80	4.9	2.8	34	21
Uganda	4,304	6,349	2.9	7.2	12.81	21.50	7.2	6.4	49	46
Ukraine	91,327	42,415	..	-10.8	50.04	49.90	2.0	1.3	15	9
United Arab Emirates	..	..	..	..	1.04	2.82	5.4	3.3	30	18
United Kingdom	975,512	1,373,612	3.2	2.2	56.33	59.10	1.9	1.7	13	12
United States	5,554,100	8,708,870	3.0	3.4	227.76	272.90	1.8	2.1	16	15
Uruguay	8,355	20,211	0.4	3.7	2.91	3.30	2.7	2.3	19	16
Uzbekistan	23,673	16,844	..	-2.0	15.95	24.50	4.8	2.7	34	23
Vanuatu	..	..	..	..	0.12	0.19	..	4.6	..	31
Venezuela	48,593	103,918	1.1	1.7	14.87	23.70	4.2	2.9	33	24

Death rate per 1,000 people		Average annual population growth %		GNP per capita		GDP per capita growth average annual real growth %	Gini index	
				$	PPP $		Survey year	
1980	1999	1980-99	1999-2015	1999	1999	1990-1999		
10	6	2.0	1.4	2,390	4,387	3.2	1996	46.2
9	6	2.3	1.6	1,020	3,815	0.9	1997	46.2
10	10	0.4	0.0	3,960	7,894	4.4	1996	32.9
10	11	0.1	0.0	10,600	15,147	2.3	1994-95	35.6
6	8	1.0	0.7	..	..	1.9	..	..
7	3	..	..	..	..	..	..	..
10	12	0.1	-0.3	1,520	5,647	-0.5	1994	28.2
11	14	0.3	-0.5	2,270	6,339	-5.9	1998	48.7
19	22	2.5	1.8	250	..	-3.0	1983-85	28.9
..	6	..	..	1,060	3,915	1.4	..	..
10	9	..	..	270	1,335	-0.9	.	..
9	4	4.0	2.9	..	..	-1.1	..	..
18	13	2.7	2.3	510	1,341	0.6	1995	41.3
7	7	..	..	6,540	10,381	1.3	..	..
29	25	2.2	1.9	130	414	-7.0	1989	62.9
5	5	2.6	1.4	29,610	27,024	4.7	..	..
10	10	0.4	0.0	3,590	9,811	1.6	1982	19.5
10	10	0.2	-0.2	9,890	15,062	2.5	1995	26.8
10	4	..	..	750	1,949	0.3	..	..
22	18	..	..	..	..	..	..	..
12	14	2.2	0.5	3,160	8,318	-0.2	1993-94	59.3
8	10	0.3	-0.2	14,000	16,730	2.0	1990	32.5
6	6	1.3	1.1	820	3,056	4.0	1995	34.4
11	12	..	..	6,420	9,801	4.9	..	..
7	7	..	..	3,770	5,022	0.9	..	..
7	7	..	..	2,700	4,667	2.6	..	..
17	11	2.3	2.1	330	1,298	..	..	..
8	7	..	..	..	..	3.3	..	..
15	13	..	..	1,360	4,200	-0.2	..	..
11	11	0.3	-0.1	25,040	20,824	1.2	1992	25.0
9	9	0.6	0.0	38,350	27,486	-0.1	1992	33.1
9	5	3.1	2.1	970	2,761	2.7	..	..
8	5	2.4	1.5	290	981	..	..	..
15	17	3.0	1.8	240	478	-0.1	1993	38.2
8	7	1.3	0.8	1,960	5,599	3.8	1998	41.4
16	15	2.9	2.0	320	1,346	-0.5	..	..
9	7	..	..	1,720	4,281	0.7	..	..
7	7	0.9	0.7	4,390	7,262	2.0	..	..
9	6	2.1	1.2	2,100	5,478	2.9	1990	40.2
10	6	1.9	1.2	2,900	6,126	2.2	1994	41.5
8	6	2.7	1.2	660	3,099	-9.6	1998	40.8
18	19	2.7	2.4	320	1,136	4.0	1992-93	39.2
11	15	0.0	-0.8	750	3,142	-10.3	1996	32.5
5	3	5.2	1.9	..	..	-1.6	..	..
12	11	0.3	0.0	22,640	20,883	2.1	1991	36.1
9	9	1.1	0.8	30,600	30,600	2.0	1997	40.8
10	10	0.7	0.6	5,900	8,280	3.0	1989	42.3
8	6	2.2	1.3	720	2,092	-3.1	1993	33.3
..	7	..	..	1,170	2,771	-0.8	..	..
6	4	2.4	1.5	3,670	5,268	-0.5	1996	48.8

Table 1.   Indicators to chapters 1–5 (continued)

COUNTRY or REGION	Gross domestic product $ millions		Average annual GDP growth %		Population millions		Fertility rate births per woman		Birth rate per 1,000 people	
	1990	1999	1980-90	1990-99	1980	1999	1980	1999	1980	1999
Vietnam	6,472	28,567	4.6	8.1	53.70	77.50	5.0	2.3	36	20
Virgin Islands (U.S.)	..	..	..	..	0.10	0.12	..	2.4	26	16
West Bank and Gaza	..	..	..	..	1.20	2.84	..	5.8	..	41
Yemen, Rep.	4,660	6,769	..	3.0	8.54	17.00	7.9	6.2	53	40
Yugoslavia, FR (Serbia, Montenegro)	..	..	..	..	9.52	10.62	2.3	1.7	18	12
Zambia	3,288	3,325	1.0	1.0	5.74	9.90	7.0	5.4	50	41
Zimbabwe	8,784	5,716	3.6	2.4	7.01	11.90	6.4	3.6	49	30
World	**21,390,644**	**30,211,993**	**3.2**	**2.5**	**4,430.20**	**5,974.70**	**3.7**	**2.7**	**27**	**22**
Low Income	889,723	1,067,242	4.4	2.4	1,612.90	2,417.00	5.3	3.7	31*	29
Middle income	3,525,445	5,488,604	3.2	3.5	2,027.90	2,666.80	3.2	2.2	28	18
Lower middle income	1,820,097*	2,575,942*	4.0*	3.4*	1 607.9*	2 093.7*	3.0	2.1	28	17
Upper middle income	1,722,041	2,918,403	2.5	3.6	419.90	573.10	3.7	2.4	28	21
Low & middle Income	4,413,061	6,557,913	3.4	3.3	3,641.00	5,083.80	4.1	2.9	30	24
East Asia & Pacific	925,765	1,888,729	8.0	7.4	1,397.80	1,836.90	3.0	2.1	22	18
Europe & Central Asia	1,240,214	1,093,237	2.4	-2.7	425.80	475.20	2.5	1.6	19	12
Latin America & Carib&	1,146,895	2,055,025	1.7	3.4	360.30	509.20	4.1	2.6	31	23
Middle East & N. Africa	402,799	590,253	2.0	3.0	174.00	290.90	6.1	3.5	41	26
South Asia	410,341	595,915	5.7	5.7	902.60	1,329.30	5.3	3.4	37	27
Sub-Saharan Africa	297,397	332,744	1.7	2.4	380.50	642.30	6.6	5.3	47	40
High Income	16,967,888	23,662,676	3.1	2.4	789.10	890.90	1.8	1.7	14	12

*indicates income-group aggregate that includes data on China.
Note: Revisions to estimates of China's GNP per Capita, made by analysts in 2000-01, caused that economy to be reclassified from low to lower middle income. As a result, for different indicators in these data tables China figures as part of one or the other income group, which considerably affects these group aggregates.

Death rate per 1,000 people		Average annual population growth %		GNP per capita		GDP per capita growth average annual real growth %	Gini index	
				$	PPP $			
1980	1999	1980-99	1999-2015	1999	1999	1990-1999	Survey year	
8	6	1.9	1.2	370	1,755	6.2	1998	36.1
..	5	..	..	..	..	..	..	..
..	4	..	3.5	1,610	..	-0.2	..	..
19	12	3.6	2.8	350	688	-0.4	1992	39.5
9	11	0.4	0.1	..	..	..	..	..
15	21	2.9	1.3	320	686	-2.4	1996	49.8
12	16	2.8	0.6	520	2,470	0.6	1990-91	56.8
10	**9**	**1.6**	**1.1**	**4,890**	**6,490**	**1.1**		
11*	11	2.1	1.5	410	1,790	1.1		
9	8	1.4	0.9	2,000	4,880	2.3		
10	8	1.4	0.8	1,200*	3,960*	2.2		
8	7	1.6	1.0	4,900	8,320	2.2		
11	9	1.8	1.2	1,240	3,410	1.9		
7	7	1.4	0.8	1,000	3,500	6.1		
10	11	0.6	0.0	2,150	5,580	-2.5		
8	7	1.8	1.3	3,840	6,280	1.8		
12	7	2.7	1.8	2,060	4,600	0.8		
14	9	2.0	1.4	440	2,030	3.6		
18	16	2.8	1.9	500	1,450	-0.4		
9	9	0.7	0.3	25,730	24,430	1.6		

Table 2. Indicators to chapters 6–7

COUNTRY or REGION	Poverty % of people living on less than $1 a day (PPP) Survey year		Prevalence of undernourishment % of population		Prevalence of child malnutrition		Cereal yield kg per hectare 2000	Agri-cultural produc-tivity 1995 US$ per worker 2000	Gross domestic investment % of GDP		Gross domestic saving % of GDP	
					Low weight for age (% of children under 5) 1993-2001	Low height for age (% of children under 5) 1993-2001						
			1990-92	1998-2000					1990	1999	1990	1999
Afghanistan	..	..	63	70	49	48	794	..	..	..	..	..
Albania	..	..	..	..	14	15	3175	1837	29	16	21	-7
Algeria	1995	<2	5	6	6	18	883	1826	29	27	27	30
American Samoa	..	..										
Andorra	..	..						..	..	..	..	
Angola	..	..	61	50	41	53	574	127	12	23	30	48
Antigua and Barbuda	..	..			..	..	1600	2621	..	..	..	..
Argentina	..	..			5	12	3454	10260	14	18	20	16
Armenia	..	..			3	13	1183	2653	47	19	36	-14
Aruba	..	..			..	..			..	..	..	..
Australia	..	..	..	..	0	0	1962	35789	21	22	21	21
Austria	..	..	..	..	..	..	5423	33217	24	25	25	25
Azerbaijan	..	..	..	..	17	20	2335	978	..	34	..	5
Bahamas, The	..	..			..	..	1950		..	..	..	..
Bahrain	..	..		..	..				..	..	..	..
Bangladesh	1996	29.1	35	35	48	45	3374	315	19	20	11	14
Barbados	..	..	..	..	..	..	2500	18912	..	..	..	..
Belarus	1998	<2	..	..	..	..	1952	2959	27	26	29	20
Belgium	..	..	..	..	..	..	7331	57556	20	18	22	22
Belize	..	..			..	..	2420	5731	..	..	..	..
Benin	..	..	19	13	23	31	1102	615	14	18	5	8
Bermuda	..	..	..	..	..	..	..	..	..	..	..	..
Bhutan	..	..	..	..	..	..	1469	158	..	..	..	..
Bolivia	1990	11.3	26	23	8	27	1646	748	13	18	11	11
Bosnia and Herzegovina	..	..	..	..	4	..	2550	7634	..	..	..	..
Botswana	1985-86	33.3	17	25	13	29	117	569	32	20	37	14
Brazil	1997	5.1	13	10	6	11	2661	4712	20	21	21	20
Brunei	..	..			..	..	1667		..	..	..	..
Bulgaria	1995	<2	..	..	..	..	2763	7959	26	16	22	12
Burkina Faso	1994	61.2	23	23	34	37	859	190	21	27	8	10
Burundi	..	..	49	69	45	..	1249	150	15	10	-5	1
Cambodia	..	..	43	36	45	45	2134	423	8	15	2	5
Cameroon	..	..	32	25	22	29	1764	1184	18	19	21	19
Canada	..	..	..	..	..	..	2812	44136	21	20	21	21
Cape Verde	..	..					795	2607	..	..	..	..
Cayman Islands	..	..	..	..	..	..	..	..	..	..	..	..
Central African Republic	1993	66.6	49	44	23	28	1088	493	12	14	-1	7
Chad	..	..	58	32	28	29	528	208	7	18	-6	0
Channel Islands	..	..							..	..	..	..
Chile	1994	4.2	8	4	1	2	4362	6039	25	24	28	23
China	1998	18.5	16	9	10	14	4789	333	35	40	38	42
Hong Kong, China	..	..	..	..	..	..	..		27	25	36	30
Macao, China	..	..							..	..	..	..
Colombia	1996	11.0	17	13	7	14	3297	3601	20	17	25	19
Comoros	..	..			..	..	1324	504	..	..	..	..

Adult illiteracy % of people 15 and above, 1998			Child labor percent of children 10–14 in the labor force		Public expenditure on education % of GNP		School enrollment % of corresponding age group						Ratio of girls to boys in primary and secondary education %
							Primary		Secondary		Tertiary		
male	fem.	total	1980	1999	1980	1997	1980	1997	1980	1997	1980	1997	2000
..	..	65	28	..	..	..	..	..	..	..	..	..	..
9	24	17	4	1	..	3.1	113	107	67	38	5	11	102
24	46	35	7	1	7.8	5.1	95	108	33	63	6	13	98
..	..	..	..	..	..	..	..	..	..	..	..	..	..
..	..	..	..	..	..	..	..	..	..	..	..	..	..
..	..	..	30	26	..	..	175	..	21	..	0	1	84
..	..	..	..	..	..	..	..	..	..	..	..	..	..
3	3	3	8	3	2.7	3.5	106	111	56	73	22	42	103
1	3	2	0	0	..	2.0	..	87	..	90	..	12	104
..	..	..	..	..	..	..	..	..	..	..	..	..	100
..	..	..	0	0	5.5	5.4	112	101	71	153	25	80	100
..	..	..	0	0	5.5	5.4	99	100	93	103	22	48	97
..	..	..	0	0	..	3.0	115	106	95	77	24	18	97
..	..	5	0	..	..	..	..	..	..	..	..	..	..
..	..	14	0	..	..	..	..	..	..	..	..	..	104
49	71	60	35	29	1.1	2.2	61	..	18	..	3	6	102
..	..	..	0	..	..	..	..	..	..	..	..	..	100
0	1	1	0	0	..	5.9	104	98	98	93	39	44	102
..	..	..	0	0	6.0	3.1	104	103	91	146	26	57	106
..	..	7	4	..	..	..	..	..	..	..	..	..	101
46	77	62	30	27	..	3.2	67	78	16	18	1	3	62
..	..	..	..	..	..	..	..	..	..	..	..	..	..
..	..	..	63	..	..	..	..	..	..	..	..	..	..
9	22	16	19	13	4.4	4.9	87	..	37	..	16	24	98
..	..	..	1	..	..	..	..	..	..	..	..	..	..
27	22	24	26	15	6.0	8.6	91	108	19	65	1	6	102
16	16	16	19	15	3.6	5.1	98	125	34	62	11	15	103
..	..	9	0	..	..	..	..	..	..	..	..	..	102
1	2	2	0	0	4.5	3.2	98	99	85	77	16	41	98
68	87	78	71	47	2.2	1.5	18	40	3	..	0	1	70
45	63	54	50	49	3.4	4.0	26	51	3	7	1	1	79
43	80	63	27	24	..	2.9	139	113	..	24	2	1	83
20	33	26	34	24	3.8	..	98	85	18	27	2	4	..
..	..	..	0	0	6.9	6.9	99	102	88	105	57	90	100
..	..	27	16	..	..	..	..	..	..	..	..	..	..
..	..	..	..	..	..	..	..	..	..	..	..	..	..
43	68	56	..	..	..	..	71	..	14	..	1	1	..
51	69	61	42	37	..	1.7	..	58	..	10	0	1	..
..	..	..	..	..	..	..	..	..	..	..	..	..	..
4	5	5	0	0	4.6	3.6	109	101	53	75	12	31	100
9	25	17	30	9	2.5	2.3	113	123	46	70	2	6	98
4	11	7	6	0	2.4	2.9	107	94	64	73	10	28	..
..	..	..	7	..	..	..	..	..	..	..	..	..	..
9	9	9	12	6	1.9	4.1	112	113	39	67	9	17	104
..	..	42	45	..	..	..	..	..	..	..	..	..	..

Table 2. Indicators to chapters 6–7 (continued)

COUNTRY or REGION	Poverty % of people living on less than $1 a day (PPP)		Prevalence of undernourishment		Prevalence of child malnutrition		Cereal yield	Agri-cultural produc-tivity 1995 US$	Gross domestic investment		Gross domestic saving	
					Low weight for age (% of children under 5)	Low height for age (% of children under 5)	kg per hectare	per worker	% of GDP		% of GDP	
	Survey year		% of population									
			1990-92	1998-2000	1993-2001	1993-2001	2000	2000	1990	1999	1990	1999
Congo, Dem. Rep.	..	..	32	73	34	45	782	220	9	8	9	9
Congo, Rep.	..	..	37	32	..	..	781	459	16	26	24	45
Costa Rica	1996	9.6	6	5	5	6	4003	5258	27	28	21	32
Cote d'Ivoire	1995	12.3	18	15	21	25	1475	1044	7	19	11	25
Croatia	..	..	..	..	1	1	3987	9383	10	23	2	14
Cuba	..	..	5	10	..	..	2526	..	..	..	..	..
Cyprus			..	..	..	..	931	..	..	..	..	..
Czech Republic	1993	<2	..	..	..	..	3908	6307	25	30	28	29
Denmark	..	..	..	..	..	..	6205	60999	20	21	25	24
Djibouti	..	..					1625	68	..	..	..	..
Dominica	..	..	..	..	..	..	1308	4314	..	..	..	..
Dominican Republic	1996	3.2	27	26	5	11	4139	3340	25	26	15	16
Ecuador	1995	20.2	8	5	14	26	2235	3303	17	15	23	20
Egypt, Arab Rep.	1995	3.1	5	4	4	19	7280	1300	29	23	16	14
El Salvador	1996	25.3	12	14	12	23	2155	1705	14	16	1	2
Equatorial Guinea	..	..						920	..	..	..	..
Eritrea	..	..	..	58	44	38	406	61	5	45	-31	-20
Estonia	1995	4.9	..	..	..	..	2115	3687	30	28	22	17
Ethiopia	1995	31.3	..	44	47	52	1115	147	12	19	7	4
Faeroe Islands	..	..	..	..	..	..	..	..	..	..	..	..
Fiji	..	..	..	..	..	..	2495	2475	..	..	..	..
Finland	..	..	..	..	..	..	3503	42454	28	17	26	26
France	..	..	..	..	..	..	7240	58018	22	17	22	21
French Polynesia	..	..	..	..	..	..			..	..	..	..
Gabon		..	11	8	12	21	1630	2048	..	..	..	..
Gambia, The	..	..	21	21	17	30	1305	297	..	..	..	..
Georgia	..	..	..	..	3	12	1362	..	31	7	25	-6
Germany	..	..	..	..	..	..	6453	32724	23	21	23	23
Ghana	..	..	35	12	25	26	1309	568	14	22	5	4
Greece	..	..	..	..	..	..	3748	13870	23	20	11	12
Greenland	..	..	..	..	..	..	..	..	..	..	..	..
Grenada	..	..	..	..	..	..	1000	2297	..	..	..	..
Guam	..	..	..	..	..	..	2000		..	..	..	..
Guatemala	1989	39.8	14	25	24	46	1773	2127	14	16	10	6
Guinea	..	..	40	32	33	41	1357	279	18	18	18	17
Guinea-Bissau	..	..	..	..	25	..	1111	325	..	..	..	..
Guyana	..	..	..	..	..	..	3819	4126	..	..	..	..
Haiti	..	..	64	50	17	23	932	..	12	11	-1	-7
Honduras	1996	40.5	23	21	17	39	1370	1043	23	26	20	9
Hungary	1993	<2	..	..	..	..	3632	4925	25	30	28	28
Iceland	.	..						49337	..	..	..	..
India	1997	44.2	25	24	53	52	2295	391	25	24	22	20
Indonesia	1999	15.2	..	6	25	42	4026	747	31	14	33	24
Iran, Islamic Rep.	..	..	4	5	11	15	1833	3684	29	16	27	16
Iraq	..	..	7	27	..	..	354		..	..	..	..

Adult illiteracy % of people 15 and above, 1998			Child labor percent of children 10–14 in the labor force		Public expenditure on education % of GNP		School enrollment % of corresponding age group						Ratio of girls to boys in primary and secondary education %
							Primary		Secondary		Tertiary		
male	fem.	total	1980	1999	1980	1997	1980	1997	1980	1997	1980	1997	2000
29	53	41	33	29	2.6	..	92	72	24	26	1	2	80
14	29	22	27	26	7.0	6.1	141	114	74	53	5	8	89
5	5	5	10	5	7.8	5.4	105	104	48	48	21	33	101
47	64	56	28	19	7.2	5.0	75	71	19	25	3	5	..
1	3	2	0	0	..	5.3	..	87	77	82	19	28	102
		4	0	..	7.2	..	106	106	81	81	17	12	100
		3	4	..	..	..	..	..	..	..	..	..	101
..	..	..	0	0	..	5.1	96	104	99	99	18	24	101
..	..	..	0	0	6.7	8.1	96	102	105	121	28	45	96
	..	38	..	..	..	..	..	..	..	..	..	..	71
..	..	..	..	..	..	..	..	..	..	..	..	..	102
17	17	17	25	14	2.2	2.3	118	94	42	54	10	23	106
8	11	9	9	5	5.6	3.5	118	127	53	50	35	26	101
35	58	46	18	10	5.7	4.8	73	101	51	78	16	23	93
19	25	22	17	14	3.9	2.5	75	97	24	37	13	18	96
..	..	19	40	..	..	..	..	..	..	..	..	..	88
34	62	48	44	39	..	1.8	..	53	..	20	..	1	79
..	..	..	0	0	..	7.2	103	94	127	104	25	45	99
58	70	64	46	42	3.1	4.0	37	43	9	12	0	1	68
..	..	..	..	..	..	..	..	..	..	..	..	..	
..	..	8	5	..	..	..	..	..	..	..	..	..	103
..	..	..	0	0	5.3	7.5	96	99	100	118	32	74	106
..	..	..	0	0	5.0	6.0	111	105	85	111	25	51	100
..	..	..	..	..	..	..	..	..	..	..	..	..	..
..	..	..	29	..	2.7	..	174	162	34	56	4	8	..
..	..	65	44	..	3.3		53	77	11	25	..	2	85
..	..	..	0	0	..	5.2	93	88	109	77	30	41	102
..	..	..	0	0	..	4.8	..	104	..	104	27	47	99
22	40	31	16	13	3.1	4.2	79	79	41	..	2	1	88
2	5	3	5	0	2.0	3.1	103	93	81	95	17	47	101
..	..	..	..	..	..	..	..	..	..	..	..	..	
..	..	..	..	..	..	..	..	..	..	..	..	..	76
..	..	..	..	..	..	..	..	..	..	..	..	..	
25	40	33	19	15	1.8	1.7	71	88	19	26	8	8	92
..	..	..	41	32	..	1.9	36	54	17	14	5	1	57
..	..	63	43	..	..	..	68	62	6	..	..	..	65
		2	2	..	..	..	..	..	..	..	..	..	..
50	54	52	33	24	1.5	..	77	..	14	..	1	1	
27	27	27	14	8	3.2	3.6	98	111	30	..	8	11	..
1	1	1	0	0	4.7	4.6	96	103	70	98	14	25	100
..	..	..	0	..	..	..	..	..	..	..	..	..	103
33	57	44	21	13	3.0	3.2	83	100	30	49	5	7	79
9	20	14	13	9	1.7	1.4	107	113	29	56	4	11	98
18	33	25	14	3	7.5	4.0	87	98	42	77	..	18	95
..	..	46	11	..	3.0	..	113	85	57	42	9	11	77

Table 2.   Indicators to chapters 6–7 (continued)

COUNTRY or REGION	Poverty % of people living on less than $1 a day (PPP) Survey year		Prevalence of undernourishment % of population 1990-92	1998-2000	Prevalence of child malnutrition Low weight for age (% of children under 5) 1993-2001	Low height for age (% of children under 5) 1993-2001	Cereal yield kg per hectare 2000	Agricultural productivity 1995 US$ per worker 2000	Gross domestic investment % of GDP 1990	1999	Gross domestic saving % of GDP 1990	1999
Ireland	..	..	..	..	..	..	7842	..	21	20	27	37
Isle of Man	..	..						..	..	..	..	..
Israel	..	..	..	..	..	..	2562	..	25	20	14	10
Italy	..	..	..	..	..	..	4994	26474	21	18	21	22
Jamaica	1996	3.2	14	9	4	4	1147	1445	28	32	24	19
Japan	..	..	..	..	..	..	6257	32015	32	29	33	30
Jordan	1997	<2	4	6	5	8	1751	1135	32	27	1	6
Kazakstan	1996	1.5	..	..	4	10	944	1598	32	15	30	15
Kenya	1994	26.2	47	44	22	33	1375	213	20	15	14	7
Kiribati	..	..					..	1001	..	..	..	..
Korea, Dem. Rep.	..	..	18	34	28	..	2367		..	..	..	..
Korea, Rep.	1993	<2	..	..	..	..	6436	13758	38	27	37	34
Kuwait	..	..	22	4	2	3	2324	..	18	12	4	22
Kyrgyz Republic	..	..	..	..	11	25	2670	1799	24	10	4	-11
Lao PDR	..	..	29	24	40	41	3006	617	..	25	..	24
Latvia	1998	<2	..	..	..	..	2172	2653	40	20	39	10
Lebanon	..	..	..	3	3	12	2363	28916	18	28	-64	-13
Lesotho	1993	43.1	27	26	18	44	944	576	53	47	-51	-35
Liberia	..	..	33	39	..	..	1278		..	..	..	..
Libya	..	..	..	..	5	15	635		..	..	..	..
Liechtenstein	..	..						..	..	..	..	..
Lithuania	1996	<2	..	..	..	..	2713	3445	33	24	24	12
Luxembourg	..	..						..	..	..	..	..
Macedonia, FYR	..	..	..	..	6	7	2560	4395	14	23	15	7
Madagascar	1993	60.2	35	40	40	48	1890	154	17	12	6	5
Malawi	..	..	40	33	25	49	1675	129	20	15	10	7
Malaysia	..	..	3	..	20	..	3038	6894	34	32	36	45
Maldives	..	..					800	..	..	..	..	..
Mali	1994	72.8	25	20	27	49	1006	261	23	20	6	8
Malta	..	..					4008					
Marshall Islands	..	..						..	..	..	..	..
Martinique	..	..						..	..	..	..	..
Mauritania	1995	3.8	14	12	32	35	864	455	20	22	5	12
Mauritius	..	..	6	5	15	10	8900	4698	..	..	..	..
Mayotte	..	..	..	..	..	..	..	..	..	..	..	..
Mexico	1995	17.9	5	5	8	18	2761	1781	23	24	22	23
Micronesia, Fed. Sts.	..	..	..	..	..	..	..	..	..	..	..	..
Moldova	1992	7.3	..	..	..	..	2033	935	25	18	23	-4
Monaco	..	..						..	..	..	..	..
Mongolia	1995	13.9	34	42	13	25	779	1432	34	26	13	20
Morocco	1990-91	<2	6	7	..	..	368	1333	25	23	16	18
Mozambique	1996	37.9	69	55	26	36	933	129	16	35	-12	11
Myanmar	..	..	10	6	43	45	3191	..	13	12	11	11
Namibia	1993	34.9	15	9	..	..	374	1630	34	20	18	9
Nepal	1995	37.7	19	19	48	51	2136	200	18	19	8	11

Adult illiteracy % of people 15 and above, 1998			Child labor percent of children 10–14 in the labor force		Public expenditure on education % of GNP		School enrollment % of corresponding age group						Ratio of girls to boys in primary and secondary education %
							Primary		Secondary		Tertiary		
male	fem.	total	1980	1999	1980	1997	1980	1997	1980	1997	1980	1997	2000
..	..	..	1	0	6.3	6.0	100	105	90	118	18	41	100
..	..	..	..	..	..	..	..	..	..	..	..	..	..
2	6	4	0	0	8.2	7.6	95	98	73	88	29	44	100
1	2	2	2	0	..	4.9	100	101	72	95	27	47	98
18	10	14	0	0	7.0	7.4	103	100	67	..	7	8	101
..	..	..	0	0	5.8	3.6	101	101	93	103	31	43	101
6	17	11	4	0	6.6	6.8	82	71	59	57	13	19	101
..	..	..	0	0	..	4.4	85	98	93	87	34	32	98
12	27	20	45	40	6.8	6.5	115	85	20	24	1	2	97
..	..	..	..	..	..	..	..	..	..	..	..	..	..
..	..	..	3	..	..	..	..	..	..	..	..	..	..
1	4	3	0	0	3.7	3.7	110	94	78	102	15	68	100
17	22	19	0	0	2.4	5.0	102	77	80	65	11	19	101
..	..	..	0	0	..	5.3	116	104	110	79	16	12	99
38	70	54	31	26	..	2.1	114	112	21	29	0	3	82
0	0	0	0	0	3.3	6.3	102	96	99	84	24	33	101
9	21	15	5	0	..	2.5	111	111	59	81	30	27	102
29	7	18	28	21	5.1	8.4	104	108	18	31	1	2	105
..	..	49	26	..	..	..	..	..	..	..	..	..	70
..	..	22	9	..	3.4	..	125	..	76	..	8	20	103
..	..	..	..	..	..	..	..	..	..	..	..	..	..
0	1	1	0	0	..	5.4	79	98	114	86	35	31	99
..	..	..	0	..	..	..	..	..	..	..	..	..	103
..	..	..	1	0	..	5.1	100	99	61	63	28	20	98
28	42	35	40	35	4.4	1.9	130	92	..	16	3	2	97
27	56	42	45	33	3.4	5.4	60	134	5	17	1	1	94
9	18	14	8	3	6.0	4.9	93	101	48	64	4	11	105
..	..	4	23	..	..	..	..	..	..	..	..	..	101
54	69	62	61	52	3.7	2.2	26	49	8	13	1	1	66
..	..	9	1	..	..	..	..	..	..	..	..	..	98
..	..	..	..	..	..	..	..	..	..	..	..	..	..
48	69	59	30	23	..	5.1	37	79	11	16	1	4	90
..	..	16	5	..	5.3	..	93	106	50	65	1	6	97
..	..	..	..	..	..	..	..	..	..	..	..	..	..
7	11	9	9	6	4.7	4.9	120	114	49	64	14	16	101
..	..	..	9	..	..	..	..	..	..	..	..	..	..
1	2	1	3	0	3.4	10.6	83	97	78	81	30	27	102
..	..	..	..	..	..	..	..	..	..	..	..	..	..
28	49	39	4	2	..	5.7	107	88	92	56	22	19	112
40	66	53	21	3	6.1	5	83	86	26	39	6	11	85
42	73	58	39	33	3.1	..	99	60	5	7	0	1	76
11	21	16	28	24	1.7	1.2	91	121	22	30	5	6	98
18	20	19	34	19	1.5	9.1	..	131	..	62	..	9	103
43	78	61	56	43	1.8	3.2	86	113	22	42	3	5	81

Table 2.   Indicators to chapters 6–7 (continued)

COUNTRY or REGION	Poverty % of people living on less than $1 a day (PPP) Survey year		Prevalence of undernourishment % of population 1990-92	1998-2000	Prevalence of child malnutrition Low weight for age (% of children under 5) 1993-2001	Low height for age (% of children under 5) 1993-2001	Cereal yield kg per hectare 2000	Agricultural productivity 1995 US$ per worker 2000	Gross domestic investment % of GDP 1990	1999	Gross domestic saving % of GDP 1990	1999
Netherlands	..	..	..	..	..	..	7627	59652	22	20	27	27
Netherlands Antilles	..	..	..	..	..	..	..	..	..	..	..	..
New Caledonia	..	..	..	..	..	..	3697	..	..	..	..	..
New Zealand	..	..	..	..	..	..	6273	28265	19	21	20	21
Nicaragua	..	..	30	29	12	25	1648	1603	19	37	-2	1
Niger	1995	61.4	42	36	40	40	290	187	8	10	1	4
Nigeria	1997	70.2	13	7	31	34	1120	716	15	11	29	0
Northern Mariana Islands	..	..	..	..	..	..	..	..	..	..	..	..
Norway	..	..	..	..	..	..	3879	36785	23	25	30	32
Oman	..	..	..	..	23	23	2321	..	..	..	..	..
Pakistan	1996	31.0	25	19	38	36	2408	733	19	15	11	11
Palau	..	..	..	..	..	..	..	..	..	..	..	..
Panama	1997	10.3	19	18	8	18	2043	2965	17	34	21	25
Papua New Guinea	..	..	25	27	..	..	4109	853	24	36	16	37
Paraguay	1995	19.4	16	14	..	..	1845	3312	22	19	16	17
Peru	1996	15.5	40	11	7	25	3086	1876	21	22	22	20
Philippines	..		26	23	32	32	2581	1440	24	21	18	16
Poland	1993	5.4	..	..	..	..	2535	1548	25	28	32	18
Portugal	1994	<2	..	..	..	..	2781	7505	29	26	21	17
Puerto Rico	..	..	..	..	..	..	1731	..	..	..	..	..
Qatar	..	..					3856	..	..	..	..	..
Romania	1994	2.8	..	..	..	..	1932	3103	30	15	21	10
Russian Federation	1998	7.1	..	..	3	13	1561	3570	30	14	30	29
Rwanda	1983-85	35.7	34	40	24	43	848	249	15	14	6	-1
Samoa	..	..						1886	..	..	..	..
Sao Tome and Principe	..	..	..	..	..	..	2230	396	..	..	..	..
Saudi Arabia	..	..	4	3	..	..	3472	15497	20	21	30	26
Senegal	1995	26.3	23	25	18	23	879	345	14	21	9	14
Seychelles	..	..						905	..	..	..	..
Sierra Leone	1989	57.0	46	47	27	..	1081	358	9	5	8	-2
Singapore	..	..	..	..	..	..	..	44213	37	33	44	52
Slovak Republic	1992	<2	..	..	..	..	..	..	33	39	24	28
Slovenia	1993	<2	..	..	..	..	4815	36170	17	25	26	24
Solomon Islands	..	..					4000	..	..	..	..	..
Somalia	..	..	67	71	26	23	497	..	..	..	..	..
South Africa	1993	11.5	..	..	8	23	2927	4061	12	16	18	18
Spain	..	..	..	..	..	..	3590	22243	25	21	21	22
Sri Lanka	1995	6.6	29	23	33	20	3338	741	22	25	14	19
St. Kitts and Nevis	..	..			..	..	..	2537	..	..	..	..
St. Lucia	..	..			..	..	..	2298	..	..	..	..
St. Vincent and the Grenadines	..	..	..	..	..	..	1667	2370	..	..	..	..
Sudan	..	..	31	21	11	34	533	..	..	..	..	..
Suriname	..	..					3897	3267	..	..	..	..
Swaziland	..	..	18	18	10	..	1528	2017	..	..	..	..
Sweden	..	..	..	..	..	..	4616	39843	21	14	22	21

Adult illiteracy % of people 15 and above, 1998			Child labor percent of children 10–14 in the labor force		Public expenditure on education % of GNP		School enrollment % of corresponding age group						Ratio of girls to boys in primary and secondary education %
							Primary		Secondary		Tertiary		
male	fem.	total	1980	1999	1980	1997	1980	1997	1980	1997	1980	1997	2000
..	..	..	0	0	7.7	5.1	100	108	93	132	29	47	97
..	..	4	0	..	..	..	..	..	..	..	..	..	96
..	..	..	..	..	..	..	..	..	..	..	..	..	..
..	..	..	0	0	5.8	7.3	111	101	83	113	27	63	103
34	31	32	19	13	3.4	3.9	94	102	41	55	12	12	105
78	93	85	48	44	3.2	2.3	25	29	5	7	0	1	68
30	48	39	29	25	6.4	0.7	109	98	18	33	3	4	..
..	..	..	..	..	..	..	..	..	..	..	..	..	..
..	..	..	0	0	6.5	7.4	100	100	94	119	26	62	101
..	..	31	6	..	2.1	..	51	76	12	67	..	8	98
42	71	56	23	16	2.1	2.7	40	..	14	..	2	4	61
..	..	..	..	..	..	..	..	..	..	..	..	..	..
8	9	9	6	3	4.9	5.1	107	106	61	69	21	32	100
29	45	37	28	18	..	..	59	80	12	14	2	3	90
6	9	7	15	7	1.5	4.0	106	111	27	47	9	10	98
6	16	11	4	2	3.1	2.9	114	123	59	73	17	26	..
5	5	5	14	6	1.7	3.4	112	117	64	78	24	35	103
0	0	0	0	0	..	7.5	100	96	77	98	18	24	98
6	11	9	8	1	3.8	5.8	123	128	37	111	11	38	102
..	..	7	0	..	..	..	..	..	..	..	42	42	..
..	..	20	0	..	..	..	..	..	..	..	..	..	103
1	3	2	0	0	3.3	3.6	104	104	94	78	12	23	100
0	1	1	0	0	3.5	3.5	102	107	96	..	46	41	..
29	43	36	43	41	2.7	..	63	..	3	..	0	1	93
..	..	20	..	..	..	..	..	..	..	..	..	..	104
..	..	..	..	..	..	..	..	..	..	..	..	..	..
17	36	25	5	0	4.1	7.5	61	76	30	61	7	16	93
55	74	65	43	29	..	3.7	46	71	11	16	3	3	84
..	..	..	..	..	..	..	..	..	..	..	..	..	101
..	..	..	19	15	3.5	..	52	..	14	..	1	2	..
4	12	8	2	0	2.8	3.0	108	94	60	74	8	39	..
..	..	..	0	0	..	5.0	..	102	..	94	18	22	101
0	0	0	0	0	..	5.7	98	98	..	92	20	36	101
..	..	..	40	..	..	..	..	..	..	..	..	..	..
..	..	..	38	..	..	..	..	..	..	..	..	..	..
15	16	15	1	0	..	7.9	90	133	..	95	5	17	100
2	4	3	0	0	2.3	5.0	109	107	87	120	23	53	102
6	12	9	4	2	2.7	3.4	103	109	55	75	3	5	102
..	..	..	..	..	..	..	..	..	..	..	..	..	123
..	..	..	..	..	..	..	..	..	..	..	..	..	107
..	..	..	..	..	..	..	..	..	..	..	..	..	104
..	..	44	33	..	4.8	..	50	51	16	21	2	4	86
..	..	..	1	..	..	..	..	..	..	..	..	..	106
..	..	..	17	..	..	..	..	..	..	..	..	..	..
..	..	..	0	0	9.0	8.3	97	107	88	140	31	50	115

Table 2. Indicators to chapters 6–7 (continued)

COUNTRY or REGION	Poverty % of people living on less than $1 a day (PPP) Survey year		Prevalence of undernourishment % of population		Prevalence of child malnutrition		Cereal yield kg per hectare	Agri-cultural produc-tivity 1995 US$ per worker	Gross domestic investment % of GDP		Gross domestic saving % of GDP	
					Low weight for age (% of children under 5)	Low height for age (% of children under 5)						
			1990-92	1998-2000	1993-2001	1993-2001	2000	2000	1990	1999	1990	1999
Switzerland	..	..	..	..	..	..	6601	..	28	20	29	25
Syrian Arab Republic	..	..	5	3	13	21	1149	2602	15	29	16	18
Tajikistan	..	..	..	..	..	31	1323	731	23	..	14	..
Tanzania	1993	19.9	36	47	29	44	1338	184	23	18	-1	14
Thailand	1998	<2	28	18	18	13	2719	847	41	21	34	32
Togo	..	..	28	23	25	22	1053	514	27	14	15	6
Tonga	..	..	..	..	..	..	..	3013	..	..	..	..
Trinidad and Tobago	..	..	13	12	..	..	2836	3075	..	..	..	..
Tunisia	1990	<2	..	..	4	8	986	3158	32	28	25	24
Turkey	1994	2.4	..	..	8	16	2311	1909	24	24	20	21
Turkmenistan	1993	20.9	..	..	12	22	1465	626	40	..	28	..
Uganda	1992	36.7	23	21	23	39	1539	342	13	17	1	6
Ukraine	1996	<2	..	..	3	16	1951	1467	27	21	26	18
United Arab Emirates	..	..	3	..	7	..	656	..	..	..	..	..
United Kingdom	..	..	..	..	..	..	7165	34516	19	16	17	15
United States	..	..	..	..	1	2	5854	54410	17	19	15	17
Uruguay	1989	<2	6	3	4	10	3696	8480	11	14	17	13
Uzbekistan	1993	3.3	..	..	19	31	2435	1424	32	19	13	19
Vanuatu	..	..					538	1395	..	..	..	..
Venezuela	1996	14.7	11	21	4	13	3244	5298	10	15	29	17
Vietnam	..	..	27	18	34	37	4113	254	13	29	6	21
Virgin Islands (U.S.)	..	..	..	..	..	..	..	..	..	..	..	..
West Bank and Gaza	..	..	..	..	15		..	..	..	..	..	..
Yemen, Rep.	1998	5.1	36	33	46	52	1085	404	15	21	9	13
Yugoslavia, FR (Serbia, Montenegro)	..	..	..	..	2	5	..	..	..	..	..	..
Zambia	1996	72.6	15	50	24	42	1462	198	17	17	17	6
Zimbabwe	1990-91	36.0	43	38	13	27	1412	380	17	18	17	15
World			**21**	**18**	..	..	**2043**	**1047**	**24**	**22**	**23**	**23**
Low Income			28*	25*	..*	..*	1324	409	24	20	21	19
Middle income			15	10	13	25	2311	805	26	24	27	26
Lower middle income			16	10	10	17	1932	700	31*	27*	30*	30*
Upper middle income			9	9	9	..	2737	3863	23	22	25	23
Low & middle Income			21	18	..	..	1751	616	26	24	26	25
East Asia & Pacific			17	11	15	14	3006	..	35	33	35	37
Europe & Central Asia			..	..	..	..	2311	2280	28	20	26	23
Latin America & Carib&			14	12	9	19	2473	3501	19	21	22	20
Middle East & N. Africa			7	8	15	..	1387	2275	24	22	22	19
South Asia			27	25	53	47	2216	405	23	22	19	19
Sub-Saharan Africa			32	33	..	..	1111	357	15	17	16	14
High Income			..	..	..	..	3868	33274	23	21	23	22

*indicates income-group aggregate that includes data on China.

Note: Revisions to estimates of China's GNP per Capita, made by analysts in 2000-01, caused that economy to be reclassified from low to lower middle income. As a result, for different indicators in these data tables China figures as part of one or the other income group, which considerably affects these group aggregates.

Adult illiteracy			Child labor percent of children 10–14 in the labor force		Public expenditure on education		School enrollment % of corresponding age group						Ratio of girls to boys in primary and secondary education
% of people 15 and above, 1998					% of GNP		Primary		Secondary		Tertiary		%
male	fem.	total	1980	1999	1980	1997	1980	1997	1980	1997	1980	1997	2000
..	..	22	0	0	4.7	5.4	84	97	94	100	18	34	96
13	42	27	14	4	4.6	3.1	100	101	46	43	17	15	92
1	1	1	0	0	..	2.2	..	95	..	78	24	20	87
17	36	26	43	38	..	..	93	67	3	6	0	1	100
3	7	5	25	14	3.4	4.8	99	89	29	59	15	21	95
28	62	45	36	28	5.6	4.5	118	120	33	27	2	4	70
..	..	..	..	..	..	..	..	..	..	..	..	..	..
..	..	7	1	..	4.0	..	99	99	69	74	4	8	102
21	42	31	6	0	5.4	7.7	102	118	27	64	5	14	100
7	25	16	21	9	2.2	2.2	96	107	35	58	5	21	84
..	..	..	0	0	..	..	..	..	..	..	23	20	..
24	46	35	49	44	1.3	2.6	50	74	5	12	1	2	89
0	1	0	0	0	5.6	7.3	102	..	94	..	42	42	98
..	..	25	0	..	1.3	..	89	89	52	80	3	12	100
..	..	..	0	0	5.6	5.3	103	116	84	129	19	52	110
..	..	..	0	0	6.7	5.4	99	102	91	97	56	81	100
3	2	2	4	1	2.3	3.3	107	109	62	85	17	30	105
7	17	12	0	0	..	7.7	81	78	106	94	29	36	..
..	..	..	..	..	..	..	..	..	..	..	..	..	..
7	9	8	4	1	4.4	5.2	93	91	21	40	21	25	104
5	9	7	22	7	..	3.0	109	114	42	57	2	7	93
..	..	..	..	..	..	..	..	..	..	..	..	..	..
..	..	..	..	..	..	..	..	..	..	..	..	..	..
34	77	56	26	19	..	7.0	..	70	..	34	4	4	56
..	..	..	0	..	..	..	..	69	..	62	18	22	101
16	31	24	19	16	4.5	2.2	90	89	16	27	2	3	..
8	17	13	37	28	5.3	..	85	112	8	50	1	7	95
18	**32**	**25**	**20**	**12**	**3.9**	**4.8**	**97**	**106**	**49**	**64**	**13**	**19**	**93**
30	49	39	24	19	3.4	3.3	94*	107*	34*	56*	3*	6*	84
10	20	15	21	7	3.8	4.8	100	106	60	66	20	25	98
10*	23*	16.4*	24*	7*	3.5*	4.8*	98	103	67	67	24	27	97
9	11	10	9	6	4.0	5.0	103	109	50	65	13	23	101
18	33	26	23	13	3.5	4.1	96	107	42	59	8	12	92
9	22	16	26	9	2.5	2.9	111	119	44	69	4	8	97
2	5	4	3	1	..	5.1	99	100	86	..	30	32	98
11	13	12	13	9	3.8	3.6	105	113	42	60	14	20	102
26	48	37	14	5	5.0	5.2	87	95	42	64	11	16	95
35	59	47	23	16	2.0	3.1	77	100	27	49	5	6	81
32	49	41	35	30	3.8	4.1	81	78	15	27	2	2	82
..	..	..	0	0	5.6	5.4	102	103	87	106	35	59	101

Table 3.   Indicators to chapters 8–9

COUNTRY or REGION	Life expectancy at birth, 1998 (years) male	fem.	total	Under-five mortality rate (per 1,000 live births) 1980	1998	Improved sanitation facilities % of total population with access 2000	% of rural population with access 2000	Improved water source % of total population with access 2000	% of rural population with access 2000	Maternal mortality ratio estimates per 100,000 live births 1995	Age dependency ratio dependents to working-age population 1980	1998
Afghanistan	..	..	46	..	..	12	8	13	11	820	0.8	..
Albania	69	75	72	57	31	91	85	97	95	31	0.7	0.6
Algeria	69	72	71	139	40	92	81	89	82	150	1	0.7
American Samoa	..	..	..	..	..	..	..	..	..	..	..	..
Andorra	..	..	..	..	..	100	100	100	100	..	..	..
Angola	45	48	47	261	204	12	8	38	40	1,300	0.9	1
Antigua and Barbuda	..	..	75	..	..	91	85	91	89	..	..	..
Argentina	70	77	73	38	22	92	81	..	..	85	0.6	0.6
Armenia	71	78	74	..	18			..	..	29	0.6	0.5
Aruba	..	..	..	..		100	100	..	..		..	..
Australia	76	82	79	13	6	100	100	100	100	6	0.5	0.5
Austria	75	81	78	17	6	100	100	100	100	11	0.6	0.5
Azerbaijan	68	75	71	..	21	81	70	78	58	37	0.7	0.6
Bahamas, The	..	..	74	..		100	100	97	86	..	0.7	..
Bahrain	..	..	73	..	..	..	..	..	..	..	0.6	..
Bangladesh	58	59	59	211	96	48	41	97	97	600	1	0.8
Barbados	..	..	76	..	..	100	100	100	100	..	0.7	..
Belarus	63	74	68	..	14	..	..	100	100	33	0.5	0.5
Belgium	75	81	78	15	6	..	..	..	..	8	0.5	0.5
Belize	..	..	75	..	..	50	25	92	82	..	1.1	..
Benin	52	55	53	214	140	23	6	63	55	880	1	1
Bermuda	..	..	..	..	..	..	..	..	..	..	..	..
Bhutan	..	..	61	..		70	70	62	60	..	0.8	..
Bolivia	60	64	62	170	78	70	42	83	64	550	0.9	0.8
Bosnia and Herzegovina	..	..	73	..		..	..	..	..	15	0.5	0.4
Botswana	45	47	46	94	105	66	43	95	90	480	1	0.8
Brazil	63	71	67	80	40	76	43	87	53	260	0.7	0.5
Brunei	..	..	76	..	..	..	..	..	..	..	0.7	..
Bulgaria	67	75	71	25	15	100	100	100	100	23	0.5	0.5
Burkina Faso	43	45	44	..	210	29	27	42	37	1400	1	1
Burundi	41	44	42	193	196	88	90	78	77	1900	0.9	0.9
Cambodia	52	55	54	330	143	17	10	30	26	590	0.7	0.8
Cameroon	53	56	54	173	150	79	66	58	39	720	0.9	0.9
Canada	76	82	79	13	7	100	99	100	99	6	0.5	0.5
Cape Verde	..	..	68	..	..	71	32	74	89	..	1.1	0.9
Cayman Islands	..	..	..	..	..	..	..	..	..	..	..	..
Central African Republic	43	46	44	..	162	25	16	70	57	1200	0.8	0.9
Chad	47	50	48	232	172	29	13	27	26	1500	0.8	1.2
Channel Islands	..	..	79	..	..	..	..	..	..	..	..	..
Chile	72	78	75	35	12	96	97	93	58	33	0.6	0.6
China	68	72	70	65	35	40	27	75	66	60	0.7	0.5
Hong Kong, China	76	82	79	..	..	..	..	..	..	..	0.5	0.4
Macao, China	..	..	78	..	..	..	..	..	..	..	..	..
Colombia	67	73	70	58	28	86	56	91	70	120	0.8	0.6
Comoros	..	..	60	..	..	98	98	96	95	..	1	..

Tuberculosis		HIV		Smoking prevalence (% of adults)		Agricul-ture	Indus-try	Ser-vices	Fixed line and mobile phone sub-scribers	Personal compu-ters	Inter-net users	Research and devel-opment expendi-ture	Scientists and engi-neers in R&D
per 100,000 people 1997	thousand of cases 1997	% of adults 1997	People infected (all ages) 1997	male 1985-98	female 1985-98	% of GDP 1999	% of GDP 1999	% of GDP 1999	per 1,000 people 2000	per 1,000 people 2000	thou-sands 2001	% of GDP 1989-2000	per million people 1990-2000
..	..	..	..	..	..	..	..	..	1	..	..	..	..
28	2	0.01	<100	50	8	54	25	21	59	8	10	..	..
44	14	0.07	..	..	..	13	54	33	61	7	60	..	..
..	..	..	..	..	..	..	..	..	..	..	..	..	..
..	..	..	..	..	..	..	..	..	740	..	..	..	..
238	56	2.1	110,000	..	..	7	70	23	7	1	60	..	..
..	..	..	..	..	..	..	..	..	786	..	..	..	..
56	30	0.69	120,000	40	23	6	32	61	389	71	3,300	0.44	713
44	2	0.0	<100	..	..	33	32	35	145	7	50	0.20	1313
..	..	..	..	..	..	..	..	..	518	..	..	..	..
8	2	0.14	11,000	29	21	..	..	..	987	470	7,200	1.51	3353
19	2	0.18	75,000	42	27	..	..	..	1245	278	2,600	1.85	2313
58	7	0.01	<100	..	..	19	43	38	156		25	0.24	2799
..	..	..	..	..	..	..	..	..	478	..	..	..	..
..	..	..	..	..	..	..	..	..	594	150	..	..	..
246	620	0.03	21,000	60	15	21	27	52	6	2	250	..	51
..	..	..	..	..	..	..	..	..	569	82	..	..	..
65	10	0.17	9,000	..	..	13	46	40	280		422	..	1893
16	2	0.14	7,500	31	19	1	28	71	1065	224	3,200	1.96	2953
..	..	..	..	..	..	..	..	..	219	125	..	..	..
220	21	2.06	54,000	..	..	38	14	48	17	2	25	..	174
		..	..	..	..	..	..	..	..	465	..	..	..
		..	..	..	..	..	..	..	22	8	..	..	..
253	27	0.07	2,600	50	21	16	31	54	133	17	150	0.29	98
81	5	0.04	..	..	..	..	..	..	231		45	0.29	..
503	9	25.1	190,000	..	..	4	45	51	204	37	50	..	..
78	194	0.63	580,000	40	25	9	29	62	319	50	8,000	0.77	323
		..	..	..	..	..	..	..	529	69	..	..	..
43	6	0.01	..	49	17	18	27	55	444	44	605	0.57	1316
155	19	7.17	370,000	..	..	32	27	41	7	1	19	0.19	16
252	16	8.3	260,000	..	..	52	17	30	5	1	6	..	21
539	101	2.4	130,000	70	10	51	15	35	12	1	10	..	..
133	35	4.89	320,000	..	..	44	20	36	16	3	45	..	..
7	2	0.33	44,000	31	29	..	..	..	944	419	13,500	1.84	2985
		..	..	..	..	..	..	..	171	57	..	..	..
		..	..	..	..	..	..	..	1072		..	..	..
237	9	10.77	180,000	..	..	55	20	25	4	2	2	..	47
205	22	2.72	87,000	..	..	38	14	48	2	1	4	..	..
		..	..	..	..	..	..	..			..	..	..
29	5	0.2	16,000	38	25	8	33	59	441	93	3,102	0.54	370
113	2721	0.06	400,000	..	..	17	50	33	178	16	33,700	1.00	545
95	6	0.08	3,100	29	3	0	15	85	1406	354	2,601	0.44	93
		..	..	..	..	..	..	..	722	159	..	..	41
55	31	0.36	72,000	35	19	14	24	61	223	35	1,154	0.25	101
		..	..	..	..	..	..	..	10	4	..	..	..

Table 3.   Indicators to chapters 8–9 (continued)

COUNTRY or REGION	Life expectancy at birth, 1998			Under-five mortality rate per 1,000 live births		Improved sanitation facilities		Improved water source		Maternal mortality ratio estimates per 100,000 live births	Age dependency ratio dependents to working-age population	
	years					% of total population with access	% of rural population with access	% of total population with access	% of rural population with access			
	male	fem.	total	1980	1998	2000	2000	2000	2000	1995	1980	1998
Congo, Dem. Rep.	49	52	51	210	141	21	6	45	26	940	1	1
Congo, Rep.	46	51	48	125	143			51	17	1100	0.9	1
Costa Rica	74	79	77	29	15	93	97	95	92	35	0.7	0.6
Cote d'Ivoire	46	47	46	170	143	52	35	81	72	1200	1	0.9
Croatia	69	77	73	23	10					18	0.5	0.5
Cuba	..	..	76	22	9	98	95	91	77	24	0.7	0.4
Cyprus	..	..	78	..	..	100	100	100	100	..	0.5	..
Czech Republic	71	78	75	19	6	..	..	..	..	14	0.6	0.4
Denmark	73	78	76	10	..	..	..	100	100	15	0.5	0.5
Djibouti	..	..	50	..	..	91	50	100	100	..	0.9	..
Dominica	..	..	76	..	..	83	75	97	90	..	..	..
Dominican Republic	69	73	71	92	47	67	60	86	78	110	0.8	0.6
Ecuador	68	73	70	101	37	86	74	85	75	210	0.9	0.6
Egypt, Arab Rep.	65	68	67	175	59	98	96	97	96	170	0.8	0.7
El Salvador	67	72	69	120	36	82	76	77	64	180	0.9	0.7
Equatorial Guinea	..	..	50	..	..	53	46	44	42	..	0.8	..
Eritrea	49	52	51	..	..	13	1	46	42	1100	..	0.9
Estonia	64	75	70	25	12	..	..	..	..	80	0.5	0.5
Ethiopia	42	44	43	213	173	12	7	24	12	1800	0.9	1
Faeroe Islands	..	..	..	..	..	..	..	..	..	..	..	..
Fiji	..	..	73	..	..	43	12	47	51	..	0.7	..
Finland	74	81	77	9	5	100	100	100	100	6	0.5	0.5
France	75	82	78	13	5	..	..	..	..	20	0.6	0.5
French Polynesia	..	..	72	..	..	..	..	..	..	..	..	..
Gabon	..	..	53	..	..	53	43	86	47	620	0.7	0.8
Gambia, The	..	..	53	..	..	37	35	62	53	1100	0.8	0.8
Georgia	69	77	73	..	20	100	99	79	61	22	0.5	0.5
Germany	74	80	77	16	6	..	..	..	..	12	0.5	0.5
Ghana	58	65	60	157	96	72	70	73	62	590	0.9	0.9
Greece	75	81	78	23	8	..	..	..	..	2	0.6	0.5
Greenland	..	..	68	..	..	..	..	..	..	..	..	..
Grenada	..	..	72	..	..	97	97	95	93	..	..	..
Guam	..	..	77	..	..	..	..	..	..	..	0.6	..
Guatemala	61	67	64	..	52	81	79	92	88	270	1	0.9
Guinea	46	47	47	299	184	58	41	48	36	1200	0.9	0.9
Guinea-Bissau	..	..	44	..	205	56	44	56	49	910	0.8	0.9
Guyana	..	..	64	..	..	87	81	94	91	..	0.8	..
Haiti	51	56	54	200	116	28	16	46	45	1100	0.9	0.8
Honduras	67	72	69	103	46	75	55	88	81	220	1	0.8
Hungary	66	75	71	26	12	99	98	99	98	23	0.5	0.5
Iceland	..	..	79	..	..	..	..	..	..	..	0.6	..
India	62	64	63	177	83	28	15	84	79	440	0.7	0.6
Indonesia	64	67	65	125	52	55	46	78	69	470	0.8	0.6
Iran, Islamic Rep.	70	72	71	126	33	83	79	92	83	130	0.9	0.7
Iraq	..	..	59	93	125	79	31	85	48	370	0.9	0.8

Tuberculosis		HIV		Smoking prevalence (% of adults)		Agriculture	Industry	Services	Fixed line and mobile phone subscribers	Personal computers	Internet users	Research and development expenditure	Scientists and engineers in R&D
per 100,000 people 1997	thousand of cases 1997	% of adults 1997	People infected (all ages) 1997	male 1985-98	female 1985-98	% of GDP 1999	% of GDP 1999	% of GDP 1999	per 1,000 people 2000	per 1,000 people 2000	thou-sands 2001	% of GDP 1989-2000	per million people 1990-2000
263	188	4.35	950,000	..	..	58	17	25	0		6	..	..
277	11	7.78	100,000	..	..	10	48	42	31	4	1		33
18	1	0.6	10,000	35	20	14	22	64	274	149	384	0.20	533
290	48	10.06	700,000	..	..	24	24	52	50	6	70	..	..
64	5	0.01	..	..	..	9	32	59	616	112	250	0.98	1187
18	2	0.02	1,400	49	25	..	..	..	44	12	120	0.49	480
				..	..				970	221		0.26	400
20	2	0.04	2,000	43	31	4	39	57	800	122	1,400	1.35	1348
11	1	0.12	3,100	37	37	..	..	..	1346	507	2,900	2.09	3474
									16	10		..	..
				..	..	..	..	..	310	71		..	..
114	14	1.89	83,000	66	14	11	35	54	187		186	..	..
165	32	0.28	18,000	..	..	12	33	55	135	22	328	0.09	83
36	35	0.03	..	..	..	17	33	50	108	13	600	0.19	493
74	7	0.58	18,000	38	12	10	28	61	218	19	50	..	47
				..	..	..	..	..	25	4		..	..
227	15	3.17	..	..	..	16	27	57	8	2	15	..	..
52	1	0.01	<100	52	24	6	27	66	750	153	430	0.76	2128
251	213	9.31	2,600,000	..	..	49	7	44	4	1	25	..	..
				..	..	..	..	..	932	..		..	..
				..	..	..	..	..	175	44		..	..
13	1	0.02	500	27	19	..	..	..	1271	396	2,235	3.37	5059
19	11	0.37	110,000	40	27	2	26	72	1070	304	15,653	2.15	2718
				..	..	..	..	..	401	322		..	..
174	4	4.25	23,000	..	..	..	..	..	130	10	17	..	..
211	4	2.24	13,000	..	..	..	..	..	30	12	18	..	..
67	5	0.01	<100	..	..	22	13	65	140	22	25	0.33	2421
15	12	0.08	35,000	37	22	1	..	36	1196	336	30,800	2.49	3161
214	67	2.38	210,000	..	..	36	25	39	18	3	41	..	..
29	3	0.14	7,500	46	28	..	..	..	1097	71	1,400	0.67	1400
				..	..	..	..	..	753	..		..	..
				..	..	..	..	..	378	127		..	..
				..	..	..	..	..	656				
85	13	0.52	27,000	38	18	23	19	58	135	11	200	..	..
171	22	2.09	74,000	..	..	23	36	41	9	4	15	..	..
181	4	2.25	12,000	..	..	..	..	..	9		4	..	..
				..	..	..	..	..	126	26		..	..
385	36	5.17	190,000	..	..	30	20	50	16		30	..	..
96	9	1.46	43,000	36	11	18	30	52	72	11	40	..	73
47	7	0.04	2,000	40	27	6	34	60	687	87	1,480	0.82	1445
				..	..	..	..	..	1448	391		2.73	6639
187	4854	0.82	4,100,000	70	..	28	25	46	36	5	7,000	1.23	157
285	1606	0.05	52,000	..	..	20	45	35	50	10	4,000	..	..
55	62	0.01	..	..	..	..	..	..	164	63	1,005	..	590
160	56	0.01	..	40	5	..	..	..	29	..	..	..	..

BEYOND ECONOMIC GROWTH

Table 3.   Indicators to chapters 8–9 (continued)

| COUNTRY or REGION | Life expectancy at birth, 1998 years | | | Under-five mortality rate per 1,000 live births | | Improved sanitation facilities | | Improved water source | | Maternal mortality ratio estimates per 100,000 live births | Age dependency ratio dependents to working-age population | |
	male	fem.	total	1980	1998	% of total population with access 2000	% of rural population with access 2000	% of total population with access 2000	% of rural population with access 2000	1995	1980	1998
Ireland	73	79	76	14	7	..	..	..	..	9	0.7	0.5
Isle of Man	..	..	..	..	..	..	..	..	..	..	..	..
Israel	76	80	78	19	8	..	..	..	..	8	0.7	0.6
Italy	75	82	78	17	6	..	..	..	..	11	0.5	0.5
Jamaica	73	77	75	39	24	99	99	92	85	120	0.9	0.6
Japan	77	84	81	11	5	..	..	..	..	12	0.5	0.5
Jordan	69	73	71	..	31	99	98	96	84	41	1.1	0.8
Kazakstan	59	70	65	..	29	99	98	91	82	80	0.6	0.5
Kenya	50	52	51	115	124	87	82	57	42	1300	1.1	0.9
Kiribati	..	..	61	..	..	48	44	48	25	..	..	..
Korea, Dem. Rep.	..	..	63	..	68	99	100	100	100	35	0.8	0.5
Korea, Rep.	69	76	73	27	11	63	4	92	71	20	0.6	0.4
Kuwait	74	80	77	35	13	..	..	77	66	25	0.7	0.6
Kyrgyz Republic	63	71	67	..	41	100	100	37	29	80	0.8	0.7
Lao PDR	52	55	54	200	..	30	19	..	..	650	0.8	0.9
Latvia	64	76	70	26	19	..	..	100	100	70	0.5	0.5
Lebanon	68	72	70	..	30	99	87	78	74	130	0.8	0.6
Lesotho	54	57	55	168	144	49	40	..	..	530	0.9	0.8
Liberia	..	..	47	235	..	..	..	72	68	..	0.9	..
Libya	..	..	70	..	27	97	96	..	..	120	1	0.7
Liechtenstein	..	..	..	..	..	..	..	..	..	..	..	..
Lithuania	67	77	72	24	12	..	..	..	..	27	0.5	0.5
Luxembourg	..	..	77	..	..	..	..	..	..	..	0.5	..
Macedonia, FYR	70	75	73	69	18	..	..	..	..	17	0.6	0.5
Madagascar	56	59	58	216	146	42	30	47	31	580	0.9	0.9
Malawi	42	42	42	265	229	76	70	57	44	580	1	1
Malaysia	70	75	72	42	12		98		94	39	0.8	0.6
Maldives	..	..	67	..	..	56	41	100	100	..	0.9	..
Mali	49	52	50	..	218	69	58	65	61	630	1	1
Malta	..	..	77	..	..	100	100	100	100	..	0.5	..
Marshall Islands	..	..	..	..	..	..	..	..	..	..	..	..
Martinique	..	..	..	..	..	..	..	..	..	..	..	..
Mauritania	52	55	54	175	140	33	19	37	40	870	0.9	0.9
Mauritius	..	..	71	..	22	99	99	100	100	45	0.6	0.5
Mayotte	..	..	..	..	..	..	..	..	..	..	..	..
Mexico	69	75	72	74	35	74	34	88	69	65	1	0.6
Micronesia, Fed. Sts.	..	..	67	..	..	..	..	..	..	..	0.9	..
Moldova	63	70	67	..	22	99	98	92	88	65	0.5	0.5
Monaco	..	..	..	..	..	100	100	100	100	..	..	..
Mongolia	65	68	66	..	60	30	2	60	30	65	0.9	0.7
Morocco	65	69	67	125	61	68	44	80	56	390	0.9	0.6
Mozambique	44	47	45	..	213	43	26	57	41	980	0.9	0.9
Myanmar	58	62	60	134	118	64	57	72	66	170	0.8	0.5
Namibia	54	55	54	114	112	41	17	77	67	370	0.9	0.8
Nepal	58	58	58	180	107	28	22	88	87	830	0.8	0.8

174

Tuberculosis per 100,000 people 1997	Tuberculosis thousand of cases 1997	HIV % of adults 1997	HIV People infected (all ages) 1997	Smoking prevalence male (% of adults) 1985-98	Smoking prevalence female (% of adults) 1985-98	Agriculture % of GDP 1999	Industry % of GDP 1999	Services % of GDP 1999	Fixed line and mobile phone subscribers per 1,000 people 2000	Personal computers per 1,000 people 2000	Internet users thousands 2001	Research and development expenditure % of GDP 1989-2000	Scientists and engineers in R&D per million people 1990-2000
21	1	0.09	1,700	29	28	..	..	..	1134	359	895	1.21	2184
				..	..							..	..
7	0	0.07	..	45	30	..	..	..	1176	254	1,800	3.62	1563
10	5	0.31	90,000	38	26	3	31	67	1211	180	16,400	1.04	1128
8	0	0.99	14,000	43	13	8	33	59	340	46	100	..	..
29	48	0.01	6,800	59	15	2	37	61	1112	315	55,930	2.98	5095
11	1	0.02	..	..	..	2	27	71	199	30	212	..	1948
104	27	0.03	2,500	..	..	10	30	60	125		100	0.29	716
297	106	11.64	1,600,000	..	..	27	17	56	15	5	500	..	..
				..	..	..	..	..	44	9			..
178	91	0.01	..	..	..	..	..	..	22		0		..
142	90	0.01	3,100	68	..	5	44	51	1060	405	24,380	2.68	2319
81	3	0.12	..	52	12	..	..	..	431	114	200	0.20	212
99	7	0.01	<100	..	..	44	22	35	79	5	151	0.19	581
167	17	0.04	1,100	62	8	53	22	25	10	3	10	..	..
82	2	0.01	<100	67	12	5	33	63	469	140	170	0.40	1078
26	1	0.09	..	..	..	12	27	61	401	53	300	..	..
407	13	8.35	85,000	38	1	18	38	44	20		5	..	..
				..	..	..	..	..	3		1		..
19	2	0.05	..	..	..	..	..	..	115	..	20	..	361
				..	..	..	..	..	915			..	..
80	5	0.01	<100	52	10	10	33	57	463	65	250	0.63	2027
				..	..	..	..	..	1446	456		..	..
47	2	0.01	<100	..	..	11	28	60	308		70	..	387
205	58	0.12	8,600	..	..	30	14	56	8	2	35	0.13	12
404	33	14.92	710,000	..	..	38	18	45	9	1	20	..	..
112	30	0.62	68,000	..	..	14	44	43	419	95	6,500	0.40	160
				..	..	..			119	37		..	..
292	58	1.67	89,000	..	..	47	17	37	5	1	30	..	..
				..	..	..	..	..	817	205		..	..
				..	..	..	..	..	84	38		..	..
				..	..	..	..	..				..	..
226	13	0.52	6,100	..	..	25	29	46	13	10	7	..	..
66	1	0.08	..	47	4	..	..	..	386	101	158	0.28	360
				..	..	..	..	..	72			..	..
41	60	0.35	180,000	38	14	5	27	68	267	58	3,636	0.43	225
				..	..	..	..	..	84			..	..
73	5	0.11	2,500	..	..	21	24	55	165	14	60	0.62	334
				..	..	..	..	..	1600			..	..
205	9	0.01	<100	40	7	33	28	40	115	13	40	..	531
122	28	0.03	..	40	9	17	32	51	131	12	400	..	..
255	66	14.17	1,200,000	..	..	32	24	44	8	4	15	..	..
171	163	1.79	440,000	58	2	53	9	38	6	2	10	..	..
527	12	19.94	150,000	..	..	13	33	55	108	42	45	..	..
211	99	0.24	26,000	69	13	41	22	37	12	3	60	..	..

Table 3.   Indicators to chapters 8–9 (continued)

COUNTRY or REGION	Life expectancy at birth, 1998 years			Under-five mortality rate per 1,000 live births		Improved sanitation facilities		Improved water source		Maternal mortality ratio estimates per 100,000 live births	Age dependency ratio dependents to working-age population	
	male	fem.	total	1980	1998	% of total population with access 2000	% of rural population with access 2000	% of total population with access 2000	% of rural population with access 2000	1995	1980	1998
Netherlands	75	81	78	11	7	100	100	100	100	10	0.5	0.5
Netherlands Antilles	..	..	76	..	..	..	..	..	..	..	0.6	..
New Caledonia	..	..	73	..	..	..	..	..	..	..	0.7	..
New Zealand	75	80	77	16	7	..	..	..	..	15	0.6	0.5
Nicaragua	66	71	68	143	42	85	72	77	59	250	1	0.9
Niger	44	48	46	317	250	20	5	59	56	920	1	1
Nigeria	52	55	53	196	119	54	45	62	49	1100	1	0.9
Northern Mariana Islands	..	..	..	..	..	..	..	..	..	..	..	..
Norway	76	81	78	11	6	..	..	100	100	9	0.6	0.5
Oman	..	..	73	..	25	92	61	39	30	120	0.9	0.9
Pakistan	61	63	62	161	120	62	43	90	87	200	0.9	0.8
Palau	..	..	71	..	..	100	100	79	20	..	..	..
Panama	72	76	74	36	25	92	83	90	79	100	0.8	0.6
Papua New Guinea	57	59	58	..	76	82	80	42	32	390	0.8	0.7
Paraguay	68	72	70	61	27	94	93	78	59	170	0.9	0.8
Peru	66	71	69	126	47	71	49	80	62	240	0.8	0.6
Philippines	67	71	69	81	40	83	69	86	79	240	0.8	0.7
Poland	69	77	73	..	11	..	..	..	..	12	0.5	0.5
Portugal	72	79	75	31	8	..	..	..	..	12	0.6	0.5
Puerto Rico	..	..	76	22	..	..	..	..	..	30	0.7	0.5
Qatar	..	..	74	..	..	..	..	..	..	..	0.5	..
Romania	66	73	69	36	25	53	10	58	16	60	0.6	0.5
Russian Federation	61	73	67	..	20	..	..	99	96	75	0.5	0.5
Rwanda	40	42	41	..	205	8	8	41	40	2300	1	0.9
Samoa	..	..	69	..	..	99	100	99	100	..	1	..
Sao Tome and Principe	..	..	64	..	..	..	..	..	..	..	..	..
Saudi Arabia	70	74	72	85	26	100	100	95	64	23	0.9	0.8
Senegal	51	54	52	..	121	70	48	78	65	1200	0.9	0.9
Seychelles	..	..	72	..	..	..	..	..	..	..	..	..
Sierra Leone	36	39	37	336	283	66	53	57	46	2100	0.9	0.9
Singapore	75	79	77	13	6	100	..	100	..	9	0.5	0.4
Slovak Republic	69	77	73	23	10	100	100	100	100	14	0.6	0.5
Slovenia	71	79	75	18	7	..	..	100	100	17	0.5	0.4
Solomon Islands	..	..	71	..	..	34	18	71	65	..	1	..
Somalia	..	..	48	..	..	..	..	..	..	..	1	..
South Africa	61	66	63	91	83	87	80	86	73	340	0.7	0.6
Spain	75	82	78	16	7					8	0.6	0.5
Sri Lanka	71	76	73	48	18	94	93	77	70	60	0.7	0.5
St. Kitts and Nevis	..	..	70	..	..	96	..	98	..	..	..	..
St. Lucia	..	..	72	..	..	89	..	98	..	..	..	..
St. Vincent and the Grenadines	..	..	73	..	..	96	93	..	..	..	..	..
Sudan	..	..	55	132	105	62	48	75	69	1500	0.9	0.7
Suriname	..	..	70	..	..	93	75	82	50	..	0.8	..
Swaziland	..	..	56	..	5	..	..	..	..	..	1	..
Sweden	77	82	79	9	5	100	100	100	100	8	0.6	0.6

Tuberculosis		HIV		Smoking prevalence (% of adults)		Agriculture	Industry	Services	Fixed line and mobile phone subscribers	Personal computers	Internet users	Research and development expenditure	Scientists and engineers in R&D
per 100,000 people 1997	thousand of cases 1997	% of adults 1997	People infected (all ages) 1997	male 1985-98	female 1985-98	% of GDP 1999	% of GDP 1999	% of GDP 1999	per 1,000 people 2000	per 1,000 people 2000	thou-sands 2001	% of GDP 1989-2000	per million people 1990-2000
10	1	0.17	14,000	36	29	..	..	..	1291	394	7,900	2.02	2572
				..	..	..	..	..	470			..	..
5	0	0.07	1,300	24	22	..	..	..	893	366	1,092	1.11	2197
95	5	0.19	4,100	..	..	26	21	53	50	24	50	0.15	73
148	32	1.45	65,000	..	..	40	17	43	2	0	12	..	..
214	442	4.12	2,300,000	24	7	41	62	-3	5	7	115	..	..
				..	..	..	..	..	452			..	..
6	0	0.06	1,300	36	36	2	32	66	1481	489	2,700	1.70	4112
13	0	0.11	..	..	..	..	..	..	152	32	120	..	4
181	583	0.09	64,000	27	4	26	25	49	24	4	500	..	69
				..	..								
57	2	0.61	9,000	..	..	8	18	74	296	37	90	0.35	124
250	30	0.19	4,500	46	28	30	46	24	14	55	50	..	..
73	5	0.13	3,200	24	6	26	22	52	201	13	60	..	..
265	70	0.56	72,000	41	13	8	39	54	117	41	3,000	0.08	229
310	481	0.06	24,000	..	..	17	31	52	124	19	2,000	..	156
44	26	0.06	12,000	51	29	4	33	63	458	69	3,800	0.70	1428
55	4	0.69	35,000	38	15	..	..	..	1095	105	2,500	0.71	1576
10	0	..	..	..	..	..	..	..	593		600		
				..	..	..	..	..	470	150		..	..
121	42	0.01	5,000	68	32	16	40	44	285	32	1,000	0.37	913
106	241	0.05	40,000	67	30	7	34	58	240	63	4,300	1.00	3481
276	17	12.75	370,000	..	..	46	20	34	7		20	..	..
				..	..	..	..	..	62	6		..	..
				..	..	..	..	..	31			..	..
46	14	0.01	..	53	..	7	48	45	201	60	300	..	..
223	33	1.77	75,000	..	..	18	25	57	48	17	100	0.01	2
				..	..	..	..	..	555	136		..	..
315	23	3.17	68,000	..	..	44	24	32	6		7	..	..
48	2	0.15	3,100	32	3	0	36	64	1168	483	1,500	1.89	4140
35	2	0.01	<100	43	26	4	32	64	520	137	674	0.69	1843
30	1	0.01	<100	35	23	4	39	57	1006	275	600	1.48	2180
				..	..	..	..	..	21	38		..	..
				..	..	..	..	..			1	..	..
394	266	12.91	2,900,000	52	17	4	32	64	304	66	3,068	..	992
61	23	0.57	120,000	48	25	4	28	69	1031	145	7,500	0.94	1921
48	14	0.07	6,900	55	1	21	28	51	65	7	150	0.18	191
				..	..	..	..	..	512	155		..	..
				..	..	..	..	..	331	142		..	..
				..	..	..	..	..	240	106		..	..
180	112	0.99	..	..	..	..	..	..	13	3	56	..	..
				..	..	..	..	..	268	..		..	..
				..	..	..	..	..	65	12	14	..	..
5	0	0.07	3,000	22	24	..	..	..	1475	507	4,600	3.80	4511

Table 3. Indicators to chapters 8–9 (continued)

COUNTRY or REGION	Life expectancy at birth, 1998 (years)			Under-five mortality rate (per 1,000 live births)		Improved sanitation facilities		Improved water source		Maternal mortality ratio (estimates per 100,000 live births)	Age dependency ratio (dependents to working-age population)	
	male	fem.	total	1980	1998	% of total population with access 2000	% of rural population with access 2000	% of total population with access 2000	% of rural population with access 2000	1995	1980	1998
Switzerland	76	82	79	11	5	100	100	100	100	8	0.5	0.5
Syrian Arab Republic	67	72	69	73	32	90	81	80	64	200	1.1	0.8
Tajikistan	66	71	69	..	33	90	88	60	47	120	0.9	0.8
Tanzania	46	48	47	176	136	90	86	68	57	1100	1	0.9
Thailand	70	75	72	58	33	96	96	84	81	44	0.8	0.5
Togo	47	50	49	188	144	34	17	54	38	980	0.9	1
Tonga	..	..	71	..	..	..	..	100	100	..	..	..
Trinidad and Tobago	..	.	73	39	18	99	..	90	..	65	0.7	0.5
Tunisia	70	74	72	100	32	84	62	80	58	70	0.8	0.6
Turkey	67	72	69	133	42	90	70	82	86	55	0.8	0.5
Turkmenistan	63	70	66	..	44	..	..	..	..	65	0.8	0.7
Uganda	42	41	42	180	170	79	77	52	47	1100	1	1
Ukraine	62	73	67	..	17	99	98	98	94	45	0.5	0.5
United Arab Emirates	..	..	75	..	10	..	..	..	..	30	0.4	0.4
United Kingdom	75	80	77	14	7	100	100	100	100	10	0.6	0.5
United States	74	80	77	15	..	100	100	100	100	12	0.5	0.5
Uruguay	70	78	74	42	19	94	85	98	93	50	0.6	0.6
Uzbekistan	66	73	69	..	29	89	85	85	79	60	0.9	0.8
Vanuatu	..	..	65	..	..	100	100	88	94	..	0.9	..
Venezuela	70	76	73	42	25	68	48	83	70	43	0.8	0.6
Vietnam	66	71	68	105	42	47	38	77	72	95	0.9	0.7
Virgin Islands (U.S.)	..	..	77	..	..	..	..	..	..	..	..	..
West Bank and Gaza	..	..	71	..	26	..	..	..	..	..	..	1
Yemen, Rep.	55	56	56	198	96	38	21	69	68	850	1.1	1.1
Yugoslavia, FR (Serbia/ Montenegro)	..	..	72	..	16	100	99	98	97	15	0.5	0.5
Zambia	43	43	43	149	192	78	64	64	48	870	1.1	0.9
Zimbabwe	50	52	51	108	125	62	57	83	73	610	1	0.8
World	**65**	**69**	**67**	**123**	**75**	**56**	**38**	**81**	**71**	**..**	**0.7**	**0.6**
Low Income	**59**	**61**	**63***	**177**	**107**	**43**	**31**	**76**	**70**	**..**	**0.8***	**0.6***
Middle income	**67**	**72**	**69**	**79**	**38**	**61**	**43**	**82**	**70**	**..**	**0.7**	**0.6**
Lower middle income	67*	72*	68	83*	39*	59	42	81	70	..	0.7	0.6
Upper middle income	67	74	71	66	35	79	64	88	77	..	0.7	0.6
Low & middle Income	63	67	65	135	79	52	36	79	70	..	0.8	0.6
East Asia & Pacific	67	71	69	82	43	47	36	76	67	..	0.7	0.5
Europe & Central Asia	65	74	69	..	26	..	..	91	83	..	0.6	0.5
Latin America & Caribbean	67	73	70	78	38	77	52	86	65	..	0.8	0.6
Middle East & N. Africa	66	69	68	136	55	85	72	88	78	..	0.9	0.7
South Asia	62	63	62	180	89	34	21	84	80	..	0.8	0.7
Sub-Saharan Africa	49	52	50	188	151	54	46	58	46	..	0.9	0.9
High Income	**75**	**81**	**78**	**15**	**6**	**..**	**..**	**..**	**..**	**..**	**0.5**	**0.5**

*indicates income-group aggregate that includes data on China.

Note: Revisions to estimates of China's GNP per Capita, made by analysts in 2000–01, caused that economy to be reclassified from low to lower middle income. As a result, for different indicators in these data tables China figures as part of one or the other income group, which considerably affects these group aggregates.

Tuberculosis per 100,000 people 1997	Tuberculosis thousand of cases 1997	HIV % of adults 1997	HIV People infected (all ages) 1997	Smoking prevalence (% of adults) male 1985-98	Smoking prevalence (% of adults) female 1985-98	Agriculture % of GDP 1999	Industry % of GDP 1999	Services % of GDP 1999	Fixed line and mobile phone subscribers per 1,000 people 2000	Personal computers per 1,000 people 2000	Internet users thousands 2001	Research and development expenditure % of GDP 1989-2000	Scientists and engineers in R&D per million people 1990-2000
11	1	0.32	12,000	36	26	..	..	..	1370	652	2,223	2.64	3592
75	17	0.01	..	..	..	..	..	..	105	15	60	0.18	29
87	9	0.01	<100	..	..	6	30	65	36		3	..	660
307	124	9.42	1,400,000	..	..	48	14	38	11	3	300	..	..
142	180	2.23	780,000	49	4	13	40	49	143	28	3,536	0.10	74
353	19	8.52	170,000	65	14	43	21	36	20	22	150	..	102
				..	..				100			..	..
11	0	0.94	6,800	..	..	..	..	..	370	62	120	0.14	145
40	6	0.04	..	..	..	13	28	59	112	23	400	0.45	336
41	42	0.01	..	63	24	18	26	56	529	38	2,500	0.64	306
74	5	0.01	<100	27	1	25	42	34	83		8	..	..
312	94	9.51	930,000	..	..	44	18	38	11	3	60	0.75	24
61	49	0.43	110,000	57	22	14	34	51	223	18	600	0.95	2118
21	1	0.18	..	..	..	..	..	..	833	136	976	..	..
18	11	0.09	25,000	28	26	..	..	..	1316	338	24,000	1.86	2666
7	15	0.76	820,000	28	23	2	26	72	1054	572	142,823	2.70	4099
31	1	0.33	5,200	41	27	9	29	62	402	105	400	0.26	219
81	29	0.01	<100	..	..	31	27	42	69		150	..	1754
				..	..	..	..	..	37	13		..	..
42	11	0.69	..	29	12	5	24	71	330	46	1,265	0.34	194
189	221	0.22	88,000	73	4	26	33	42	42	8	1,010	..	274
				..	..	..	..	..	951			..	..
26	1	..	..	..	..	..	..	..	142	..	60	..	..
111	31	0.01	..	..	..	17	49	34	21	2	17	..	..
51	8	0.01	..	..	..	..	..	..	349	23	600	..	2389
576	61	19.07	770,000	..	..	17	26	57	18	7	25	..	
543	74	25.84	1,500,000	36	15	19	24	56	49	17	100	..	..
136	**16,146**	**0.95**		..	..	**4**	**32**	**61**	**215**	**80**	**501,478**	**2.38**	**..**
180		1.22		..*	..*	27	30	43	26	5	15,932		..
241		0.71		50	21	10	36	55	192	31	96,658		778
101		0.92		..	..	15*	40*	46*	162	26	60,355	0.72	818
64		0.41		46	22	7	32	61	337	72	36,303	..	453
157		1.06		..	..	12	35	54	98	19	112,591	..	..
151		0.2		..	..	13	46	41	101	16	50,902	1.00	545
75		0.08		60	27	10	32	58	276	53	18,778	0.80	2074
81		0.59		39	20	8	29	63	216	49	26,282	..	287
67		0.03		..	..	..	..	..	107	29	3,356	..	..
193		0.66		..	..	28	25	47	30	4	7,973		158
267		7.28		..	..	18	32	50	19	10	5,300	..	..
18		0.36		37	23	2	30	64	1081	391	388,888	2.61	3281

Table 4. Indicators to chapters 10–13

COUNTRY or REGION	Urban population % of total population		Motor vehicles per 1,000 people		Passenger cars per 1,000 people		Central government expenditure % of GDP		State-owned enterprises share in GDP, %	State-owned enterprises share in Gross domestic investment, %	Proceeds from privatization $ millions	Military expenditures % of GNP		Trade in goods % of PPP GDP		Net private capital flows $ millions	
	1980	1999	1980	1998	1980	1998	1980	1998	1990-97	1990-97	1990-99	1992	1997	1989	1999	1990	1999
Afghanistan	..		..	..	..	..	..	..			..	..		..	..	..	..
Albania	34	41	..	40	..	27	..	29.8	..	..	28.5	4.7	1.4	6.7	13.9	31	37
Algeria	44	60	..	52	30	25	..	29.2	..	..	55.1	1.8	3.9	16.4	14.3	-424	-1,486
American Samoa	..	..	..	..	..	..	..	..	..	..	..	..		..	..	..	..
Andorra	..	..	..	..	..	..	..	..	..	..	..	..		..	..	..	..
Angola	21	34	..	20		18	..	..	..	..	6.2	24.2	20.5	31.1	16	235	2,373
Antigua and Barbuda	31		..	..	..	..	..	..	..	..	..	..		..	65	..	..
Argentina	83	90	155	176	..	137	18.2	15.3	1.3	3.1	44,588.00	1.9	1.2	5.1	10.9	-203	32,296
Armenia	66	70	..	2	..	0	..	..	..	..	219.2	3.5	3.5	..	13.3	0	122
Aruba	..	..	..	..	..	..	..	..	..	..	..	..		..	..	..	..
Australia	86	85	502	605	401	488	22.7	24.5	..	12	..	2.5	2.2	28.2	26.9	..	..
Austria	65	65	330	521	297	481	36.6	40.5	..	..	..	1	0.9	50.8	65.1	..	..
Azerbaijan	53	57	..	47	..	36	..	25.1	..	..	15.8	2.9	1.9	..	8.6	..	596
Bahamas, The	..	..	..	..	..	..	..	..	..	..	..	..		..	..	..	..
Bahrain	81	..	..	..	..	..	..	..	..	..	..	..		..	..	..	..
Bangladesh	14	24	..	1	..	1	7.4	..	2.5	11.9	59.6	1.3	1.4	4.1	6.8	70	198
Barbados	40	..	..	..	..	..	..	..	..	..	..	..		..	..	..	..
Belarus	57	71	..	112	..	..	..	32.2	..	..	10.8	1.9	1.7	..	18.2	..	394
Belgium	95	97	349	485	..	435	50.1	46.6	..	..	..	1.8	1.5	..	129.6	..	..
Belize	49	..	..	..	..	..	..	..	..	..	..	..		..	..	..	..
Benin	27	42	..	8	..	7	..	..	..	..	39	1.3	1.3	19.8	18.1	1	31
Bermuda	100	..	..	..	..	..	..	..	..	..	..	..		..	..	..	..
Bhutan	..	..	..	..	..	..	..	..	..	..	..	..		..	..	..	..
Bolivia	46	62	19	52	..	32	..	21.9	11.4	18	1,045.40	2.2	1.9	12.5	14.6	3	1,016
Bosnia and Herzegovina	36	..	..	26	..	23	..	..	..	..	..	..		..	..	..	0
Botswana	15	50	27	45	9	15	29.8	35.3	5.5	12.4	..	4.4	5.1	54.7	44	77	36
Brazil	66	81	85	77	75	..	20.2	..	7.4	8.2	69,607.70	1.1	1.8	6.3	8.4	562	22,793
Brunei	60	..	..	..	..	..	..	..	..	..	..	..		..	..	..	..
Bulgaria	61	69	..	252	92	220	..	48.1	..	..	3,199.00	3.3	3	59.7	22.9	-42	1,112
Burkina Faso	9	18	..	5	..	4	12.2	..	..	..	7.5	2.4	2.8	6.6	8.7	0	10
Burundi	4	9	..	..	..	..	21.5	24	..	..	4.2	2.7	6.1	7	4.5	-5	0
Cambodia	12	16	..	6		5	..	..	..	..	..	4.9	4.1	2	6.7	0	122
Cameroon	31	..	8	12	..	7	15.7	12.7	5.4	6.8	133.1	1.6	3	15.4	12.7	-125	-13
Canada	76	77	548	560	417	455	21.1	24.7	..	..	..	2	1.3	43.5	57.3	..	..
Cape Verde	24	..	..	..	..	..	..	..	..	..	..	..		..	..	..	..
Cayman Islands	..	..	..	..	..	..	..	..	..	..	..	..		..	..	..	..
Central African Republic	35	41	8	1	..	0	22	..	..	..	..	2	3.9	8.9	12	0	13
Chad	19	23	..	8	..	3	..	..	..	..	..	4	2.7	8.7	9.8	-1	14
Channel Islands	32	..	..	..	..	..	..	..	..	..	..	..		..	..	..	..
Chile	81	85	61	110	45	71	28	21.6	8.3	6.7	2,138.40	2.5	3.9	24	23.7	2,098	11,851

Foreign direct investment						Portfolio investment				Aid dependency							
$ millions		% of gross domestic investment		% of PPP GDP		Bonds $ millions		Equity $ millions		$ millions		Aid per capita $		Aid as % of GNP		Aid as % of gross domestic investment	
1990	1999	1990	1999	1989	1999	1990	1999	1990	1999	1994	1999	1994	1999	1994	1999	1994	1999
..	..	..	..	..	..	..	..	..	..	..	..	..	..	..	..	..	..
0	41	0.0	6.6	0.0	0.4	0	0	0	0	164.8	479.7	51.7	142.1	8.4	12.8	46.4	77.7
0	7	0.0	0.1	0.0	..	-16	0	0	3	419.4	88.9	15.3	3.0	1.0	0.2	3.1	0.7
..	..	..	..	..	..	..	..	..	..	..	..	..	..	..	..	..	..
-335	2,471	-27.9	71.9	1.4	..	0	0	0	0	449.6	387.5	42.3	31.4	23.1	13.1	66.7	..
..	..	..	..	..	..	..	..	..	..	..	..	..	..	..	..	..	..
1,836	23,929	9.3	44.2	0.4	5.5	-857	8,000	13	404	146.8	91.3	4.3	2.5	0.1	0.0	0.3	0.2
0	122	..	34.0	..	2.6	0	0	0	0	191.3	208.5	51.0	54.7	8.1	..	34.6	58.0
..	..	..	..	..	..	..	..	..	..	..	..	..	..	..	..	..	..
7,456	5,655	10.9	6.7	4.5	2.9	..	..	..	..	..	..	..	..	..	..	..	..
653	2,834	1.7	5.6	1.0	3.0	..	..	..	..	..	..	..	..	..	..	..	..
..	510	..	32.2	..	2.2	..	0	..	0	147.4	162.0	19.4	20.3	4.5	4.7	29.2	10.2
..	..	..	..	..	..	..	..	..	..	..	..	..	..	..	..	..	..
..	..	..	..	..	..	..	..	..	..	..	..	..	..	..	..	..	..
3	179	0.1	1.8	0.0	0.1	0	0	0	4	1,751.7	1,203.1	14.9	9.4	5.0	2.5	28.2	11.8
..	..	..	..	..	..	..	..	..	..	..	..	..	..	..	..	..	..
..	225	..	3.5	..	0.3	..	0	..	0	119.1	24.0	11.6	2.4	0.6	0.1	1.8	0.4
..	38,392	..	..	..	..	..	..	..	..	..	..	..	..	..	..	..	..
..	..	..	..	..	..	..	..	..	..	..	..	..	..	..	..	..	..
1	31	0.4	7.9	2.0	1.0	0	0	0	0	256.0	210.8	48.1	34.5	17.5	9.0	108.5	50.4
..	..	..	..	..	..	..	..	..	..	..	..	..	..	..	..	..	..
27	1,016	4.4	64.7	0.7	5.3	0	0	0	0	568.5	568.6	78.6	69.9	9.8	7.0	66.1	36.2
..	0	..	0.0	..	..	..	0	..	0	390.6	1,063.0	107.5	273.9	..	22.8	..	69.4
95	37	8.0	3.1	0.7	0.6	0	0	0	0	85.6	60.9	60.1	38.3	2.0	1.1	7.2	5.2
989	32,659	1.1	21.3	0.2	2.9	129	2,683	0	1961	252.8	183.6	1.6	1.1	0.0	0.0	0.2	0.1
..	..	..	..	..	..	..	..	..	..	..	..	..	..	..	..	..	..
4	806	0.1	34.1	0.0	2.1	65	18	0	102	158.0	264.8	18.7	32.3	1.6	2.1	17.2	11.2
0	10	0.0	0.1	0.1	..	0	0	0	0	432.6	398.1	44.4	36.2	23.5	15.5	113.4	55.4
1	0	0.6	0.3	0.0	0.0	0	0	0	0	312.1	74.2	51.8	11.1	34.2	10.5	319.3	114.0
0	126	0.0	28.1	..	0.9	0	0	0	0	326.6	278.9	31.5	23.7	13.6	9.0	73.3	..
-113	40	-5.7	3.0	0.6	..	0	0	0	0	730.3	433.8	57.0	29.5	10.0	5.0	60.6	24.3
7,581	25,129	6.4	19.6	2.4	6.0	..	..	..	..	..	..	..	..	..	..	..	..
..	..	..	..	..	..	..	..	..	..	..	..	..	..	..	..	..	..
..	..	..	..	..	..	..	..	..	..	..	..	..	..	..	..	..	..
1	13	0.5	3.3	0.2	..	0	0	0	0	165.3	117.2	51.3	33.1	19.9	11.3	165.6	77.9
0	15	0.0	9.5	0.8	..	0	0	0	0	213.0	187.8	33.0	25.1	18.5	12.4	108.5	118.7
..	..	..	..	..	..	..	..	..	..	..	..	..	..	..	..	..	..
590	9,221	7.8	62.8	2.0	10.8	-7	862	320	18	151.2	69.1	10.8	4.6	0.3	0.1	1.2	0.5

Table 4.   Indicators to chapters 10–13 (continued)

COUNTRY or REGION	Urban population % of total population		Motor vehicles per 1,000 people		Passenger cars per 1,000 people		Central government expenditure % of GDP		State-owned enterprises share in GDP, %	State-owned enterprises share in Gross domestic investment, %	Proceeds from privatization $ millions	Military expenditures % of GNP		Trade in goods % of PPP GDP		Net private capital flows $ millions	
	1980	1999	1980	1998	1980	1998	1980	1998	1990-97	1990-97	1990-99	1992	1997	1989	1999	1990	1999
China	20	32	2	8	..	3	..	9.3	..	27.6	20,593.20	2.8	2.2	7.3	8	8,107	40,632
Hong Kong, China	92	100	54	77	41	56			..	..	..	..	..	165.4	239.2	..	..
Macao, China	..	..	..	..	..	..			..	..	..	..	..	..	..	..	..
Colombia	64	73	..	40	11	21	11.5	16	..	..	5,979.50	2.4	3.7	6.7	9.3	345	3,635
Comoros	21	..	..	..	..	..	..	..	..	..	..	..	..	..	..	..	..
Congo, Dem. Rep.	29	..	..	..	..	..	12.4	10.4	..	..	..	3	5	4	2.4	-24	1
Congo, Rep.	41	62	..	20	..	14	49.4	38.4	..	..	..	5.7	4.1	88.8	104.5	-100	5
Costa Rica	43	48	..	130	20	85	25	30.1	..	11.5	50.8	1.4	0.6	19.9	40.6	23	924
Cote d'Ivoire	35	46	24	28	..	18	31.7	24	..	..	597.4	1.5	1.1	26.9	28.6	57	74
Croatia	50	57	..	..	..	..	..	45.6	..	..	1,318.30	7.7	6.3	..	36.5	..	2,392
Cuba	68	..	..	32	..	16	..	..	..	..	706	..	..	..	..	..	..
Cyprus	46	..	..	..	..	..	..	..	..	..	..	..	..	..	..	..	..
Czech Republic	75	75	..	402	..	358	..	35	..	..	5,633.10	2.7	1.9	..	41.6	876	4,837
Denmark	84	85	322	413	271	355	38.6	41.4	..	..	..	2	1.7	58.3	67.8	..	..
Djibouti	74	..	..	..	..	..	..	..	..	..	..	..	..	..	..	..	..
Dominica	..	..	..	..	..	..	..	..	..	..	..	..	..	..	..	..	..
Dominican Republic	51	64	36	45	20	27	16.9	16.7	..	..	643.4	0.9	1.1	21.4	29	130	1,404
Ecuador	47	64	..	45	28	41	14.2	..	..	13.9	169.3	3.5	4	15.5	20.1	183	944
Egypt, Arab Rep.	44	45	..	30	8	23	50.3	30.6	..	..	2,905.40	3.7	2.8	8.2	9.1	698	1,558
El Salvador	42	46	..	61	16	30	..	..	..	..	1,070.10	2.1	0.9	11.4	16.1	8	360
Equatorial Guinea	27	..	..	..	..	..	..	..	..	..	..	..	..	..	..	..	..
Eritrea	14	18	..	2	..	2	..	..	..	..	2	..	7.8	..	..	..	0
Estonia	70	69	..	372	..	312	..	32.9	..	..	778.2	0.5	1.5	..	58.5	104	569
Ethiopia	11	17	2	2	1	1	19.9	..	..	..	172	3.7	1.9	..	5.5	-45	78
Faeroe Islands	..	..	..	..	..	..	..	..	..	..	..	..	..	..	..	..	..
Fiji	38	..	..	..	..	..	..	..	..	..	..	..	..	..	..	..	..
Finland	60	67	288	448	256	392	28.1	35.5	..	..	..	2.2	1.7	54.2	61.3	..	..
France	73	75	402	530	355	442	39.5	46.6	..	..	..	3.4	3	37.6	44	..	..
French Polynesia	60	..	..	..	..	..	..	..	..	..	..	..	..	..	..	..	..
Gabon	36	..	..	29	..	17	36.5	..	..	..	..	..	..	52.8	52.2	..	209
Gambia, The	18	..	..	17	11	8	31.7	..	..	..	..	..	..	14.5	14.9	..	14
Georgia	52	60	..	87	..	80	..	8.6	..	..	..	2.4	1.4	..	6.3	21	86
Germany	83	87	399	552	297	506	..	32.9	..	..	..	2.1	1.6	51.9	52	..	..
Ghana	31	38	..	7	..	5	10.9	..	..	..	888.4	0.8	0.7	11.3	15.1	-5	-16
Greece	58	60	134	328	91	238	29.3	34	..	..	..	4.4	4.6	20.7	25.5	..	..
Greenland	..	..	..	..	..	..	..	..	..	..	..	..	..	..	..	..	..
Grenada	..	..	..	..	..	..	..	..	..	..	..	..	..	..	..	..	..
Guam	40	..	..	..	..	..	..	..	..	..	..	..	..	..	..	..	..
Guatemala	37	39	..	17	..	9	14.3	..	2	4.8	1,351.20	1.5	1.4	11.5	16.6	44	98
Guinea	19	32	..	5	..	2	..	16.9	..	..	45	1.4	1.5	13.9	14.1	-1	63

Foreign direct investment						Portfolio investment				Aid dependency							
$ millions		% of gross domestic investment		% of PPP GDP		Bonds $ millions		Equity $ millions		$ millions		Aid per capita $		Aid as % of GNP		Aid as % of gross domestic investment	
1990	1999	1990	1999	1989	1999	1990	1999	1990	1999	1994	1999	1994	1999	1994	1999	1994	1999
3,487	38,753	2.8	10.5	0.3	1.0	-48	660	0	3732	3,225.2	2,323.8	2.7	1.9	0.6	0.2	1.4	0.6
..	..	..	..	..	35.3	..	..	..	..	26.9	3.7	4.5	0.6	0.0	0.0	0.1	0.0
..	..	..	..	..	..	..	..	..	..								
500	1,109	6.7	10.1	0.4	0.8	-4	1,235	0	25	77.4	301.3	2.0	7.3	0.1	0.4	0.4	2.7
..	..	..	..	..	..	..	..	..	..	..	..	..	..	..	..	..	..
-12	1	-1.4	0.2	..	..	0	0	0	0	245.5	132.3	5.8	2.7	4.8	..	53.4	..
0	5	0.0	0.0	0.0	0.0	0	0	0	0	362.1	140.3	145.5	49.1	23.9	8.4	37.6	28.4
163	669	8.3	25.5	0.7	2.1	-42	283	0	0	73.3	-9.8	22.5	-2.7	0.7	-0.1	3.3	-0.4
48	350	6.6	19.2	0.1	1.8	-1	-46	0	8	1,593.5	447.0	118.0	29.0	23.1	4.3	165.7	24.5
..	1,408	..	29.2	..	4.8	..	539	..	0	110.3	48.2	23.7	10.8	0.9	0.2	5.2	1.0
..	..	..	..	..	..	..	..	..	..	47.1	58.1	4.3	5.2	..	..	..	..
..	..	..	..	..	..	..	..	..	..	..	..	..	..	..	..	..	..
207	5,093	2.4	33.7	..	4.0	0	175	0	500	148.3	318.1	14.3	30.9	0.4	0.6	1.2	2.1
1,132	8,482	4.2	24.8	3.2	13.3	..	..	..	..	..	..	..	..	..	..	..	..
..	..	..	..	..	..	..	..	..	..	..	..	..	..	..	..	..	..
..	..	..	..	..	..	..	..	..	..	..	..	..	..	..	..	..	..
133	1,338	7.5	30.6	0.4	2.9	0	-4	0	0	60.5	194.7	7.9	23.2	0.6	1.2	2.7	4.5
126	690	6.7	28.1	0.6	1.9	0	-19	0	0	211.6	145.6	18.9	11.7	1.4	0.8	6.7	5.9
734	1,065	5.9	5.2	1.0	0.5	-1	100	0	550	2,689.8	1,579.0	47.1	25.2	5.2	1.8	31.3	7.8
2	231	0.3	11.4	0.3	0.9	0	150	0	0	304.7	182.7	55.0	29.7	3.8	1.5	19.0	9.0
..	..	..	..	..	..	..	..	..	..	..	..	..	..	..	..	..	..
..	0	..	0.0	..	..	..	0	..	0	157.2	148.5	45.1	37.2	23.7	19.5	173.5	48.6
82	305	7.2	23.8	..	3.6	..	45	..	191	43.9	82.7	29.3	57.3	1.1	1.6	4.0	6.4
12	90	1.5	0.2	0.0	..	0	0	0	0	1,071.0	633.4	19.5	10.1	22.2	9.9	144.4	54.4
..	..	..	..	..	..	..	..	..	..	..	..	..	..	..	..	..	..
812	4,754	2.0	18.7	4.2	14.3	..	..	..	..	..	..	..	..	..	..	..	..
13,183	38,828	4.6	14.3	3.0	10.9	..	..	..	..	..	..	..	..	..	..	..	..
..	..	..	..	..	..	..	..	..	..	..	..	..	..	..	..	..	..
..	200	5.7	16.4	2.5	..	0	0	0	0	181.1	47.6	169.1	39.3	4.9	1.2	19.8	3.9
..	14	0.0	20.0	1.1	0.7	0	0	0	0	69.6	33.1	64.7	26.5	19.5	8.6	105.9	47.3
..	82	0.0	17.8	..	0.6	..	0	..	0	176.5	238.6	32.5	43.8	..	8.4	..	51.8
2,532	52,232	1.0	11.2	1.8	7.8	..	..	..	..	..	..	..	..	..	..	..	..
15	17	1.8	0.9	0.1	0.0	0	0	0	19	546.0	607.5	32.8	32.3	10.2	8.0	41.9	33.7
1,005	984	5.2	3.9	0.7	0.7	..	..	..	..	..	..	..	..	..	..	..	..
..	..	..	..	..	..	..	..	..	..	..	..	..	..	..	..	..	..
..	..	..	..	..	..	..	..	..	..	..	..	..	..	..	..	..	..
..	..	..	..	..	..	..	..	..	..	..	..	..	..	..	..	..	..
48	155	4.6	4.9	0.3	4.2	-11	-31	0	0	217.2	292.9	22.4	26.4	1.7	1.6	10.7	9.2
18	63	3.6	10.0	0.1	0.5	0	0	0	0	359.0	237.6	55.9	32.8	10.7	7.0	67.9	39.0

Table 4.   Indicators to chapters 10–13 (continued)

COUNTRY or REGION	Urban population % of total population 1980	1999	Motor vehicles per 1,000 people 1980	1998	Passenger cars per 1,000 people 1980	1998	Central government expenditure % of GDP 1980	1998	State-owned enterprises share in GDP, % 1990-97	State-owned enterprises share in Gross domestic investment, % 1990-97	Proceeds from privatization $ millions 1990-99	Military expenditures % of GNP 1992	1997	Trade in goods % of PPP GDP 1989	1999	Net private capital flows $ millions 1990	1999
Guinea-Bissau	17	..	..	10	..	6	..	..	..	..	0.5	..	..	12.8	17.9	..	3
Guyana	31	..	..	..	..	..	..	..	..	..	..	..	..	..	..	..	..
Haiti	24	35	..	7	..	4	17.4	..	..	..	16.5	1.5	..	4	10.7	8	30
Honduras	35	52	..	37	..	..	..	..	..	..	74.1	1.4	1.3	18.4	26.9	77	251
Hungary	57	64	108	268	95	229	56.2	43.4	..	..	13,998.90	2.1	1.9	18.2	46.1	-308	4,961
Iceland	88	..	..	..	..	..	..	..	..	..	..	..	..	..	..	..	..
India	23	28	2	7	..	5	12.3	14.4	13.4	32.4	8,983.40	2.5	2.8	3.2	3.6	1,873	1,813
Indonesia	22	40	8	22	..	12	22.1	17.9	..	15.7	6,134.80	1.4	2.3	12.1	12.3	3,235	-8,416
Iran, Islamic Rep.	50	61	..	36	..	26	35.7	26.7	..	..	..	3	3	12.6	8.4	-392	-1,385
Iraq	66	..	..	56	..	39	..	..	..	..	..	..	..	..	..	..	..
Ireland	55	..	236	314	216	279	45.1	35.5	..	..	..	1.4	1.2	92.1	120.1	..	..
Isle of Man	..	..	..	..	..	..	..	..	..	..	..	..	..	..	..	..	..
Israel	89	91	123	264	107	215	72.8	49	..	..	..	11.7	9.7	43.3	52.4	..	..
Italy	67	67	334	591	303	539	41.3	44.6	..	..	..	2.1	2	30.5	35	..	..
Jamaica	47	56	..	48	..	40	41.5	..	..	..	385.5	1	0.9	36.5	40.2	92	425
Japan	76	79	323	560	203	394	18.4	..	..	6.5	..	1	1	20.8	23.2	..	..
Jordan	60	74	56	66	41	48	41.3	34	..	..	63.8	8.8	9	30.9	29.4	254	112
Kazakstan	54	56	..	82	..	62	..	..	..	..	6,375.90	2.9	1.3	..	12.5	117	1,477
Kenya	16	32	8	14	7	11	25.3	29	..	..	318.3	3	2.1	14.4	15.6	122	-51
Kiribati	..	..	..	..	..	..	..	..	..	..	..	..	..	..	..	..	..
Korea, Dem. Rep.	57	..	..	..	..	..	..	..	..	..	..	..	..	..	..	..	..
Korea, Rep.	57	81	14	226	7	163	17.3	17.4	..	..	..	3.7	3.4	35.7	35.9	1,056	6,409
Kuwait	90	97	390	462	..	359	27.7	50.9	..	..	..	77	7.5	86.8	..	..	..
Kyrgyz Republic	38	34	..	32	..	32	..	..	..	..	139.5	0.7	1.6	..	8.4	..	-16
Lao PDR	13	23	..	4	..	3	..	..	..	..	32	9.8	3.4	7.3	11.2	6	79
Latvia	68	69	..	237	..	198	..	33	..	..	490.9	1.6	0.9	..	30.7	43	303
Lebanon	74	89	..	..	..	..	..	32.1	..	..	..	4	3	53.2	39	12	1,771
Lesotho	13	27	10	17	3	6	45.3	55.8	..	..	16.2	3.6	2.5	39.4	28.4	17	168
Liberia	35	..	..	..	..	..	..	..	..	..	..	..	..	..	..	..	..
Libya	70	..	..	209	..	154	..	..	..	..	..	..	..	..	..	..	..
Liechtenstein	..	..	..	..	..	..	..	..	..	..	..	..	..	..	..	..	..
Lithuania	61	68	..	293	..	265	..	30.4	..	..	1,535.60	0.7	0.8	..	..	-3	1,148
Luxembourg	79	..	..	..	..	..	..	..	..	..	..	..	..	..	..	..	..
Macedonia, FYR	54	62	..	156	..	142	..	..	..	..	679.3	2.2	2.5	..	33.1	..	51
Madagascar	18	29	..	5	..	4	..	17.3	..	..	9	1.1	1.5	6.9	6.7	7	52
Malawi	9	24	5	5	2	2	34.6	..	..	..	18.9	1.1	1	20.1	16.6	2	60
Malaysia	42	57	..	172	52	145	28.5	19.7	..	25.7	10,159.60	3.2	2.2	59.3	80.2	769	3,247
Maldives	22	..	..	..	..	..	..	..	..	..	..	..	..	..	..	..	..
Mali	19	29	..	5	..	3	19.4	..	..	..	21.9	2.3	1.7	14.9	16.1	-8	19
Malta	83	..	..	..	..	..	..	..	..	..	..	..	..	..	..	..	..

Foreign direct investment						Portfolio investment				Aid dependency							
$ millions		% of gross domestic investment		% of PPP GDP		Bonds $ millions		Equity $ millions		$ millions		Aid per capita $		Aid as % of GNP		Aid as % of gross domestic investment	
1990	1999	1990	1999	1989	1999	1990	1999	1990	1999	1994	1999	1994	1999	1994	1999	1994	1999
..	3	2.7	1.1	0.0	..	0	0	0	0	172.1	52.4	162.4	44.2	77.7	25.7	335.5	147.1
..	..	..	..	..	..	..	..	..	..	..	..	..	..	..	..	..	..
8	30	2.2	1.9	0.5	0.1	0	0	0	0	601.1	262.8	85.8	33.7	30.7	6.1	899.8	55.5
44	230	6.3	13.0		1.6	0	0	0	0	293.3	816.9	53.4	129.3	9.1	15.6	22.7	46.1
0	1,950	0.0	14.0	0.0	2.0	921	605	150	592	200.5	247.6	19.5	24.6	0.5	0.5	2.2	1.8
..	..	..	..	..	..	..	..	..	..	..	..	..	..	..	..	..	..
162	2,169	0.2	2.1	0.0	0.1	147	-1,126	105	1302	2,324.3	1,484.4	2.5	1.5	0.7	0.3	3.1	1.4
1,093	-2,745	3.1	-9.2	0.2	0.9	26	-1,458	312	1273	1,638.7	2,206.3	8.6	10.7	1.0	1.7	3.0	6.5
-362	85	-1.1	0.3	0.0	0.0	0	0	0	0	130.3	161.4	2.2	2.6	0.2	0.1	0.8	0.8
..	..	..	..	..	..	..	..	..	..	259.2	75.8	12.8	3.3	..	..	..	..
627	19,091	6.3	87.6	0.2	25.2	..	..	..	..	..	..	..	..	..	..	..	..
..	..	..	..	..	..	..	..	..	..	..	..	..	..	..	..	..	..
129	2,363	1.1	11.1	0.4	3.1	..	..	..	..	1,237.2	905.7	229.1	148.3	1.7	0.9	6.9	4.3
6,411	6,783	2.6	2.8	0.4	1.2	..	..	..	..	..	..	..	..	..	..	..	..
138	524	11.7	28.9	0.9	6.7	0	-65	0	0	109.1	-22.6	43.7	-8.7	2.7	-0.3	7.7	-1.2
1,777	12,308	0.2	1.1	2.0	1.2	..	..	..	..	..	..	..	..	..	..	..	..
38	158	3.0	9.4	0.2	0.9	0	-9	0	11	368.7	430.0	90.8	90.7	6.2	5.4	17.8	25.6
100	1,587	1.2	56.8	..	2.2	..	-200	..	0	48.3	161.0	3.0	10.8	0.2	1.1	0.9	5.8
57	14	3.4	1.0	0.3	0.0	0	0	0	5	675.3	308.0	25.7	10.5	10.0	2.9	57.5	21.4
..	..	..	..	..	..	..	..	..	..	..	..	..	..	..	..	..	..
..	..	..	..	..	..	..	..	..	..	5.8	200.7	0.3	8.6	..	..	..	..
788	9,333	0.8	8.5	0.5	2.1	168	-1,414	518	12426	-114.2	-55.2	-2.6	-1.2	0.0	0.0	-0.1	-0.1
..	72	..	2.0	4.9	..	..	..	..	..	3.4	7.2	2.3	3.8	0.0	0.0	0.1	0.2
..	36	..	15.7	..	0.3	..	0	..	0	172.0	266.6	37.9	54.8	5.5	22.7	59.7	118.2
6	79	..	14.7	0.1	1.1	0	0	0	0	215.9	293.8	48.1	57.7	14.0	21.1	..	..
29	348	1.1	21.1	..	2.4	..	240	..	0	52.6	96.4	20.6	39.7	1.0	1.6	5.0	5.8
6	250	1.2	4.2	..	..	0	-114	0	3	235.2	193.9	59.9	45.4	2.5	1.2	8.0	..
17	163	5.1	64.1	0.8	4.2	0	0	0	0	116.0	31.1	61.5	14.8	9.5	2.8	24.9	..
..	..	..	..	..	..	..	..	..	..	..	..	..	..	..	..	..	..
..	..	..	..	..	..	..	..	..	..	4.0	7.3	0.8	1.3	..	..	..	..
..	487	0.0	20.0	..	2.7	..	505	..	0	71.4	128.9	19.2	34.9	1.2	1.2	6.6	5.3
..	..	..	..	..	..	..	..	..	..	..	..	..	..	..	..	..	..
..	30	..	4.1	..	0.3	..	0	..	0	104.3	273.0	53.5	135.1	4.4	8.0	27.6	37.0
22	58	4.2	2.9	0.1	0.1	0	0	0	0	289.2	358.2	22.4	23.8	10.2	9.8	89.1	74.6
0	60	0.0	22.4	0.0	..	0	0	0	0	466.6	445.8	49.2	41.3	41.0	25.1	135.7	166.2
2,333	1,553	16.4	8.8	2.1	0.8	-1,239	747	293	522	65.9	142.6	3.3	6.3	0.1	0.2	0.2	0.8
..	..	..	..	..	..	..	..	..	..	..	..	..	..	..	..	..	..
-7	19	-1.3	3.4	0.1	0.5	0	0	0	0	440.7	354.0	46.9	33.4	25.3	14.0	91.5	65.0
..	..	..	..	..	..	..	..	..	..	..	..	..	..	..	..	..	..

Table 4. Indicators to chapters 10–13 (continued)

COUNTRY or REGION	Urban population % of total population		Motor vehicles per 1,000 people		Passenger cars per 1,000 people		Central government expenditure % of GDP		State-owned enterprises share in GDP, %	share in Gross domestic investment, %	Proceeds from privatization $ millions	Military expenditures % of GNP		Trade in goods % of PPP GDP		Net private capital flows $ millions	
	1980	1999	1980	1998	1980	1998	1980	1998	1990-97	1990-97	1990-99	1992	1997	1989	1999	1990	1999
Marshall Islands	..	..	..	..	..	..	..	..	..	..	..	..	..	..	..	..	..
Martinique	..	..	..	..	..	..	..	..	..	..	..	..	..	..	..	..	..
Mauritania	27	56	..	12	..	8	..	..	..	..	1.1	3.5	2.3	32.4	18.8	6	0
Mauritius	42	..	44	92	27	71	27.2	22.4	..	..	..	..	..	41.8	34.4	..	102
Mayotte	..	..	..	..	..	..	..	..	..	..	..	..	..	..	..	..	..
Mexico	66	74	..	144	60	97	15.7	16.3	4.9	10.3	28,593.00	0.5	1.1	14.1	35.6	8,253	26,780
Micronesia, Fed. Sts.	25	..	..	..	..	..	..	..	..	..	..	..	..	..	..	..	..
Moldova	40	46	..	65	..	46	..	..	..	..	26.6	0.5	1	..	11.9	..	12
Monaco	..	..	..	..	..	..	..	..	..	..	..	..	..	..	..	..	..
Mongolia	52	63	..	30	..	16	..	23	..	..	..	2.6	1.9	43.4	18.7	28	28
Morocco	41	55	..	48	..	38	33.1	33.3	..	..	3,102.20	4.5	4.3	13.1	18.6	341	-118
Mozambique	13	39	..	1	..	0	..	..	..	..	138.2	7.6	2.8	11.8	8.7	35	374
Myanmar	24	27	..	1	..	1	15.8	8.9	..	..	..	8.3	7.6	..	..	153	203
Namibia	23	30	..	82	..	46	..	..	..	..	..	2.2	2.7	38.7	36	..	..
Nepal	7	12	..	..	..	..	14.3	17.5	..	..	15.1	1	0.8	4.6	6.8	-8	-8
Netherlands	88	89	343	421	322	391	52.9	47.6	..	..	..	2.5	1.9	85.4	101.4	..	..
Netherlands Antilles	68	..	..	..	..	..	..	..	..	..	..	..	..	..	..	..	..
New Caledonia	57	..	..	..	..	..	..	..	..	..	..	..	..	..	..	..	..
New Zealand	83	86	492	579	420	470	38.3	33.4	..	..	..	1.6	1.3	35.8	36.7	..	..
Nicaragua	50	56	..	34	8	18	30.4	33.2	..	..	130.3	3.1	1.5	11	21.3	21	382
Niger	13	20	6	5	5	4	18.6	..	..	..	..	1.3	1.1	10.9	8.5	9	-8
Nigeria	27	43	4	26	3	9	..	..	..	..	730.2	2.6	1.4	21.3	20.5	467	860
Northern Mariana Islands	..	..	..	..	..	..	..	..	..	..	..	..	..	..	..	..	..
Norway	71	75	342	498	302	402	34.4	35.7	..	..	..	3.1	2.1	62.7	62.2	..	..
Oman	8	..	..	152	..	103	38.5	31.6	..	..	60.1	..	..	..	..	..	-413
Pakistan	28	36	2	8	2	5	17.5	21.4	..	28.2	1,992.30	7.4	5.7	8.5	8	182	53
Palau	..	..	..	..	..	..	..	..	..	..	..	..	..	..	..	..	..
Panama	50	56	..	102	..	79	30.5	27	7.3	4.6	1,427.30	1.3	1.4	15.1	26.3	127	620
Papua New Guinea	13	17	..	27	..	7	34.4	..	..	..	223.6	1.5	1.3	46.1	27.5	204	499
Paraguay	42	55	..	24	..	14	9.9	..	4.6	5.5	42	1.8	1.3	11	12.8	67	109
Peru	65	72	..	42	..	26	19.5	16.4	5.1	4.5	8,134.40	1.8	2.1	7.5	12.2	59	3,140
Philippines	38	58	..	31	6	10	13.4	19.3	2.2	9.9	3,960.00	1.9	1.5	9.5	24.5	639	4,915
Poland	58	65	86	273	67	230	..	37.7	..	..	12,171.90	2.3	2.3	11.5	22.4	71	10,452
Portugal	29	63	145	347	..	309	33.1	40.8	..	..	..	2.7	2.4	29.9	38.9	..	..
Puerto Rico	67	..	..	280	..	229	..	..	..	..	..	..	..	..	..	..	..
Qatar	86	..	..	..	..	..	..	..	..	..	..	..	..	..	..	..	..
Romania	49	56	..	135	..	116	44.8	31.9	63	72.9	1,865.70	3.3	2.4	12.4	13.9	4	714
Russian Federation	70	77	..	154	..	120	..	25.4	..	..	2,671.60	8	5.8	..	10.6	5,562	3,780
Rwanda	5	6	2	3	1	1	14.3	..	..	..	..	4.4	4.4	6.2	4.6	6	2
Samoa	21	..	..	..	..	..	..	..	..	..	..	..	..	..	..	..	..

		Foreign direct investment						Portfolio investment				Aid dependency							
$ millions		% of gross domestic investment		% of PPP GDP		Bonds $ millions		Equity $ millions		$ millions		Aid per capita $		Aid as % of GNP		Aid as % of gross domestic investment	
1990	1999	1990	1999	1989	1999	1990	1999	1990	1999	1994	1999	1994	1999	1994	1999	1994	1999
..	..	..	..	..	..	..	..	..	..	..	..	..	..	..	..	..	..
..	..	..	..	..	..	..	..	..	..	..	..	..	..	..	..	..	..
7	2	3.4	3.5	0.1	0.0	0	0	0	0	267.2	218.5	118.0	84.1	27.4	23.6	125.5	128.2
..	49	5.0	4.2	0.7	0.5	0	0	0	6	14.2	41.5	12.8	35.3	0.4	1.0	1.3	3.5
..	..	..	..	..	..	..	..	..	..	..	..	..	..	..	..	..	..
2,634	11,786	4.3	10.5	0.6	1.5	661	5621	563	1129	424.9	34.5	4.7	0.4	0.1	0.0	0.5	0.0
..	34	0.0	13.1	..	0.6	..	0	..	0	53.6	102.1	12.3	23.8	2.0	8.5	6.8	39.9
2	30	..	12.7	0.0	0.7	..	0	..	0	182.4	218.6	81.3	91.9	27.6	25.4	107.2	91.3
165	3	2.5	0.0	0.2	0.9	0	-35	0	91	631.1	678.0	24.3	24.0	2.2	2.0	9.7	8.0
9	384	2.3	29.6	0.0	1.6	0	0	0	0	1,199.9	118.4	77.8	6.8	58.1	3.2	267.2	9.1
161	216	..	..	..	..	0	0	0	0	161.4	73.2	3.8	1.6	..	..	..	..
..	..	..	..	2.0	1.4	..	..	..	..	137.1	177.6	91.2	104.4	4.5	5.7	19.3	28.7
6	4	0.9	0.4	0.0	0.0	0	0	0	0	447.9	343.7	21.6	14.7	10.9	6.7	49.4	34.0
12,352	34,154	14.8	39.4	9.4	20.3	..	..	..	..	..	..	..	..	..	..	..	..
..	..	..	..	..	..	..	..	..	..	..	..	..	..	..	..	..	..
..	..	..	..	..	..	..	..	..	..	..	..	..	..	..	..	..	..
1,735	745	21.3	7.4	7.1	12.0	..	..	..	..	..	..	..	..	..	..	..	..
0	300	0.0	30.7	0.0	2.7	0	0	0	0	596.9	674.7	138.7	137.2	46.5	33.0	143.9	69.1
-1	15	-0.5	7.3	0.1	..	0	0	0	0	376.8	187.1	42.6	17.8	24.6	9.4	231.9	90.7
588	1,005	14.0	11.8	2.8	1.0	0	0	0	2	190.1	151.6	1.8	1.2	0.9	0.5	4.1	1.8
..	..	..	..	..	..	..	..	..	..	..	..	..	..	..	..	..	..
1,003	3,597	3.7	8.6	3.6	7.3	..	..	..	..	..	..	..	..	..	..	..	..
..	60	10.2	..	..	..	0	0	0	11	95.2	39.9	45.8	17.0	1.0	..	5.0	..
244	530	3.2	4.3	0.2	0.3	0	-75	0	0	1,605.1	732.0	13.4	5.4	3.0	1.2	15.8	8.4
..	..	..	..	..	..	..	..	..	..	..	..	..	..	..	..	..	..
132	22	14.8	0.7	1.8	5.0	-2	381	0	0	30.6	13.6	11.8	4.8	0.4	0.2	1.5	0.4
155	297	19.7	46.3	3.5	2.7	0	0	0	232	322.1	215.7	76.7	45.8	6.3	6.3	28.1	33.7
76	72	6.3	5.3	0.1	0.6	0	0	0	0	93.3	77.6	19.8	14.5	1.2	1.0	5.1	4.3
41	1,969	0.9	17.3	0.1	1.7	0	-255	0	289	336.2	452.2	14.5	17.9	0.8	0.9	3.4	4.0
530	573	5.0	4.0	0.3	0.3	395	3895	0	422	1,057.2	690.2	15.8	9.3	1.6	0.9	6.9	4.9
89	7,270	0.6	17.8	0.0	2.6	0	1096	0	721	1,805.8	983.8	46.9	25.5	1.8	0.6	10.1	2.4
2,610	1,112	13.6	10.8	1.7	3.2	..	..	..	..	..	..	..	..	..	..	..	..
..	..	..	..	..	..	..	..	..	..	..	..	..	..	..	..	..	..
..	..	..	..	..	..	..	-681	..	..	..	..	..	..	..	..	..	..
0	1,041	0.0	15.4	0.0	0.8	0	0	0	0	143.8	373.4	6.3	16.6	0.5	1.1	2.1	5.5
..	3,309	0.0	5.3	..	0.5	310	..	0	644	1,847.3	1,816.3	12.5	12.4	0.6	0.5	2.2	2.9
8	2	2.1	0.6	0.2	0.0	0	0	0	0	714.0	372.9	114.6	44.9	95.3	19.2	809.8	133.8
..	..	..	..	..	..	..	..	..	..	..	..	..	..	..	..	..	..

Table 4.   Indicators to chapters 10–13 (continued)

COUNTRY or REGION	Urban population % of total population		Motor vehicles per 1,000 people		Passenger cars per 1,000 people		Central government expenditure % of GDP		State-owned enterprises share in GDP, %	share in Gross domestic investment, %	Proceeds from privatization $ millions	Military expenditures % of GNP		Trade in goods % of PPP GDP		Net private capital flows $ millions	
	1980	1999	1980	1998	1980	1998	1980	1998	1990-97	1990-97	1990-99	1992	1997	1989	1999	1990	1999
Sao Tome and Principe	32	..	..	..	..	..	..	..	..	..	..	..	..	..	..	..	..
Saudi Arabia	66	85	163	166	67	98	..	..	..	..	..	26.8	14.5	37.5	36	..	..
Senegal	36	47	19	14	..	10	23.3	..	..	..	410.7	2.8	1.6	22.4	19.3	42	54
Seychelles	43	..	..	..	..	..	..	..	..	..	..	..	..	..	..	..	..
Sierra Leone	24	36	..	6	..	5	26.5	17.7	..	..	1.6	3.2	5.9	10.6	4.3	36	1
Singapore	100	100	..	168	71	108	20	16.8	..	..	..	5.2	5.7	264.5	275.1	..	..
Slovak Republic	52	57	..	253	..	222	..	..	..	..	1,979.40	2.2	2.1	..	37.6	278	281
Slovenia	48	50	..	440	..	403	..	..	..	..	521.1	2.1	1.7	..	58.5	..	..
Solomon Islands	11	..	..	..	..	..	..	..	..	..	..	..	..	..	..	..	..
Somalia	19	..	..	..	..	..	..	..	..	..	..	..	..	..	..	..	..
South Africa	48	52	133	..	85	85	21.6	29.7	..	..	2,964.20	3.2	1.8	14	14.2	..	4,533
Spain	73	77	239	467	202	385	26.5	36.1	..	..	..	1.6	1.5	24.2	35.8	..	..
Sri Lanka	22	23	..	34	8	15	41.4	25	..	..	804.5	3.8	5.1	11.5	16.9	54	109
St. Kitts and Nevis	36	..	..	..	..	..	..	..	..	..	..	..	..	..	..	..	..
St. Lucia	42	..	..	..	..	..	..	..	..	..	..	..	..	..	..	..	..
St. Vincent and the Grenadines	27	..	..	..	..	..	..	..	..	..	..	..	..	..	..	..	..
Sudan	20	..	..	10	..	9	17.4	..	..	..	..	..	..	..	..	..	371
Suriname	45	..	..	..	..	..	..	..	..	..	..	..	..	..	..	..	..
Swaziland	18	..	..	..	..	..	..	..	..	..	..	..	..	..	..	..	..
Sweden	83	83	370	468	347	428	39.3	42.7	..	8.7	..	2.6	2.5	66.1	76.5	..	..
Switzerland	57	68	383	516	356	477	19.2	27.9	..	..	..	1.8	1.4	70.9	82.7	..	..
Syrian Arab Republic	47	54	..	27	..	9	48.2	24.6	..	..	..	9.7	5.6	18.1	10.4	18	87
Tajikistan	34	28	..	2	..	0	..	..	..	..	..	0.3	1.7	..	..	..	10
Tanzania	15	32	3	5	2	1	..	..	8.6	22.9	272.3	2.2	1.3	12.6	14.3	4	171
Thailand	17	21	13	103	9	27	18.8	18.6	..	10	2,985.80	2.6	2.3	23.9	29.4	4,399	2,471
Togo	23	33	..	27	..	19	30.8	..	..	..	38.1	2.9	2	14.5	13	0	30
Tonga	24	..	..	..	..	..	..	..	..	..	..	..	..	..	..	..	..
Trinidad and Tobago	63	..	..	108	..	90	30.9	28.2	..	..	276.2	..	..	38.4	44.6	..	713
Tunisia	52	65	38	64	20	30	31.6	32.6	..	..	523	2.4	2	24.5	25.5	-122	739
Turkey	44	74	23	81	..	64	21.3	29.9	5	13.8	4,654.40	3.8	4	11.1	16.2	1,782	8,667
Turkmenistan	47	45	..	..	..	..	..	..	..	..	..	..	4.6	..	16.8	..	-54
Uganda	9	14	1	4	1	2	6.2	..	..	..	174.4	2.4	4.2	4.8	7.4	16	221
Ukraine	62	68	..	94	..	..	..	..	..	..	31.5	1.9	3.7	..	13.6	369	371
United Arab Emirates	72	..	..	14	..	11	12.1	11	..	..	..	..	..	78.3	106.7	..	..
United Kingdom	89	89	303	439	268	375	38.3	37.9	2.8	4.6	..	3.8	2.7	36.8	44.8	..	..
United States	74	77	..	767	536	483	22	21.1	..	4	..	4.8	3.3	14.9	19.8	..	..
Uruguay	85	91	..	169	..	154	21.8	33.3	..	..	17	2.3	1.4	14.6	19	-192	65
Uzbekistan	41	37	..	..	..	..	..	..	..	..	212	2.7	2.5	..	7.7	40	658
Vanuatu	..	..	..	..	..	..	..	..	..	..	..	..	..	..	..	..	..
Venezuela	79	87	112	..	91	69	18.7	19.8	..	..	6,072.00	2.6	2.2	22.6	26.6	-126	3,130

Foreign direct investment						Portfolio investment				Aid dependency							
$ millions		% of gross domestic investment		% of PPP GDP		Bonds $ millions		Equity $ millions		$ millions		Aid per capita $		Aid as % of GNP		Aid as % of gross domestic investment	
1990	1999	1990	1999	1989	1999	1990	1999	1990	1999	1994	1999	1994	1999	1994	1999	1994	1999
..	..	..	..	..	..	..	..	..	..	..	..	..	..	..	..	..	..
..	..	..	..	0.5	0.4	..	0	..	..	16.3	28.8	0.9	1.4	0.0	0.0	0.1	0.1
57	60	7.2	4.0	0.4	1.5	0	..	0	0	640.0	534.3	78.9	57.5	18.3	11.4	94.7	59.1
..	..	..	..	..	..	..	..	..	..	..	..	..	..	..	..	..	..
32	1	37.9	51.0	0.7	..	0	..	0	0	275.4	73.5	62.6	14.9	33.9	11.3	348.6	3,751.0
5,575	6,984	41.5	25.1	10.6	13.3	..	..	..	..	16.9	-1.1	5.0	-0.3	0.0	0.0	0.1	0.0
0	354	0.0	5.6	..	1.3	0	415	0	0	78.5	318.3	14.7	59.0	0.5	1.6	2.4	5.1
..	181	5.0	3.2	..	0.7	..	..	..	..	31.7	31.0	15.9	15.6	0.2	0.2	1.1	0.6
..	..	..	..	..	..	..	..	..	..	..	..	..	..	..	..	..	..
..	..	..	..	..	..	..	..	..	..	..	..	..	..	..	..	..	..
..	1,376	..	6.7	0.2	0.7	..	234	..	3855	294.6	539.2	7.7	12.8	0.2	0.4	1.4	2.6
13,984	9,321	10.1	6.5	2.1	6.4	..	..	..	..	..	..	..	..	..	..	..	..
43	177	2.4	4.1	0.1	0.4	0	0	0	6	595.2	251.4	33.3	13.2	5.2	1.6	18.8	5.8
..	..	..	..	..	..	..	..	..	..	..	..	..	..	..	..	..	..
..	..	..	..	..	..	..	..	..	..	..	..	..	..	..	..	..	..
..	..	..	..	..	..	..	..	..	..	..	..	..	..	..	..	..	..
..	371	..	..	..	..	0	0	0	0	409.8	242.9	15.7	8.4	5.6	2.8	..	..
..	..	..	..	..	..	..	..	..	..	..	..	..	..	..	..	..	..
..	..	..	..	..	..	..	..	..	..	..	..	..	..	..	..	..	..
1,982	59,386	3.5	147.2	8.0	39.4	..	..	..	..	..	..	..	..	..	..	..	..
4,961	9,944	9.3	14.2	8.7	22.9	..	..	..	..	..	..	..	..	..	..	..	..
71	91	3.7	1.6	0.0	0.4	0	0	0	0	744.6	228.2	54.3	14.5	4.8	1.5	16.4	4.0
..	24	..	14.9	..	..	..	0	..	0	66.7	122.0	11.6	19.6	..	6.6	..	75.9
0	183	0.0	12.1	0.0	1.1	0	0	0	0	965.3	989.6	33.5	30.1	22.2	11.3	86.8	66.4
2,444	6,213	6.9	23.8	1.0	1.8	-87	-1,358	449	2527	577.8	1,003.3	9.9	16.7	0.4	0.8	1.0	3.8
0	30	0.0	15.9	0.2	0.9	0	0	0	0	125.3	71.3	31.4	15.6	13.5	5.2	84.7	37.8
..	..	..	..	..	..	..	..	..	..	..	..	..	..	..	..	..	..
..	633	17.1	44.0	2.0	7.5	-52	230	0	0	21.2	26.2	16.9	20.3	0.5	0.4	2.1	1.8
76	350	1.9	6.3	0.3	0.6	-60	240	0	0	106.2	244.5	12.0	25.9	0.7	1.2	2.8	4.4
684	783	1.9	1.8	0.3	0.3	597	3223	35	800	159.3	-9.7	2.7	-0.2	0.1	0.0	0.6	0.0
..	80	..	5.4	..	0.9	..	0	..	0	25.0	20.9	5.7	4.4	0.8	0.7	..	1.4
0	222	0.0	21.1	0.0	0.9	0	0	0	0	749.5	589.8	40.3	27.5	19.0	9.2	127.7	56.1
..	496	0.0	6.5	..	0.3	..	187	..	0	289.8	479.8	5.6	9.6	0.6	1.3	1.6	6.3
..	..	..	..	..	..	..	..	..	..	-8.1	4.2	-3.5	1.5	0.0	..	-0.1	..
32,518	84,812	16.3	33.4	7.4	23.0	..	..	..	..	..	..	..	..	..	..	..	..
48,954	275,535	4.8	10.6	2.5	5.2	..	..	..	..	..	..	..	..	..	..	..	..
0	229	0.0	7.2	0.0	0.8	-16	-137	0	0	74.3	21.7	23.3	6.5	0.5	0.1	2.9	0.7
40	113	1.5	7.1	..	..	..	0	..	0	27.7	133.9	1.2	5.5	0.1	0.8	0.7	5.0
..	..	..	..	..	..	..	..	..	..	..	..	..	..	..	..	..	..
451	3,187	9.1	20.0	0.4	2.8	345	134	0	67	27.0	43.5	1.3	1.8	0.0	0.0	0.3	0.3

Table 4. Indicators to chapters 10–13 (continued)

COUNTRY or REGION	Urban population % of total population 1980	1999	Motor vehicles per 1,000 people 1980	1998	Passenger cars per 1,000 people 1980	1998	Central government expenditure % of GDP 1980	1998	State-owned enterprises share in GDP, % 1990-97	share in Gross domestic investment, % 1990-97	Proceeds from privatization $ millions 1990-99	Military expenditures % of GNP 1992	1997	Trade in goods % of PPP GDP 1989	1999	Net private capital flows $ millions 1990	1999
Vietnam	19	20	..	..	..	..	..	20.1	..	..	7.6	3.4	2.8	7.4	16	16	828
Virgin Islands (U.S.)	46	..	..	..	..	..	..	..	..	..	..	..	..	..	..	..	..
West Bank and Gaza	..	..	..	..	..	..	..	..	..	..	..	..	..	..	..	..	..
Yemen, Rep.	19	24	..	32	8	14	..	42.2	..	..	..	9.4	8.1	25.9	34.1	30	-150
Yugoslavia, FR (Serbia/ Montenegro)	46	..	118	188	..	173	..	..	..	..	921.7	..	..	..	..	..	0
Zambia	40	40	..	23	..	15	37.1	..	..	..	826	3.3	1.1	33.9	18.7	194	151
Zimbabwe	22	35	..	31	..	28	27.9	35.7	9.2	..	217.8	3.8	3.8	14.9	14.4	85	70
World	**40**	**46**	**72**	**116**	**..**	**91**	**25.3**	**28.7**	**..**	**..**	**..**	**3.2**	**2.5**	**22.5**	**27.4**	**..**	**..**
Low Income	24	31	3*	9*	..	5*	..*	12.4*	..	..	..	2.7	2.9	7.2	7.8	6,630	2,083
Middle income	38	50	..	104	..	79	20.9	..	..	..	..	4	2.9	14.1	16.9	36,030	216,992
Lower middle income	31*	43*	..	78	..	55	..	24	..	..	..	4.2*	3.2*	11.5	11.7	20,673	83,086
Upper middle income	64	76	77	173	62	140	19.5	..	..	..	..	3.8	2.8	17.2	26	15,357	133,906
Low & middle Income	32	41	14	38	..	25	20.1	18.9	..	..	..	3.8	2.9	12.3	14.7	43,645	219,076
East Asia & Pacific	22	34	3	21	..	11	..	13.8	..	..	..	2.9	2.5	14.5	15.3	19,405	51,062
Europe & Central Asia	59	67	..	157	..	138	..	29.1	..	..	..	5.2	4	..	17.7	7,667	43,164
Latin America & Caribbean	65	75	93	89	62	67	19	..	..	..	..	1.4	1.8	10.2	18.2	12,626	111,367
Middle East & N. Africa	48	58	..	65	..	45	..	..	..	..	..	14.4	7	19.4	16.8	399	979
South Asia	22	28	2	6	..	4	13.5	15.8	..	..	..	3.1	3.1	4	4.6	2,173	2,054
Sub-Saharan Africa	23	34	21	21	14	13	22.1	..	..	..	..	3.1	2.3	15.9	16.3	1,374	10,449
High Income	**75**	**77**	**321**	**585**	**355**	**429**	**26.4**	**31.2**	**..**	**..**	**..**	**3.1**	**2.4**	**28.5**	**37.4**	**..**	**..**

*indicates income-group aggregate that includes data on China.

Note: Revisions to estimates of China's GNP per Capita, made by analysts in 2000-01, caused that economy to be reclassified from low to lower middle income. As a result, for different indicators in these data tables China figures as part of one or the other income group, which considerably affects these group aggregates.

Foreign direct investment						Portfolio investment				Aid dependency							
$ millions		% of gross domestic investment		% of PPP GDP		Bonds $ millions		Equity $ millions		$ millions		Aid per capita $		Aid as % of GNP		Aid as % of gross domestic investment	
1990	1999	1990	1999	1989	1999	1990	1999	1990	1999	1994	1999	1994	1999	1994	1999	1994	1999
16	1,609	1.9	22.1	..	..	0	0	0	0	890.8	1,420.6	12.4	18.3	5.7	5.0	22.5	19.5
..	..	..	..	..	..	..	..	..	..	459.8	511.8	196.5	180.3	12.6	10.2	44.8	30.9
-131	-150	-19.2	-11.8	1.5	1.7	0	0	0	0	170.0	456.4	11.5	26.8	5.2	7.4	23.0	36.0
..	0	..	..	..	..	..	0	..	0	49.2	638.5	4.7	60.1	..	..	..	..
203	163	35.7	29.6	2.5	..	0	0	0	0	718.1	623.4	82.2	63.1	23.1	20.8	260.4	113.3
-12	59	-0.8	9.2	0.0	..	-30	-30	0	4	560.4	244.2	52.0	20.5	8.5	4.7	27.9	38.0
200,479	**884,452**	**4.2**	**10.2**	**2.0**	**4.6**	..	..	..	..	67,506.0	59,125.4	12.1	**9.9**	0.3	0.2	1.1	**0.9**
2,201	9,830	1.1	3.0	0.2	0.3	142	-2,548	417*	2,616	29,422.4	22,399.1	13.4	9.3	2.9	2.2	13.8	10.0
22,064	175,577	2.3	14.0	0.4	1.6	1,018	27,993	2,341	31,839	24,531.4	22,923.9	9.7	8.6	0.6	0.4	2.1	1.7
9,584	66,214	1.8	9.7	0.3	1.0	1,099	8,126	484	13,289	18,315.1	17,816.4	9.2	8.5	0.9	0.7	3.3	2.6
12,480	109,364	3.0	17.8	0.5	2.6	-81	19,868	1,857	18,550	4,932.9	3,848.0	9.2	6.7	0.2	0.1	0.9	0.6
24,265	185,408	2.1	12.4	0.3	1.3	1160	25,446	3,743	34,456	58,475.2	48,472.8	12.4	9.5	1.1	0.8	4.3	3.1
11,135	56,041	3.5	9.6	0.4	1.1	-802	1,072	2,290	21,133	9,431.5	9,811.2	5.4	5.3	0.7	0.5	1.7	1.7
1,051	26,534	0.3	11.6	..	1.1	1893	6,167	235	3,550	9,728.0	10,878.3	20.6	22.9	1.0	1.0	4.6	4.7
8,188	90,352	3.8	22.3	0.4	3.0	101	19,067	1,111	3,893	5,683.7	5,855.7	12.1	11.5	0.4	0.3	1.6	1.4
2,504	1,461	2.3	0.8	0.3	0.5	-148	182	0	669	7,194.0	5,127.7	27.4	17.7	1.6	0.9	7.0	3.9
464	3,070	0.5	2.4	0.0	0.1	147	-1,201	105	1,312	7,057.1	4,254.3	5.8	3.2	1.6	0.7	7.2	3.3
923	7,949	2.0	9.3	0.6	0.7	-31	158	0	3,899	19,380.9	12,545.6	34.4	19.5	7.2	4.1	39.4	22.0
176,213	699,045	4.8	9.6	2.9	7.2	..	..	..	..	2,197.3	1,823.2	2.5	2.0	0.0	0.0	0.0	0.0

Table 5.   Indicators to chapters 14–16

| COUNTRY or REGION | Commercial energy use | | | | GDP per unit of energy use | |
| | Total, thousand metric tons of oil equivalent | | per capita, kg of oil equivalent | | PPP $ per kg of oil equivalent | |
	1990	1997	1990	1997	1990	1997
Afghanistan	..	..	..	..	..	..
Albania	2,567	1,048	782	317	3.4	8.5
Algeria	23,959	26,497	958	912	4.7	5.3
American Samoa	..	..	..	..	..	..
Andorra	..	..	..	..	..	..
Angola	5,617	6,848	609	587	3.1	2.6
Antigua and Barbuda	..	..	..	..	..	..
Argentina	43,313	61,710	1,332	1,730	5.6	6.9
Armenia	7,941	1,804	2,240	476	1.5	4.3
Aruba	..	..	..	..	..	..
Australia	87,155	101,626	5,107	5,484	3.2	4.0
Austria	25,699	27,761	3,326	3,439	5.5	6.7
Azerbaijan	22,841	11,987	3,191	1,529	1.5	1.3
Bahamas, The	..	..	..	..	..	..
Bahrain	..	..	..	..	..	..
Bangladesh	20,936	24,327	190	197	5.0	6.8
Barbados	..	..	..	..	..	..
Belarus	43,050	25,142	4,196	2,449	1.6	2.4
Belgium	48,426	57,125	4,858	5,611	3.8	4.1
Belize	..	..	..	..	..	..
Benin	1,678	2,182	354	377	1.9	2.3
Bermuda	..	..	..	..	..	..
Bhutan	..	..	..	..	..	..
Bolivia	2,896	4,254	441	548	4.0	4.1
Bosnia and Herzegovina	..	..	..	..	..	..
Botswana	..	..	..	..	..	..
Brazil	136,131	172,030	920	1,051	5.8	6.5
Brunei	..	..	..	..	..	..
Bulgaria	27,126	20,616	3,111	2,480	1.7	1.9
Burkina Faso	..	..	..	..	..	..
Burundi	..	..	..	..	..	..
Cambodia	..	..	..	..	..	..
Cameroon	5,058	5,756	441	413	3.5	3.6
Canada	209,712	237,983	7,546	7,930	2.6	3.0
Cape Verde	..	..	..	..	..	..
Cayman Islands	..	..	..	..	..	..
Central African Republic	..	..	..	..	..	..
Chad	..	..	..	..	..	..
Channel Islands	..	..	..	..	..	..
Chile	13,876	23,012	1,059	1,574	4.5	5.7
China	866,666	1,113,050	763	907	1.8	3.3
Hong Kong, China	10,455	14,121	1,833	2,172	8.7	10.6
Macao, China	..	..	..	..	..	..
Colombia	26,762	30,481	765	761	7.4	8.2
Comoros	..	..	..	..	..	..
Congo, Dem. Rep.	11,858	14,539	317	311	4.5	2.7
Congo, Rep.	1,117	1,242	503	459	2.0	2.2
Costa Rica	2,025	2,663	676	769	6.8	7.7
Cote d'Ivoire	4,596	5,597	395	394	3.5	4.0
Croatia	..	7,650	..	1,687	..	4.0

| CO₂ emissions | | | | | | Forest area | Human Development Index | HDI rank | PPP GNP per capita rank | Genuine domestic savings |
| total, million, metric tons | | per capita, metric tons | | kg per PPP $ of GDP | | thousand sq.km | | | | % of GDP |
1990	1996	1990	1996	1980	1996	1995	1998	1998	1999	1998
..	1.2	..	..	..	..	..	..	..	..	..
8.4	1.9	2.6	0.6	..	0.2	10	0.713	94	137	-13.4
80.4	94.3	3.2	3.3	1.1	0.7	19	0.683	107	101	5.6
..	0.3	..	..	..	..	..	..	..	..	..
..	..	..	..	..	..	..	..	..	..	..
4.6	5.1	0.5	0.5	..	0.3	222	0.405	160	199	10.4
..	0.3	..	..	0.8	..	..	0.833	37	..	..
109.7	129.9	3.4	3.7	0.6	0.3	339	0.837	35	56	4.8
3.7	3.7	1.0	1.0	..	0.5	3	0.721	93	150	-21.0
..	1.5	..	..	..	..	..	..	..	..	..
266.0	306.6	15.6	16.7	1.4	0.8	409	0.929	4	20	12.2
57.4	59.3	7.4	7.4	0.7	0.3	39	0.908	16	15	21.1
47.1	30.0	6.4	3.9	..	0.2	10	0.722	90	146	-29.5
..	1.707	..	..	3.7	..	..	0.844	33	..	..
..	10.578	..	..	2.0	..	..	0.820	41	..	..
15.4	23.0	0.1	0.2	0.2	0.1	10	0.461	146	168	10.0
..	0.835	..	..	0.5	..	..	0.858	30	..	..
94.3	61.7	9.1	6.0	..	1.1	74	0.781	57	79	14.4
97.4	106.0	9.8	10.4	1.3	0.5	..	0.925	7	13	..
..	0.355	..	..	0.8	..	..	0.777	58	..	..
0.6	0.7	0.1	0.1	0.3	0.1	46	0.411	157	189	2.7
..	0.462	..	..	..	..	..	..	..	..	..
..	0.260	..	..	0.1	..	..	0.483	142	..	..
5.5	10.1	0.8	1.3	..	0.6	483	0.643	114	151	4.7
..	3.111	..	..	..	..	27	..	..	..	..
2.2	2.1	1.7	1.4	0.7	0.2	139	0.593	122	84	14.5
202.6	273.4	1.4	1.7	0.4	0.3	5,511	0.747	74	81	11.9
..	5.071	..	..	2.1	..	..	0.848	32	..	..
75.3	55.3	8.6	6.6	3.1	1.3	32	0.772	60	99	4.6
1.0	1.0	0.1	0.1	0.1	0.1	43	0.303	172	187	2.3
0.2	0.2	0.0	0.0	0.1	..	3	..	..	..	-14.8
0.5	0.5	0.0	0.0	..	0.0	98	0.512	136	176	0.2
1.5	3.5	0.1	0.3	0.5	0.2	196	0.528	134	169	10.4
409.6	409.4	14.7	13.8	1.5	0.6	2,446	0.935	1	16	13.2
..	0.121	..	..	1.0	..	..	0.688	105	..	..
..	0.282	..	..	..	..	..	..	..	..	..
0.2	0.2	0.1	0.1	0.1	0.1	299	0.371	166	180	-1.3
0.1	0.1	0.0	0.0	0.1	0.0	110	0.367	167	190	-2.3
..	..	..	..	..	..	..	..	..	..	..
36.3	48.8	2.8	3.4	1.0	0.4	79	0.826	38	68	13.6
2,401.7	3,363.5	2.1	2.8	3.6	1.0	1,333	0.706	99	128	32.0
26.2	23.1	4.6	3.7	0.5	0.2	..	0.872	26	26	20.8
..	1.4	..	..	..	..	..	..	..	..	..
55.9	65.3	1.6	1.7	0.4	0.3	530	0.764	68	88	4.1
..	0.055	..	..	0.3	..	..	0.510	137	..	..
4.1	2.3	0.1	0.1	0.1	0.1	..	0.430	152	..	..
2.0	5.0	0.9	1.9	0.4	1.8	195	0.507	139	188	5.4
2.9	4.7	1.0	1.4	0.3	0.2	12	0.797	48	87	20.6
9.9	13.1	0.9	0.9	0.5	0.6	55	0.420	154	163	19.4
..	17.5	..	3.9	..	0.6	18	0.795	49	78	..

Table 5. Indicators to chapters 14–16 (continued)

COUNTRY or REGION	Commercial energy use				GDP per unit of energy use	
	Total, thousand metric tons of oil equivalent		per capita, kg of oil equivalent		PPP $ per kg of oil equivalent	
	1990	1997	1990	1997	1990	1997
Cuba	..	..	..	..	..	..
Cyprus	..	..	..	..	..	..
Czech Republic	45,020	40,576	4,344	3,938	2.8	3.3
Denmark	18,282	21,107	3,557	3,994	5.0	6.0
Djibouti	..	..	..	..	..	..
Dominica	..	..	..	..	..	..
Dominican Republic	3,973	5,453	559	673	5.6	6.6
Ecuador	6,558	8,513	639	713	4.1	4.6
Egypt, Arab Rep.	31,895	39,581	608	656	3.9	4.7
El Salvador	2,695	4,095	527	691	5.5	5.9
Equatorial Guinea	..	..	..	..	..	..
Eritrea	..	..	..	..	..	..
Estonia	10,163	5,556	6,469	3,811	1.2	2.0
Ethiopia	15,208	17,131	297	287	1.6	2.1
Faeroe Islands	..	..	..	..	..	..
Fiji	..	..	..	..	..	..
Finland	28,813	33,075	5,779	6,435	3.0	3.2
France	227,600	247,534	4,012	4,224	4.3	5.0
French Polynesia	..	..	..	..	..	..
Gabon	..	..	..	..	..	..
Gambia, The	..	..	..	..	..	..
Georgia	10,590	2,295	1,940	423	4.3	7.9
Germany	355,732	347,272	4,478	4,231	4.3	5.2
Ghana	5,233	6,896	352	383	4.0	4.5
Greece	22,056	25,556	2,171	2,435	5.1	5.7
Greenland	..	..	..	..	..	..
Grenada	..	..	..	..	..	..
Guam	..	..	..	..	..	..
Guatemala	4,377	5,633	500	536	5.5	6.5
Guinea	..	..	..	..	..	..
Guinea-Bissau	..	..	..	..	..	..
Guyana	..	..	..	..	..	..
Haiti	1,585	1,779	245	237	6.5	5.9
Honduras	2,442	3,182	501	532	4.1	4.7
Hungary	28,463	25,311	2,746	2,492	3.3	4.0
Iceland	..	..	..	..	..	..
India	359,846	461,032	424	479	3.3	4.2
Indonesia	98,846	138,779	555	693	3.4	4.5
Iran, Islamic Rep.	72,342	108,289	1,330	1,777	2.9	3.0
Iraq	..	..	..	..	..	..
Ireland	10,463	12,491	2,984	3,412	3.8	6.0
Isle of Man	..	..	..	..	..	..
Israel	11,923	17,591	2,559	3,014	5.1	5.8
Italy	153,316	163,315	2,703	2,839	6.3	7.3
Jamaica	3,037	3,963	1,264	1,552	2.5	2.2
Japan	438,797	514,898	3,552	4,084	5.4	6.0
Jordan	3,445	4,795	1,087	1,081	2.1	3.3
Kazakstan	106,028	38,418	6,486	2,439	1.0	1.8
Kenya	12,479	14,138	530	494	1.8	2.0
Kiribati	..	..	..	..	..	..

| CO$_2$ emissions | | | | | | Forest area | Human Development Index | HDI rank | PPP GNP per capita rank | Genuine domestic savings |
| total, million, metric tons | | per capita, metric tons | | kg per PPP $ of GDP | | thousand sq.km | | | | % of GDP |
1990	1996	1990	1996	1980	1996	1995	1998	1998	1999	1998
..	31.170	..	..	..	..	18	0.783	56	..	..
..	5.379	..	..	1.3	..	..	0.886	22	..	..
141.7	126.7	13.7	12.3	..	0.9	26	0.843	34	52	21.2
50.7	56.6	9.9	10.7	1.3	0.5	4	0.911	15	12	17.6
..	0.366	..	..	..	..	..	0.447	149	..	..
..	0.081	..	..	0.4	..	..	0.793	51	..	..
9.4	12.9	1.3	1.6	0.6	0.4	16	0.729	87	103	11.9
16.6	24.5	1.6	2.1	0.9	0.6	111	0.722	91	141	5.9
75.4	97.9	1.4	1.7	1.0	0.6	0	0.623	119	127	10.0
2.6	4.0	0.5	0.7	0.2	0.2	1	0.696	104	114	-4.5
..	0.143	..	..	..	..	..	0.555	131	..	..
..	..	..	..	..	..	3	0.408	159	183	-33.9
21.4	16.4	13.8	11.2	..	1.6	20	0.801	46	74	12.8
3.0	3.4	0.1	0.1	0.1	0.1	136	0.309	171	200	-8.7
..	0.630	..	..	..	..	..	..	..	..	..
..	0.762	..	..	0.7	..	..	0.769	66	..	..
51.1	59.2	10.2	11.5	1.3	0.6	200	0.917	11	25	19.6
353.2	361.8	6.2	6.2	0.9	0.3	150	0.917	12	24	14.8
..	0.561	..	..	..	..	..	..	..	..	..
..	3.7	..	..	1.6	0.5	179	0.592	123	..	25.4
..	0.216	..	..	0.3	0.1	1	0.396	161	..	-6.1
15.2	3.0	2.8	0.5	..	0.2	30	0.762	70	122	-10.5
889.2	861.2	11.1	10.5	..	0.5	107	0.911	14	21	15.8
3.5	4.0	0.2	0.2	0.2	0.1	90	0.556	129	157	1.4
72.2	80.6	7.1	7.7	0.8	0.6	65	0.875	25	50	..
..	0.5	..	..	..	..	..	..	..	..	..
..	0.161	..	..	0.4	..	..	0.785	54	..	..
..	4.1	..	..	..	..	..	..	..	..	..
5.1	6.8	0.6	0.7	0.3	0.2	38	0.619	120	125	-2.3
1.0	1.1	0.2	0.2	..	0.1	64	0.394	162	158	8.7
..	0.23	..	..	0.5	0.2	23	0.331	169	..	-13.5
..	0.953	..	..	4.0	..	..	0.709	96	..	..
1.0	1.1	0.2	0.1	0.1	0.1	0	0.440	150	170	20.1
2.6	4.0	0.5	0.7	0.4	0.3	41	0.653	113	148	20.1
64.1	59.5	6.2	5.8	1.5	0.6	17	0.817	43	60	21.3
..	2.195	..	..	0.4	..	..	0.927	5	..	..
675.3	997.4	0.8	1.1	0.8	0.5	650	0.563	128	153	10.3
165.2	245.1	0.9	1.2	0.8	0.4	1,098	0.670	109	143	5.9
212.4	266.7	3.9	4.4	1.1	0.9	15	0.709	97	95	-7.9
..	91.4	..	..	0.5	..	1	0.583	126	..	..
29.8	34.9	8.5	9.6	1.4	0.5	6	0.907	18	34	..
..	..	..	..	..	..	..	..	..	..	..
34.6	52.3	7.4	9.2	0.7	0.5	1	0.883	23	..	0.1
398.9	403.2	7.0	7.0	0.7	0.3	65	0.903	19	29	13.9
8.0	10.1	3.3	4.0	2.1	1.1	2	0.735	83	129	12.8
1,070.7	1,167.7	8.7	9.3	0.9	0.4	251	0.924	9	14	20.1
..	..	..	..	..	..	0	0.721	92	124	-1.8
292.7	173.8	17.7	10.9	..	2.5	105	0.754	73	106	-7.8
5.8	6.8	0.2	0.2	0.6	0.2	13	0.508	138	185	-2.7
..	0.022	..	..	1.2	..	..	..	..	..	..

Table 5.   Indicators to chapters 14–16 (continued)

COUNTRY or REGION	Commercial energy use				GDP per unit of energy use	
	Total, thousand metric tons of oil equivalent		per capita, kg of oil equivalent		PPP $ per kg of oil equivalent	
	1990	1997	1990	1997	1990	1997
Korea, Dem. Rep.	..	..	..	..	..	..
Korea, Rep.	91,402	176,351	2,132	3,834	4.0	3.9
Kuwait	13,132	16,165	6,180	8,936	..	..
Kyrgyz Republic	1,875	2,793	427	603	8.3	3.8
Lao PDR	..	..	..	..	..	..
Latvia	3,274	4,460	1,226	1,806	6.6	3.1
Lebanon	2,297	5,244	632	1,265	3.2	3.3
Lesotho	..	..	..	..	..	..
Liberia	..	..	..	..	..	..
Libya	..	..	..	..	..	..
Liechtenstein	..	..	..	..	..	..
Lithuania	17,224	8,806	4,628	2,376	..	2.6
Luxembourg	..	..	..	..	..	..
Macedonia, FYR	..	..	..	..	..	..
Madagascar	..	..	..	..	..	..
Malawi	..	..	..	..	..	..
Malaysia	23,974	48,473	1,317	2,237	4.0	4.0
Maldives	..	..	..	..	..	..
Mali	..	..	..	..	..	..
Malta	..	..	..	..	..	..
Marshall Islands	..	..	..	..	..	..
Martinique	..	..	..	..	..	..
Mauritania	..	..	..	..	..	..
Mauritius	..	..	..	..	..	..
Mayotte	..	..	..	..	..	..
Mexico	124,187	141,520	1,492	1,501	4.2	5.1
Micronesia, Fed. Sts.	..	..	..	..	..	..
Moldova	9,959	4,436	2,283	1,029	2.0	2.1
Monaco	..	..	..	..	..	..
Mongolia	..	..	..	..	..	..
Morocco	6,745	9,275	281	340	9.9	9.5
Mozambique	7,318	7,664	517	461	1.0	1.6
Myanmar	10,787	13,009	266	296	..	..
Namibia	..	..	..	..	..	..
Nepal	5,834	7,160	311	321	2.8	3.7
Netherlands	66,593	74,910	4,454	4,800	3.8	4.6
Netherlands Antilles	..	..	..	..	..	..
New Caledonia	..	..	..	..	..	..
New Zealand	14,157	16,679	4,120	4,435	3.4	4.0
Nicaragua	2,174	2,573	568	551	2.8	3.9
Niger	..	..	..	..	..	..
Nigeria	70,905	88,652	737	753	1.0	1.1
Northern Mariana Islands	..	..	..	..	..	..
Norway	21,456	24,226	5,059	5,501	3.6	4.8
Oman	..	..	..	..	..	..
Pakistan	43,238	56,818	400	442	3.3	3.9
Palau	..	..	..	..	..	..
Panama	1,535	2,328	640	856	5.8	6.1
Papua New Guinea	..	..	..	..	..	..
Paraguay	3,097	4,191	734	824	5.3	5.5

CO$_2$ emissions total, million, metric tons		CO$_2$ emissions per capita, metric tons		CO$_2$ emissions kg per PPP $ of GDP		Forest area thousand sq.km	Human Development Index	HDI rank	PPP GNP per capita rank	Genuine domestic savings % of GDP
1990	1996	1990	1996	1980	1996	1995	1998	1998	1999	1998
..	254.3	..	..	..	..	62	..	..	..	..
241.2	408.1	5.6	9.0	1.2	0.6	76	0.854	31	49	25.9
..	..	..	..	1.0	..	0	0.836	36	..	-31.2
11.8	6.1	2.6	1.3	..	0.6	7	0.706	98	149	-2.7
0.2	0.3	0.1	0.1	..	0.0	..	0.484	140	161	18.5
13.1	9.3	5.0	3.7	..	0.7	29	0.771	63	85	5.4
9.1	14.2	2.5	3.5	..	0.9	1	0.735	82	113	-22.0
..	..	..	..	..	..	0	0.569	127	155	-44.5
..	0.326	..	..	1.6	..	..	..	..	..	..
..	40.6	..	..	0.7	..	4	0.760	72	..	..
..	..	..	..	..	..	..	..	..	..	..
21.4	13.8	5.7	3.7	..	0.6	20	0.789	52	83	6.8
..	8.3	..	..	1.9	..	..	0.908	17	..	..
..	12.7	..	6.4	..	1.5	10	0.763	69	108	..
0.9	1.2	0.1	0.1	0.3	0.1	151	0.483	141	192	-0.2
0.6	0.7	0.1	0.1	0.3	0.1	33	0.385	163	203	-8.2
55.3	119.1	3.0	5.6	0.8	0.6	155	0.772	61	72	36.8
..	0.297	..	..	..	..	..	0.725	89	..	..
0.4	0.5	0.0	0.0	0.1	0.1	116	0.380	165	196	5.2
..	1.75	..	..	0.7	..	..	37	0.865	27	..
..	..	..	..	..	..	100	..	..	..	..
..	..	..	..	..	..	86	..	..	..	..
2.6	2.9	1.3	1.2	0.4	0.8	6	0.451	147	164	-18.5
..	1.744	..	..	0.5	..	0	0.761	71	..	16.8
..	..	..	..	0.3	0.2	..	..	..	..	..
295.0	348.1	3.5	3.8	0.9	0.5	554	0.784	55	75	12.4
..	..	..	..	..	..	..	..	..	..	..
21.8	12.1	5.0	2.8	..	1.3	4	0.700	102	144	-5.2
..	..	..	..	..	..	..	..	..	..	..
10.0	8.9	4.5	3.6	3.8	2.4	94	0.628	117	166	..
23.5	27.9	1.0	1.0	0.5	0.3	38	0.589	124	131	9.7
1.0	1.0	0.1	0.1	0.6	0.1	169	0.341	168	191	-4.3
4.1	7.3	0.1	0.2	..	..	272	0.585	125	..	..
..	..	..	..	..	..	124	0.632	115	92	13.2
0.6	1.6	0.0	0.1	0.1	0.1	48	0.474	144	177	-1.8
138.9	155.2	9.3	10.0	1.1	0.5	3	0.925	8	17	20.3
..	6.4	..	..	..	..	..	..	..	..	..
..	1.8	..	..	..	..	..	..	..	..	..
23.6	29.8	6.9	8.0	0.6	0.4	79	0.903	20	42	15.9
2.6	2.9	0.7	0.6	0.4	0.3	56	0.631	116	152	-5.2
1.0	1.1	0.1	0.1	0.2	0.2	26	0.293	173	194	-4.9
88.7	83.3	0.9	0.7	1.9	0.9	138	0.439	151	193	-14.2
..	..	..	..	..	..	..	..	..	..	..
47.7	67.0	11.2	15.3	2.2	0.6	81	0.934	2	8	23.1
..	15.1	..	..	1.5	..	0	0.730	86	..	..
67.9	94.3	0.6	0.8	0.6	0.4	17	0.522	135	159	4.0
..	0.2	..	..	..	..	..	..	..	..	..
3.1	6.7	1.3	2.5	0.7	0.5	28	0.776	59	98	20.5
2.4	2.4	0.6	0.5	0.5	0.2	369	0.542	133	147	..
2.3	3.7	0.5	0.7	0.2	0.2	115	0.736	81	111	10.6

Table 5.   Indicators to chapters 14–16 (continued)

| COUNTRY or REGION | Commercial energy use | | | | GDP per unit of energy use | |
| | Total, thousand metric tons of oil equivalent | | per capita, kg of oil equivalent | | PPP $ per kg of oil equivalent | |
	1990	1997	1990	1997	1990	1997
Peru	11,549	15,127	535	621	5.3	7.3
Philippines	28,294	38,251	452	520	6.8	7.2
Poland	100,114	105,155	2,626	2,721	2.1	2.7
Portugal	16,419	20,400	1,659	2,051	6.6	7.1
Puerto Rico	..	..	..	..	..	..
Qatar	..	..	..	..	..	..
Romania	61,117	44,135	2,634	1,957	2.3	3.2
Russian Federation	906,433	591,982	6,112	4,019	1.6	1.7
Rwanda	..	..	..	..	..	..
Samoa	..	..	..	..	..	..
Sao Tome and Principe	..	..	..	..	..	..
Saudi Arabia	63,275	98,449	4,004	4,906	2.5	2.1
Senegal	2,213	2,770	302	315	3.8	4.1
Seychelles	..	..	..	..	..	..
Sierra Leone	..	..	..	..	..	..
Singapore	13,357	26,878	4,938	8,661	2.8	2.9
Slovak Republic	21,363	17,216	4,044	3,198	2.1	3.0
Slovenia	5,250	..	2,627	..	..	4.4
Solomon Islands	..	..	..	..	..	..
Somalia	..	..	..	..	..	..
South Africa	91,229	107,220	2,592	2,636	3.1	3.3
Spain	90,552	107,328	2,332	2,729	5.3	5.9
Sri Lanka	5,476	7,159	322	386	6.2	7.6
St. Kitts and Nevis	..	..	..	..	..	..
St. Lucia	..	..	..	..	..	..
St. Vincent and the Grenadines	..	..	..	..	..	..
Sudan	..	..	..	..	..	..
Suriname	..	..	..	..	..	..
Swaziland	..	..	..	..	..	..
Sweden	47,747	51,934	5,579	5,869	3.1	3.5
Switzerland	24,998	26,218	3,724	3,699	6.2	6.9
Syrian Arab Republic	11,928	14,642	984	983	2.4	3.0
Tajikistan	3,268	3,384	616	562	4.0	1.6
Tanzania	12,529	14,258	492	455	0.9	1.0
Thailand	43,706	79,963	786	1,319	4.9	4.7
Togo	..	..	..	..	..	..
Tonga	..	..	..	..	..	..
Trinidad and Tobago	..	..	..	..	..	..
Tunisia	5,683	6,805	697	738	5.5	7.2
Turkey	52,498	71,273	935	1,142	5.0	5.7
Turkmenistan	18,923	12,181	5,159	2,615	1.1	1.0
Uganda	..	..	..	..	..	..
Ukraine	252,631	150,059	4,868	2,960	1.3	1.1
United Arab Emirates	..	..	..	..	..	..
United Kingdom	213,090	227,977	3,702	3,863	4.4	5.3
United States	1,925,680	2,162,190	7,720	8,076	2.9	3.6
Uruguay	2,233	2,883	719	883	8.2	9.7
Uzbekistan	43,697	42,553	2,130	1,798	1.1	1.1
Vanuatu	..	..	..	..	..	..
Venezuela	40,851	57,530	2,095	2,526	2.4	2.4

CO₂ emissions						Forest area	Human Development Index	HDI rank	PPP GNP per capita rank	Genuine domestic savings
total, million, metric tons		per capita, metric tons		kg per PPP $ of GDP		thousand sq.km				% of GDP
1990	1996	1990	1996	1980	1996	1995	1998	1998	1999	1998
22.2	26.2	1.0	1.1	0.5	0.3	676	0.737	80	107	11.1
44.3	63.2	0.7	0.9	0.3	0.2	68	0.744	77	118	7.6
347.6	356.8	9.1	9.2	7.3	1.3	87	0.814	44	73	14.6
42.3	47.9	4.3	4.8	0.5	0.3	29	0.864	28	45	15.0
..	15.8	..	..	0.7	..	3	..	..	..	..
..	29.1	..	..	..	..	..	0.819	42	..	..
155.1	119.3	6.7	5.3	2.1	0.8	62	0.770	64	89	0.4
1,954.4	1,579.5	13.1	10.7	..	1.5	7,635	0.771	62	80	-3.3
0.5	0.5	0.1	0.1	0.1	..	3	0.382	164	..	-10.4
..	..	..	..	..	..	..	0.711	95	..	..
..	0.1	..	..	0.6	..	..	0.547	132	..	..
177.1	267.8	11.2	13.8	1.3	1.3	2	0.747	75	..	-11.0
2.9	3.1	0.4	0.4	0.7	0.3	74	0.416	155	173	9.9
..	0.2	..	..	0.4	..	..	0.786	53	..	..
0.3	0.4	0.1	0.1	0.3	0.2	13	0.252	174	206	-10.6
41.9	65.8	15.5	21.6	2.4	0.9	0	0.881	24	7	40.7
43.0	39.6	8.1	7.4	..	0.8	20	0.825	40	64	21.1
..	13.0	..	6.5	..	0.5	11	0.861	29	47	12.0
..	0.2	..	..	1.0	..	..	75	0.614	121	..
..	0.015	..	..	0.7	..	..	..	100	..	..
291.1	292.7	8.3	7.3	1.3	0.8	85	0.697	103	69	7.9
211.7	232.5	5.5	5.9	0.8	0.4	84	0.899	21	41	16.0
3.9	7.1	0.2	0.4	0.2	0.1	18	0.733	84	136	14.8
..	0.1	..	..	..	..	..	0.798	47	..	..
..	0.2	..	..	..	..	..	0.728	88	..	..
..	0.1	..	..	0.4	..	..	0.738	79	..	..
..	3.5	..	..	0.3	0.1	416	0.477	143	..	..
..	2.1	..	..	5.5	..	..	0.766	67	..	..
..	0.3	..	..	1.2	..	..	0.665	112	..	..
48.5	54.1	5.7	6.1	0.9	0.3	244	0.926	6	28	19.0
42.7	44.2	6.4	6.3	0.5	0.2	11	0.915	13	6	18.2
35.8	44.3	3.0	3.1	1.3	1.0	?	0.660	111	139	..
21.3	5.8	3.8	1.0	..	1.0	4	0.663	110	184	..
2.3	2.4	0.1	0.1	..	0.2	325	0.415	156	205	4.5
95.7	205.4	1.7	3.4	0.6	0.5	116	0.745	76	90	33.7
0.7	0.8	0.2	0.2	0.2	0.1	12	0.471	145	172	-1.6
..	0.1	..	..	..	..	..	..	..	..	..
..	22.2	..	..	3.1	2.4	2	0.793	50	..	-5.7
13.3	16.2	1.6	1.8	0.6	0.3	6	0.703	101	91	18.0
143.8	178.3	2.6	2.9	0.7	0.5	89	0.732	85	82	17.1
34.2	34.2	8.5	7.4	..	2.4	38	0.704	100	134	..
0.8	1.0	0.1	0.1	0.1	0.0	61	0.409	158	179	-1.8
631.1	397.3	12.1	7.8	..	2.3	92	0.744	78	133	6.6
..	81.8	..	..	1.5	1.6	1	0.810	45	..	..
563.3	557.0	9.8	9.5	1.2	0.5	24	0.918	10	27	8.2
4,824.0	5,301.0	19.3	20.0	1.6	0.7	2,125	0.929	3	4	8.4
3.9	5.6	1.3	1.7	0.4	0.2	8	0.825	39	70	7.1
106.5	95.0	5.0	4.1	..	2.0	91	0.686	106	154	2.9
..	0.1	..	..	0.7	..	..	0.623	118	..	..
113.6	144.5	5.8	6.5	1.5	1.1	440	0.77	65	94	4.4

Table 5. Indicators to chapters 14–16 (continued)

COUNTRY or REGION	Commercial energy use				GDP per unit of energy use	
	Total, thousand metric tons of oil equivalent		per capita, kg of oil equivalent		PPP $ per kg of oil equivalent	
	1990	1997	1990	1997	1990	1997
Vietnam	24,451	39,306	369	521	2.7	3.2
Virgin Islands (U.S.)	..	..	..	..	..	..
West Bank and Gaza	..	..	..	..	..	..
Yemen, Rep.	2,665	3,355	224	208	3.0	3.5
Yugoslavia, FR (Serbia,Montenegro)	..	..	..	..	..	..
Zambia	5,220	5,987	671	634	1.1	1.2
Zimbabwe	8,934	9,926	917	866	2.6	3.1
World	**8,608,411**	**9,431,190**	**1,705**	**1,692**	..	..
Low Income	1,122,683	1,194,696	607	563	..	..
Middle income	3,297,830	3,523,253	1,397	1,368	..	..
Lower middle income	2,426 917*	2 384 856*	1,302*	1,178*	..	..
Upper middle income	870,913	1,138,397	1,753	2,068	..	..
Low & middle Income	4,420,513	4,717,949	1,049	1,005	..	..
East Asia & Pacific	1,188,126	1,647,182	743	942	..	..
Europe & Central Asia	1,799,838	1,240,586	3,966	2,690	1.8	2.2
Latin America & Caribbean	457,439	575,389	1,057	1,181	..	..
Middle East & N. Africa	266,687	374,375	1,134	1,354	3.3	3.3
South Asia	435,330	556,496	394	443	..	..
Sub-Saharan Africa	273,093	323,921	705	695	..	..
High Income	4,187,901	4,713,241	4,996	5,369	..	..

*indicates income-group aggregate that includes data on China.

Note: Revisions to estimates of China's GNP per Capita, made by analysts in 2000-01, caused that economy to be reclassified from low to lower middle income. As a result, for different indicators in these data tables China figures as part of one or the other income group, which considerably affects these group aggregates.

| CO$_2$ emissions | | | | | | Forest area | Human Development Index | HDI rank | PPP GNP per capita rank | Genuine domestic savings |
| total, million, metric tons | | per capita, metric tons | | kg per PPP $ of GDP | | thousand sq.km | | | | % of GDP |
1990	1996	1990	1996	1980	1996	1995	1998	1998	1999	1998
22.5	37.6	0.3	0.5	..	0.3	91	0.671	108	160	10.3
..	12.9	..	..	..	..	..	..	..	..	..
..	..	..	..	..	..	..	..	..	..	..
..	..	..	..	..	..	0	0.448	148	197	-26.3
..	36.2	..	..	..	..	18	..	..	..	..
2.4	2.4	0.3	0.3	1.0	0.3	314	0.420	153	198	-3.6
16.6	18.4	1.7	1.6	1.0	0.6	87	0.555	130	142	12.3
16,183.1	**22,690.1**	**3.3**	**4.0**	**1.2**	**0.6**	**32,712**	**0.712**			**13.3**
1,376.8	2,433.8	0.7	1.1	1.6*	0.7*	7,379*	..	..	..	20*
5,772.8	9,524.1	2.7	3.7	1.0	0.7	18,898	..	..	..	10.6
3,721.6*	6,734.6*	2.2*	3.3*	1.0	0.9	11,101	..	..	..	5.9
2,051.2	2,789.6	4.3	5.1	1.0	0.6	7,797	..	..	..	12.9
7,150.8	11,959.5	1.8	2.5	1.2	0.7	26,277		..	..	13.5
3,289.6	4,717.5	2.0	2.7	2.1	0.8	3,832		..	..	28.3
924.8	3,448.9	9.1	7.3	2.2	1.3	8,579		..	..	8.3
966.4	1,207.5	2.2	2.5	0.6	0.4	9,064		..	..	9.8
737.6	987.2	3.3	3.9	1.1	0.8	89		..	..	-2.2
765.9	1,125.1	0.7	0.9	0.7	0.5	744		..	..	9.6
465.3	471.7	0.9	0.8	1.0	0.5	3,969		..	..	3.7
9,033.5	10,732.1	11.9	12.3	1.2	0.5	6,436		..	..	13.3

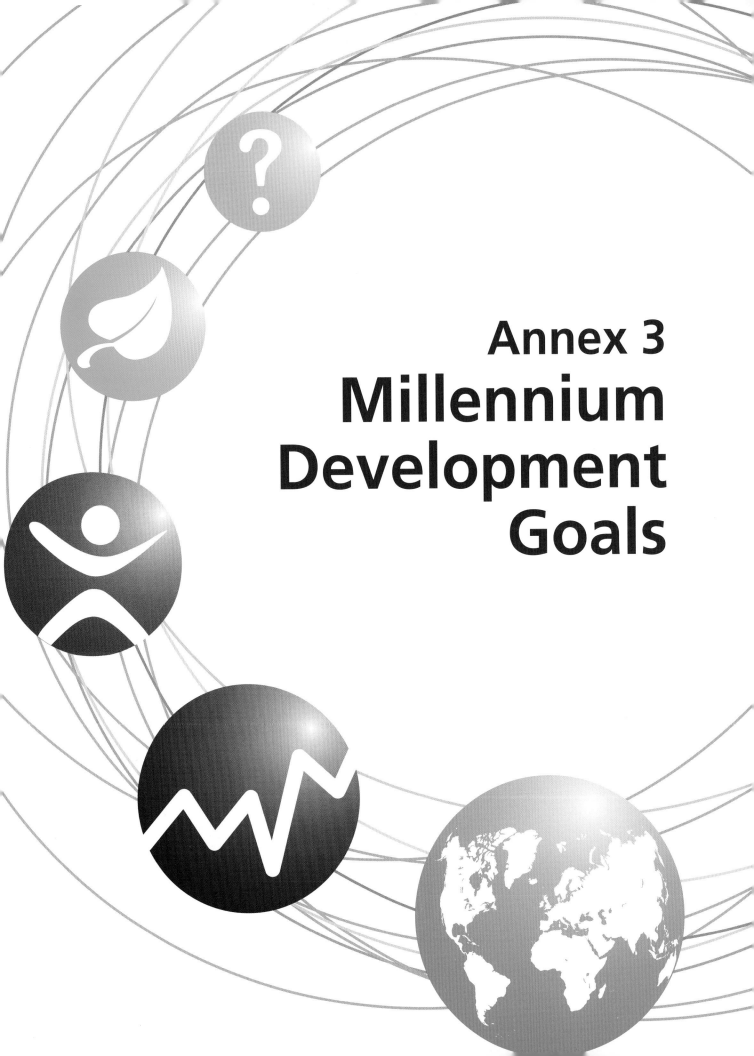

Annex 3
Millennium Development Goals

Millennium Development Goals (MDGs)

	Goals and Targets	Indicators
Goal 1:	**Eradicate extreme poverty and hunger**	
Target 1:	Halve, between 1990 and 2015, the proportion of people whose income is less than one dollar a day	1. Proportion of population below $1 per day 2. Poverty gap ratio [incidence x depth of poverty] 3. Share of poorest quintile in national consumption
Target 2:	Halve, between 1990 and 2015, the proportion of people who suffer from hunger	4. Prevalence of underweight children (under five years of age) 5. Proportion of population below minimum level of dietary energy consumption
Goal 2:	**Achieve universal primary education**	
Target 3:	Ensure that, by 2015, children everywhere, boys and girls alike, will be able to complete a full course of primary schooling	6. Net enrollment ratio in primary education 7. Proportion of pupils starting grade 1 who reach grade 5 8. Literacy rate of 15–24 year olds.
Goal 3:	**Promote gender equality and empower women**	
Target 4:	Eliminate gender disparity in primary and secondary education preferably by 2005 and to all levels of education no later than 2015	9. Ratio of girls to boys in primary, secondary and tertiary education 10. Ratio of literate females to males of 15–24 year olds 11. Share of women in wage employment in the non-agricultural sector 12. Proportion of seats held by women in national parliament
Goal 4:	**Reduce child mortality**	
Target 5:	Reduce by two-thirds, between 1990 and 2015, the under-five mortality rate	13. Under-five mortality rate 14. Infant mortality rate
		15. Proportion of 1 year old children immunized against measles
Goal 5:	**Improve maternal health**	
Target 6:	Reduce by three-quarters, between 1990 and 2015, the maternal mortality rate	16. Maternal mortality rate 17. proportion of births attended by skilled health personnel
Goal 6:	**Combat HIV/AIDS, malaria and other diseases**	
Target 7:	Have halted by 2015, and begun to reverse, the spread of HIV/AIDS	18. HIV prevalence among 15–24 year old pregnant women 19. Contraceptive prevalence rate 20. Number of children orphaned by HIV/AIDS
Target 8:	Have halted by 2015, and begun to reverse, the incidence of malaria and other major diseases	21. Prevalence and death rates associated with malaria 22. Proportion of population in malaria risk areas using effective malaria prevention and treatment measures 23. Prevalence and death rates associated with tuberculosis 24. Proportion of TB cases detected and cured under DOTS (Directly Observed Treatment Short Course)

Goals and Targets	Indicators
Goal 7: **Ensure environmental sustainability***	
Target 9: Integrate the principles of sustainable development into country policies and programmes and reverse the loss of environmental resources	25. Proportion of land area covered by forest 26. Land area protected to maintain biological diversity 27. GDP per unit of energy use (as proxy for energy efficiency) 28. Carbon dioxide emissions (per capita)
Target 10: Halve by 2015, the proportion of people without sustainable access to safe drinking water	29. Proportion of population with sustainable access to an improved water source
Target 11: By 2020, to have achieved a significant improvement in the lives of at least 100 million slum dwellers	30. Proportion of people with access to improved sanitation 31. Proportion of people with access to secure tenure
Goal 8: **Develop a Global Partnership for Development***	
Target 12: Develop further an open, rule-based, predictable, non-discriminatory trading and financial system Includes a commitment to good governance, development, and poverty reduction—both nationally and internationally	**Official Development Assistance**** 1. Net ODA as percentage of Development Assistance Committee donors' GNP [targets of 0.7% in total and 0.15% for Least Developed Countries] 2. Proportion of ODA to basic social services (basic education, primary health care, nutrition, safe water and sanitation) 3. Proportion of ODA that is untied 4. Proportion of ODA for environment in small island developing states 5. Proportion of ODA for transport sector in land-locked contries
Target 13: Address the Special Needs of the Least Developed Countries Includes: tariff- and quota-free access for LDC exports; enhanced programme of debt relief for HIPC, cancellation of official bilateral debt; and more generous ODA for countries committed to poverty reduction	**Market Access** 6. Proportion of exports (by value and excluding arms) admitted free of duties and quotas 7. Average tariffs and quotas on agricultural products and textiles and clothing 8. Domestic and export agricultural subsidies in OECD countries 9. Proportion of ODA provided to help build trade capacity
Target 14: Address the Special Needs of landlocked countries and small island developing states **Target 15:** Deal comprehensively with the debt problems of developing countries through national and international measures in order to make debt sustainable in the long term	*Debt Sustainability* 10. Proportion of official bilateral HIPC debt cancelled 11. Debt service as a percentage of exports of goods and services 12. Proportion of ODA provided as debt relief 13. Numbers of countries reaching HIPC decision and completion points
Target 16: In cooperation with developing countries, develop and implement strategies for decent and productive work for youth	14. Unemployment rate of 15–24 year olds
Target 17: In cooperation with pharmaceutical companies, provide access to affordable essential drugs in developing countries	15. Proportion of population with access to affordable essential drugs on a sustainable basis
Target 18: In cooperation with the private sector, make available the benefits of new technologies, especially information and communications	16. Telephone lines per 1000 people 17. Personal computers per 1000 people **Other indicators to be determined**

*Source: 2002 World Development Indicators, p. 16–17 (<<http://www.worldbank.org/data/wdi2002/2worldview.pdf>>).

**Note: Some of the indicators will be monitored separately for the Least Developed Countries (LDCs), Africa, landlocked countries and small island developing states.

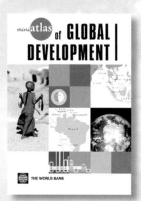

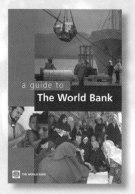